An Introduction to Gaelic Fiction

T0322391

An Introduction to Gaelic Fiction

Moray Watson

Edinburgh University Press

© Moray Watson, 2011

Edinburgh University Press Ltd
22 George Square, Edinburgh

www.euppublishing.com

Typeset in Minion Pro, and
printed and bound in Great Britain by
CPI Antony Rowe, Chippenham and Eastbourne

A CIP record for this book is available from the British Library

ISBN 978 0 7486 3663 1 (hardback)
ISBN 978 0 7486 3664 8 (paperback)

Contents

Abbreviations

AC	*An Aghaidh Choimheach*
BA	*Bùrn is Aran*
BiS	*Books in Scotland*
CG	*The Celtic Garland*
CGS	*The Companion to Gaelic Scotland*
CnG	*Caraid nan Gaidheal*
DA	*Dùn-àluinn*
G	*Gairm*
GA	*An Guth Aoibhneach*
LS	*Lìontan Sgaoilte*
NG	*Na Guthan*
NT	*An naidheachd bhon taigh*
OM	*An t-Ogha Mór*

This book is dedicated to my parents and my sister, with thanks for all the things families do, but especially for making a home where reading mattered.

Introduction

In an important paper that appears in *Aiste*, the new journal on Gaelic literature, Derick Thomson writes: 'We could do with a detailed critical account of the history of Gaelic fiction in the twentieth century' (Thomson 2007: 7). In fact, there is really no account of the history of Gaelic fiction in the twentieth century, critical, detailed or otherwise, aside from a portion of one article published over thirty years ago (MacLeod 1977). Although that article is an important cornerstone of modern Gaelic literary studies, the part dealing with Gaelic fiction in the twentieth century is rather short, and so it amounts to little more than a brief overview. Its author, Donald John MacLeod, also wrote a comprehensive bibliography of Gaelic publications in the century, which was connected with his PhD thesis on Gaelic prose writing in the century. It seems that Thomson was influential in guiding MacLeod towards this work, and that he might well have gone on to produce the kind of detailed critical history that Thomson was still requesting in 2007. However, MacLeod left academia before much more of his extensive knowledge could find its way into print, and the ever-busy Thomson never undertook the task for himself. More than three decades later, the present book attempts to go some way towards filling the gap that Thomson has identified.

In 2006, William Gillies published a paper titled 'On the Study of Gaelic Literature' (Gillies 2006), in which he surveyed the state of Gaelic literary criticism. Even as recently as 2006, Gillies felt justified in using the word *literature* as a synonym for *poetry*: that is to say, he found so little to say about the criticism of Gaelic prose fiction or drama (or other conceivable forms) that he had no need to be more specific with the terminology of his title. As he explained it himself:

> my title uses the word 'literature', but I shall be talking almost
> exclusively about poetry, because most of it *is* poetry (Gillies 2006: 3)

It is fair to say that the bulk of literary items that have been produced in the Gaelic language are poems or songs. However, as the present book shows, there is no shortage of prose literature in Gaelic, and the same might be said of drama, although that form is outside the scope of this survey. What is more telling is the lack of writing about fiction. It is not so much, then, that there was no prose literature on which Gillies could comment, but rather that there was an extreme dearth of criticism of fiction that he could analyse or cite. Each new book of short stories and each new novel that is published (at least since the 1950s) tends to receive at least one review, among other places in the leading Gaelic magazines or papers of the day, such as *Gairm* or *Gath*. Some of them are given lengthier treatments in newspaper critique columns or on radio programmes or elsewhere. However, aside from reviews, surveys and overviews, there was almost a complete avoidance of literary criticism of prose fiction throughout the twentieth century. This chapter explores this phenomenon in an effort to establish why this is the case, why it is now changing, and how the critics may influence the writing, either directly or indirectly.

In the first place, it is important to understand what kind of subject Gaelic is at university level, since the universities train or employ most of the literary critics. From its inception as a university subject, Gaelic was studied within the broader framework of Celtic Studies: that is to say, Gaelic was not regarded as a discipline in its own right, but as a subset of another area of study. Celtic Studies was introduced to Edinburgh University in the nineteenth century, then Glasgow and Aberdeen Universities early in the twentieth century. In all three institutions, the subject was heavily influenced by the study of the Classics (see Watson 2010 for a fuller discussion of this). Lecturers within the field, and other academics who took an active interest in Celtic, were often Classics scholars. Celtic Studies outside of Scotland had been strongly connected with comparative philology even before the subject took root in the universities here. Thus, Celticists in Scotland tended to focus on linguistic interests rather more than on literary criticism. When their focus turned to literature, it went primarily to literary works in Gaelic most akin to the works of the Classical authors: thus, they followed the example of Celticists elsewhere in concentrating on either the medieval or early modern literatures. As Thomson himself has put it, '[t]here was almost an assumption that students would be fluent and literate in Gaelic and should explore other matters at university' (Thomson 1994: 291). Such matters would include 'the study of grammar and comparative philology' (291), but only a little work on modern Gaelic literature. A much greater emphasis would be placed on the study of the medieval and early modern languages and literatures. Indeed, at the heart of the literature produced in the Early Modern Gaelic language is the syllabic, bardic poetry that is often known as Classical Gaelic poetry. The very name scholars have given it tends to account for the privileged position it has occupied in Celtic Studies both within Scotland and elsewhere, and it is without question that the bardic poetry does represent some kind of literary apogee in the Goedelic languages. If Celtic scholars remarked upon literature other than the medieval or early modern work, they tended to take interest in the vernacular poetry and song that was emerging at the end of the Classical Gaelic period, illustrating that the people's professional social structures might have been dismantled by political exigencies but that their creative ingenuity remained intact.

Up to the nineteenth century, Gaelic largely failed to produce creative written prose. By contrast, there was a long tradition of oral myth, legend and folk tales, and there was also a long tradition of writing down some of this material. Therefore, if a scholar was to apply any academic tools to a study of anything other than the language itself and outside of the rightly-vaunted poetry, that scholar would find plenty of scope for working within the fields of myth and folklore and little or nothing within the field of prose fiction.[1] The poetry of the nineteenth century has generally been regarded as significantly below the standard of what had gone before it (see Watson 1918, and suggested in Thomson 1990, for instance), although this view – once almost universally held – is now being reconsidered (see Meek 2003 and 2007b as examples of this). Thus, when Gaelic at university came into being, in the form of Celtic Studies, it was perhaps adjudged that there was little of note in the then-modern literature and that a scholar with a critical mindset should set about working on either the literatures of the earlier forms of the language or else the highly-acclaimed vernacular poetry of the seventeenth and, especially, eighteenth centuries (see Blackie 1876, Maclean 1904, MacNeil 1892, and Watson 1915 and 1918 for insights into scholars' perceptions of the literature that was, to them, contemporary).

When Magnus Maclean wrote his two series of lectures on literature at the beginning of the twentieth century, he found almost nothing to say about the contemporary literature, and certainly nothing to note about prose fiction of his day. Maclean was Professor in Electrical Engineering at Glasgow Technical College, and he became the first Celtic lecturer at Glasgow University in 1900. Maclean's lectures were collected and published as *The Literature of the Celts* (1902) and *The Literature of the Highlands* (1904). According to Thomson, the former is more successful than the latter (Thomson 2007: 2–3). *The Literature of the Celts* does seem more assured, responding to an existing critical tradition, including the similarly-titled and much-discussed work by Matthew Arnold (1910; Gillies 2006 also deliberately employs a similar title). Maclean's *The Literature of the Highlands* deals with the important poets of the seventeenth and eighteenth centuries, and attempts to establish their significance. It also turns its attention to the Ossianic controversy, which it never quite manages to handle adequately (the matter of Ossian was never satisfactorily treated until Thomson himself published *The Gaelic Sources of Macpherson's Ossian* in 1951, which allowed scholars to approach the text with more confidence). When Maclean looks to prose, he finds only some Gaelic proverbs and some travel and historical writing, much of it in English. Similarly, Donald MacLean responded to a perceived need for an accessible introduction to Gaelic literature following his namesake's foray into the field, and also wrote almost exclusively about poetry in his *The Literature of the Scottish Gael* (1912). A slimmer volume, aimed at the less affluent student of the literature, *The Literature of the Scottish Gael* covers much of the same ground as Magnus Maclean's work.

Donald MacKinnon of Colonsay, the first professor of Celtic in Scotland, was a prolific writer in Gaelic, and is regarded as one of the most positive influences on the development of our modern prose registers. His writings were collected by Lachlan MacKinnon, on behalf of the Scottish Gaelic Texts Society (MacKinnon 1956). MacKinnon's critical essays concentrated almost entirely on poetry, but created a model for the kind of critical writing that has only recently resumed through the medium of Gaelic. For much of the century, only reviews and short survey articles appeared in the language, leading to a situation whereby most of the extended criticism of Gaelic literature was conducted through the medium of English. To a large extent, this is more of a sociolinguistic issue than a literary one, but it does speak to a certain lack of shared confidence within the literary milieu that may go some way towards explaining some of the long delays and hiatuses in developments in the literature itself. It may be regretted that MacKinnon's work did not provide the inspiration for entire generations of Gaelic-medium literary critics. One of the few major voices to follow MacKinnon closely and write criticism in clear and confident Gaelic was his fellow Argyll-man, Donald Lamont of Tiree. Lamont is described in Thomson's encyclopaedia by Roderick MacLeod as '[a]rguably the greatest Gaelic prose writer of all time' (CGS 1994: 146). Like his friend and one-time teacher, Donald MacKinnon, Lamont wrote what could be loosely described as cultural criticism. Also like MacKinnon, Lamont's writing was collected for the Scottish Gaelic Texts Society (Murchison 1960). The editor, Thomas M. Murchison, gave a clear and concise description of the state of Gaelic prose writing in Lamont's time:

> Gaelic prose literature has come down to us in two streams. There
> is the older stream of 'oral prose'—that vast corpus of *sgeulachd* and
> *seanchas*, folk-tale and anecdote, of anonymous authorship, passed
> on, subtly and unconsciously revised, from generation to generation,
> in castle hall and by the ceilidh fire, both by professional story-tellers
> and by ordinary folk relating what they had heard from those before
> them. (Murchison 1960: xvi)

The second stream is what Murchison terms 'literary prose', which is 'of known origin or authorship' (xvi). Original prose is a subsection within Murchison's 'literary prose' genre. This original prose was new and 'comparatively meagre' in Lamont's time. Nevertheless, Lamont himself contributed more than two million words to the corpus (CGS 1994: 146). Among those contributions were his fictional tales about an imaginary parish called Cille-Sgumain, which Murchison describes as 'sketches' (Murchison 1960: xx). Both MacLeod and Murchison found much to commend in Lamont's writing style:

> He wrote in a flowing, natural, idiomatic style. (CGS 1994: 146)

> Dr Lamont's writing is simple and never subtle. It is straightforward and crystal-clear. There is no seeking after an elaboration which too often conceals rather than conveys the meaning. He steers a middle course between pedantry and extreme colloquialism. His concern is to convey his thoughts and ideas, and not to air his learning. He dislikes the verbosity that uses four words where one will serve. (Murchison 1960: xix)

Unfortunately, Lamont's fiction never really developed into what we might call short stories and his cultural commentary never crossed over into true literary criticism: specifically, criticism of the 'meagre' amount of prose fiction that did exist in his day.

It is perfectly possible that scholars of Gaelic studies might have begun analysing fiction earlier if the universities had employed more of them. As it was, all three universities in Scotland with Celtic departments were single-person departments for many years (CGS 1994: 290–2). Even in more recent decades, the numbers have remained modest. Consequently, scholars outside of the Scottish universities have made at least as much of a contribution to the literary criticism of fiction as those within those institutions. Linked to the small numbers of scholars, and to the facts outlined above with regard to Gaelic's place within a wider Celtic academic world, it has not always been obvious where to publish pure literary criticism on modern Gaelic. Most academic journals tended to focus on philological and linguistic issues, with any literary-orientated space dedicated to those questions most akin to linguistic ones and dedicated most commonly to the literature of the medieval and early modern periods (see Watson 2010). As a result, when important work is being done on the literature, it can take some time to appear in print. For instance, at the major Rannsachadh na Gàidhlig conference held at Aberdeen University in 2000, only three (at most) of more than sixty papers read there dealt with fiction. The two papers most clearly relevant to the current discussion both failed to appear in print within the subsequent five years.

So far, I have perhaps given the impression that only those with university Celtic posts contribute to the literary criticism, but this is clearly not the case. While the criticism of modern literature remains relatively scant, compared to work on some other areas, there have been contributions from critics from a range of backgrounds, involved in various occupations. We may hope that this will continue and will expand: it enhances our general appreciation of the literature and brings a breadth of perspectives to our understanding.

It is not uncommon for scholars outside of Celtic and Gaelic circles to write histories or general discussions of Scottish literature. In some cases, these critics touch on Gaelic work (sometimes, perhaps, without knowing the language, or without knowing it at all well), and, in some cases, they do not. Sometimes when they do not deal with Gaelic work, they attempt to justify this in one of a number of related ways, and sometimes they completely ignore the existence of Gaelic or make the assumption that they need not mention it at all. An example of this last treatment is Maurice Lindsay's *History of Scottish Literature* (1992). The reader might assume from the title that a broad spread of the literature of Scotland would be discussed. Moreover, Lindsay writes that it is the purpose of the book 'to present to the general reader a full account of Scottish literature' (7). He immediately retracts this claim, however:

> It is, of course, necessary to qualify this statement, since Gaelic
> literature does not come within the compass of the survey except in
> so far as where, briefly in the latter part of the eighteenth century and
> rather more extensively in our own day, the traditions of the Gaelic
> speakers of Scotland and the literature of the non-Gaelic speakers
> have impinged upon each other. (7)

Lindsay's use of the phrase *of course* is telling. It suggests that he believes there is no need even to question his decision to leave out Gaelic literature from his 'full account of Scottish literature'. Further, he does not go on to explain this decision: it is presented as a *fait accompli* and merits no discussion. Similarly, there is no discussion of why it is relevant to deal with those instances of 'the traditions of the Gaelic speakers of Scotland' and the other literature of Scotland coming into contact with each other, when it is not otherwise relevant to deal with Gaelic at all. He maintains this unexplained invisible division when writing about Iain Crichton Smith: 'As far as the novels and stories of Iain Crichton Smith (and, indeed, the plays) are concerned, those in Gaelic do not come within the bounds of this survey' (432). When discussing the literature of medieval Scotland, Lindsay does mention Gaelic in passing, albeit only to say that most of the Gaelic manuscripts that survive from the Dark Ages have 'found their way to places of preservation in Europe' (9). (It is perhaps more accurate to imagine that most of these manuscripts were scribed on the continent by clerics who had made their way there to be educated.) Lindsay goes on to discuss Macpherson briefly (243), and then to give every impression of having an unfavourable opinion of Gaels and Gaelic generally:

Whatever may be later reactions to his Gael-mongering . . . (245)

[. . .]

The barrier of Gaelic that for so long had separated Highlands and Lowlands was already receding in Scott's times. To the Romantic mind, the old Highland ways were an irresistible attraction. (281)

A perfectly reasonable explanation for Lindsay's choices in the book might be that his command of Gaelic was not sufficient to allow him to deal critically with the literature in any reasonable depth. If that were the case, though, it might be more appropriate simply to say so, rather than to suggest (sometimes forcefully) that he was giving a comprehensive account.

This approach, as exemplified by Lindsay, has been adopted by several writers, ranging from highly scholarly and academic researchers to those writing for general, popular or younger readers. For instance, Duncan Glen's *Scottish Literature: A New History from 1299 to 1999* (1999) is written for schools or the general reader. Like Lindsay's *History*, its title suggests that its coverage would be inclusive, and, again like Lindsay's, it begins with a brief discussion of Celtic languages in Scotland. However, by page 6, Glen indicates that the book is actually about 'Lowland Scottish literature'. There is no explanation of why this is the case and no justification for either that or the broader implications of the title. As with Lindsay's book, there is some room for a few brief nods in a Gaelic direction, with the ubiquitous Macpherson being discussed briefly (48).[2] In one section of the book, Glen ponders who are the significant writers of the twentieth century, and seems to find only MacDiarmid to fit that bill (Glen 1999: 111). And yet, when he lists Sorley Maclean, George Campbell Hay, Iain Crichton Smith and Derick Thomson in this context as writers who have come to prominence (Glen 1999: 112), he makes no mention of the fact that their work is largely or exclusively Gaelic. Nor indeed does he acknowledge that Maclean is often considered to be a poet at least as great as MacDiarmid.

There is nothing wrong with writing a book about Lowland Scottish literature. For anyone who is unable to read Gaelic, for example, that may be the only realistic or desirable option. Culturally, linguistically, or practically, in fact, it may be preferable in many cases to write separately about

Lowland and Gaelic literature. Difficulties arise, however, when authors forget that there is also non-Gaelic Highland-based literature (and that they are calling this 'Lowland Scottish') or when authors imply that there is no contradiction in suggesting inclusion or comprehensiveness in a Scottish context while energetically excluding and, in some cases, dismissing Gaelic or Highland literature. This is a form of cultural imperialism, a dismissive casualness to which Scots are already much-accustomed, albeit more commonly coming from a different direction.

There are several writers who have been aware of these difficulties and who have made efforts to include reference to Gaelic in their surveys or discussions of Scottish literature. The second edition of Roderick Watson's *The Literature of Scotland* (2006),[3] for instance, makes a convincing effort to be inclusive. *The Literature of Scotland* deals with all three indigenous languages of Scotland (*viz.* Gaelic, Scots and English), and also includes Latin, which has formerly been a medium of significant writing in the country. Usefully, Watson interweaves criticism and history of the three main languages in a way that creates a sense of an engaging, overarching narrative. In this way, the reader is given an integrated sense of the development of literature in Scotland which is usually lacking in other treatments (including this present book). Perhaps inspired by Cairns Craig's Aberdeen series in the late 1980s (Craig 1987–9), many of the more recent general collections of essays on Scottish literature have included substantial Gaelic contributions (see for instance Brown et al. 2006).

The end of the twentieth century and beginning of the twenty-first have seen a sudden and marked shift in the way prose fiction has been treated by critics. Furthermore, there is a clear sense that Gaelic academia is now taking the criticism of modern literature seriously: this is evidenced not only by the establishment of the journal *Aiste*, based at Glasgow University, but also by the increased numbers of literary crictical papers being read at conferences and their subsequent appearance in proceedings volumes and elsewhere. What was for so long a specialist interest, or a hobby for a scholar of another area, has now become part of the mainstream in modern Gaelic studies. At the same time, the writing and publishing of prose has arrived at a paradoxical position that entirely contradicts that which pertained from the 1950s to the 1990s. In the earlier period, the short story was flourishing, largely thanks to the quarterly magazine *Gairm* (as discussed in Chapter 3), but also in other outlets, and there were numerous accomplished authors of the form. Novels modulated between scarcity and non-production throughout the same period, although a few years in the 1990s saw modest increases. The demise of *Gairm* in 2002 saw the end of regular publication of separate Gaelic short stories (to date),[4] but the following year marked the appearance of *An Oidhche Mus do Sheòl Sinn* by

Aonghas Pàdraig Caimbeul. This was the first novel in a significant pub-lishing venture known as Ùr-Sgeul organised by the Gaelic Books Council. Although the Ùr-Sgeul initiative has published some collections of short stories, including a set of small multi-author books, the emphasis has largely been on single-author novels, and the lack of a regular magazine perhaps endangers the future of short fiction in the language. Despite this, the number of novels published since 2003 makes the first decade of the twenty-first century the most productive one so far for Gaelic novels. Some of these novels have been published by new or relatively new authors, but others are the work of previously-established writers. Caimbeul has followed his first with three more, and some of the other authors have also written more than one. At the time of writing, there is no sign of the production slowing down, and the Ùr-Sgeul website suggests that more of the same is to come.

An issue that has exercised scholars in recent years is the 'almost complete absence of critical discourse in Gaelic' (Gillies 2006: 12). The effect of this is that there is danger of a sense of disengagement between the literature and its criticism. There is, furthermore, a failure to develop the terms and methods of enquiry within the language, which means that Gaelic literature is understood and interpreted almost always through the medium of a different language. This, in turn, threatens to encourage authors to write for an audience that will understand and interpret their work through the medium of English (as is the case with this book, which may well be read by people who have not read the fiction it discusses). The implications of this for Gaelic cultural expression may or may not be serious, but it is nevertheless important to be aware of the situation. Reviews of new books and discussions of established authors did appear in Gaelic in the magazine *Gairm*, but, while often insightful, these rarely had the space to examine issues in any real depth: of the articles dealing with prose writing or writers, Donald Meek's one on Cailein T. MacCoinnich in *Gairm* 123 is among the longest, at only ten pages. It may be, however, that the situation described is in the process of changing. In recent scholarly books, there seems to be a growing willingess to engage with theoretical and analytical questions through the medium of Gaelic, and this willingness extends to literature as well as to the other areas of study in the language. It remains to be seen whether this will indeed turn out to be a trend or merely a brief foray.

Prior to the present book, there was no volume that dealt with prose fic-tion in Gaelic. Articles and chapters appearing in books about more general subjects, or multi-authored volumes have also been scarce. As was men-tioned at the beginning of this chapter, the best-known and most-quoted article dealing with Gaelic prose is undoubtedly Donald John MacLeod's contribution to the *Transactions of the Gaelic Society of Inverness*, which appeared in 1977. MacLeod's article is well-researched and thorough, but it surveys four hundred years of publishing in around thirty pages. The entire twentieth century – which, as this book will demonstrate, encompasses almost the entire range of what we would normally think of as 'fiction' – is dealt with in a matter of thirteen pages. MacLeod's 1987 contribution to the Aberdeen *History of Scottish Literature* is an updated, much shorter, version of some of the ground covered in the former article.

Another survey article dealing with prose fiction is the 2007 contribution that Michelle Macleod and I published in the third volume of the *Edinburgh History of Scottish Literature*. Again, though, this is limited in length and scope, and deals with both fiction and drama, in around five thousand words. Although we were able to update the situation still further than MacLeod's 1987 article, and mention authors and works pertinent to the past two decades, the format of a survey like that means that even the most significant writers could be given scarcely more than a paragraph or two.

Besides these few general works on the fiction, there are small numbers of articles and chapters now appearing in scholarly publications, and it would appear that fiction is beginning to take its place alongside poetry as a mode that critics consider seriously. Mark Wringe, who has a role within the Ùr-Sgeul project, has made several scholarly contributions about fiction at recent conferences. He also hosts a regular radio programme that discusses literature in general, through the medium of Gaelic. Máire Ní Annracháin has written a number of papers about Gaelic fiction, especially the novels. Her 'Television and the Novel: *Cùmhnantan* and *An Claíomh Solais*' (2006) compares a Gaelic novel with an Irish one, whereas her 'Shifting Boundaries: Scottish Gaelic Literature after Devolution' (2007) compares the effects (or lack thereof) of the new Scottish constitution on Gaelic prose and poetry in the past decade. Along with a few others, Ní Annracháin has succeeded in (rather rapidly and without much precedent) placing the criticism of Gaelic fiction on a contemporary footing. Her articles situate the criticism of the fiction within a framework that incorporates the advances made within literary theories during the past century, but also provides an understanding and appreciation of the unique culture-specific aspects of the Gaelic literature. A similar movement has already taken place in the criticism of Gaelic poetry (actuated by critics like Christopher Whyte and Ní Annracháin herself), meaning that Gaelic poetry now benefits from both scholarly research and theoretical criticism: if, as seems likely, the analysis of prose fiction is heading in the same direction, this can only be a good thing for our understanding both of the literature itself and also of Gaelic culture in general. There is a growing sense that Gaelic writers have now learnt how to manipulate the language in a manner that is effective in prose fiction. Ní Annracháin has written that: 'The novel in Irish is more developed and numerous, although Scottish Gaelic often compensated in quality for what it lacked in quantity' (2006: 138).

Like Ní Annracháin, Michelle Macleod has brought a more theoretical focus to bear on a reading of the novels. In NicLeòid (2007), she considers the Jungian concept of the *puer aeternus* in relation to main characters in a number of the modern novels. Published in the same year, her article on Iain Crichton Smith's short stories applies a more general existentialist reading (Macleod 2007). Both of these articles draw on theoretical readings of fiction from her PhD work (Macleod 1999). In my own writing, I have brought in some basic concepts of postcolonial thinking (Watson 2006, forthcoming b) as well as using some of the techniques of stylistics and Conversation Analysis to explore the dynamics of the use of the language in fiction (Watson 2007, 2008, 2010, forthcoming a). It is my intention to develop both of these areas in much greater depth in the future, and it is to be hoped that other commentators will also continue to be attracted to the area of Gaelic prose fiction, and that the body of work, both scholarly and theoretical, will continue to grow in the coming years.

Chapter 1

The Origin of Gaelic Fiction

In this chapter, I address the question of where Gaelic fiction comes from. Specifically, I have stated that Gaelic fiction was 'invented' or 'imported' during a seventy-year period at the end of the nineteenth and beginning of the twentieth centuries (Watson 2008). This is not new knowledge, as Donald John MacLeod (1977), among others, had already made similar statements (for instance, see also Murchison 1960: xvi). It is necessary here, however, to go beyond these kinds of tantalising statements and provide some evidence for them, so that we may come to a fuller understanding of how Gaelic fiction then weathered the various storms of the twentieth century and came to be in the form which it currently takes at the beginning of the twenty-first. Among the questions to be posed here, we may consider what are the fiction's origins, both in direct and indirect terms. From this, we begin to discover how the form links both to the literary and oral past in Gaelic culture and also to the contemporary literary and social scene. The chapter considers the kinds of authors who were involved in the evolution of fiction and the ways in which their backgrounds can be seen to have influenced the type of prose that emerged. Similarly, we consider how the networks of authors, editors and publishers were influenced by other literature that was being produced around them: since much of the Gaelic prose being written between the middle of the nineteenth century and the early twentieth century was being composed or published in the cities, it is reasonable to imagine that the agents of the prose revolution had access to the other magazines of the day, and further research will undoubtedly prove this to be the case. Finally, the chapter takes a literary critical approach to discussing how the prose fiction developed, in structural, thematic, figurative and linguistic terms.

The origins of Gaelic prose – from myth to folk tale

A question we might ask would be why it took so long for Gaelic fiction to emerge at all. Gaelic, in the broadest definition, has been a written language, in one form or another, for perhaps 1,500 years (see Ó Baoill 2010) and scholars often argue that a specifically Scottish variety of Gaelic has been written since at least the tenth century. Further, Gaelic has existed within polities that have prized both literacy and education for many centuries. While the education and literacy of Gaels, and, specifically, through and in the Gaelic language, have not always been a priority, there has nevertheless always been an awareness of writing as a practice throughout the Gaelic community. Gaelic has also co-existed for over a thousand years with Scots and English, which have been the basis for centuries-long traditions of written fiction. Writing was a highly-respected profession in Gaelic during the Early Modern period – from around the twelfth century until the seventeenth or eighteenth century – and the court poet had a status at least on a par with a physician during much of that time. The printing press has been in long use in the production of Gaelic books, the first book having been printed in 1567. Therefore, one might wonder, with some justification, how it could be that it would take so long for prose fiction to become a feature of the literature. Moreover, given the lateness of its development, we might even question how or why it is that it has emerged at all.

When one begins to look at the Gaelic myths and legends, it quickly becomes clear that the lateness of the emergence of fiction is not due to a lack of imagination within the culture. The several arcs of tales, known as 'cycles', for instance, display a wide range of flights of fancy that would compare favourably with the likes of Greek mythology. Then, in the Gaelic folk tradition, stories can be found that match up to a very broad spectrum of international tale types. Examples include 'The Tailor and his Wife', which is a version of AT 1730, 'The Butler's Son', which is a version of AT 1525, and 'The King's Three Questions' which is a version of AT 922 (all Bruford and MacDonald 2003). Although Gaelic versions of the international tale types have their own variations and emphases, there is no doubt that they cover a breadth of imaginative experience that matches well with any other culture. The 'story' is, therefore, clearly and unequivocally as much a part of Gaelic tradition as the song. Rather than pointing towards a lack of creative imagination or a distaste for the fictitious, the Gaelic storytelling tradition might suggest another, different reason for the slow emergence of a written prose fiction. The Jacobite adventures marked the end of the professional stratum of Gaelic society, and the old professions quickly withered away in the absence of a social infrastructure that could support them. This may be one reason why literacy did not initially evolve into a means of entertainment and escapism in the way that it did in cultures that found themselves with a portion of their population that had spare time and money.[1] At the same time, storytelling retained its place within the community that remained. Indeed, the oral tradition survived well into the twentieth century, which is likely to be another reason that written fiction did not emerge until very recently: that is, the taste for stories was already being satisfied at one level, and those with a talent for stories were already exercising that talent. It was only when the Gaelic community became increasingly urbanised and scattered – a process that began before the nineteenth century but reached a tipping point at the end of the nineteenth and beginning of the twentieth centuries – that imaginative writing began to become popular (see Macleod 2010 on the social developments alluded to here). Thus, when Henry Whyte compiled his books of *cèilidh* 'readings', he was catering to what was a relatively new audience, an audience that would gradually come to justify, if not demand, the writing of original prose works of an imaginative nature.

The origins of Gaelic prose – from sermon to conversation

When, in 1567, John Carswell wrote a Gaelic version of the *Book of Common Order*, he provided the model for the next two hundred years of publishing in the language.[2] As Donald John MacLeod has noted (1977: 200), all but one of the seven volumes printed between Carswell's book and the 1745 Jacobite Rising were translations of religious works. The reasons for the small numbers of books being published were doubtless manifold, and we might expect that they were, for the most part, the same reasons why books have not always been abundant in any other language: issues of cost, distribution, audience, literacy levels, poverty, confidence, and so on are not in any way unique to Gaelic (O'Leary 1994). Perhaps more telling is the matter of register differentiation, which MacLeod identified (1977: 200) as having been problematic (see also Watson 2007 and Murchison 1960: xv–xxi). The situation was that an upper register form of the language did exist, but, in common with upper registers in other languages, it was conservative by nature and closely associated with the educated and wealthy classes. By the time *Foirm na n-Urrnuidheadh* (1567) made it to the printing press, the upper register was already at best unfamiliar to all but the most scholarly few, and may well have been all but inscrutable to the 'ordinary person'. This upper register was based on the professional poetry written in Scotland and Ireland between the twelfth and eighteenth centuries, and the language must have been closer to the way Gaelic was spoken in the earlier half of that period than in the latter. Syntactic structures, verb forms and vocabulary that were obsolete in the vernacular by the eighteenth century are still the norm in the upper register language used by Carswell. We may consider the following extract as an example:

> Acht atā ni cheana, is mōr an leathrom agas an uireasbhuidh atā riamh orainde, Gaoidhil Alban agas Eireand, tar an gcuid eile don domhan, gan ar gcanamhna Gaoidheilge do chur a gcló riamh mar atāid a gcanamhna agas a dteangtha féin a gcló ag gach uile chinēl dhaoine oile sa domhan. (Carswell 10)

Carswell is here addressing the reader of his book, and begins a long justification of why he has undertaken to translate it into Gaelic, stating (in the part quoted here) that Gaelic has long suffered from the disadvantage of not being seen in print, and that this compares unfavourably with the situation for other peoples' languages (with a little hyperbole, as he claims that all other peoples' languages appear in print). The verb forms *atá* and *atáid* were more than likely obsolete in Scottish Gaelic long before this period, as indeed was the use of synthetic verb forms in almost any situation. The marking of eclipsis (the 'eclipsing' of the *c* at the beginning of *cuid* with a *g*) is a feature that is not recognised as modern Scottish Gaelic. Similarly, the plural forms in *canamhna* and *teangtha* differentiate this passage from the vernacular of Carswell's own time.

Although secular works did begin to appear from the middle of the eighteenth century onwards (most notably, the vocabulary book and poems of Alasdair Mac Mhaighstir Alasdair), Gaelic publishing was dominated by the activities of the clergy for many more years, and most particularly by the translation of religious works (Watson 2010). By the nineteenth century, however, the range of printed materials was beginning to widen, and the number of items being produced beginning to increase markedly. There has previously been a tendency for scholars to view the nineteenth century as a time of creative poverty in Gaelic literature, at least in comparison with the achievements of the preceding centuries, but, as was mentioned already in this book, this view has been successfully challenged recently. Further, as Meek has noted, the nineteenth century was the period in which Gaels truly began to explore genre development in print (Meek 2007: 253). As a result, the production of books increased to the point where several were being published each year (MacLeod 1977: 202 gives further detail).

There is little doubt that the two most salient advances in terms of preparing the ground for the arrival of what we would recognise as fiction in the language took place in the nineteenth century. The first of these was the fashion for periodical magazines, and the second, related innovation was the advent of the so-called 'readings'. In very much a similar vein to what was happening throughout urban Scotland and elsewhere at the same time, short-run periodicals began appearing in Gaelic from time to time right from the beginning of the century. A few, notably some of those of the Rev. Dr Norman MacLeod, were more lasting. MacLeod has been described as 'one of the most important figures in the history of Gaelic prose' by Donald John MacLeod (1977: 203), and 'the father of prose literature' in one of my own articles (Watson 2008: 573). According to Edward MacCurdy, MacLeod occupies 'the premier position among the writers of Gaelic', due to the 'perfect lucidity of his prose' (MacCurdy 1949–50: 229), and

Murchison wrote that his writing was considered 'the standard of Gaelic prose style' (Murchison 1960: xvi). At any rate, it is beyond question that MacLeod's activities as a writer and editor played a crucial role in shaping the prose literature for at least a century after his floruit.

MacLeod's periodical *An Teachdaire Gaelach* (1829–31) popularised the dialogue or conversation as a literary form. According to Donald Meek, the conversation was the 'backbone' of this important phase in the development of the literature (Meek 2007: 258). I have argued that the conversation was of particular importance in paving the way for prose fiction, as it provided stylistic models that were previously almost non-existent (Watson 2010 and forthcoming a). If we bear in mind that, just as there was essentially no prose fiction in the early nineteenth century, there was also no drama, it should be clear that the composition of fictive dialogue was therefore relatively unexplored at this point. It may be that dialogue is not strictly a *sine qua non* of fiction, but a brief glance at the novels and stories the Gaelic literati might have been reading in, say, English, Scots and French should reveal that dialogue was ordinarily intrinsic to fiction of that period. The conversations gave Norman MacLeod and others a chance to address the vernacular more than ever before. We might find the dialogue in these conversations stilted, dry and, as I have suggested, 'narratistic' at times, but it is evident that MacLeod and the other writers were trying to capture something of the flavour of everyday conversation as they perceived it, and the language is therefore closer to everyday speech than the bulk of the printed Gaelic that had gone before. In particular, the first few turns in each conversation, and then the utterances at the opening and, sometimes, closing of a turn, give the impression of a level of colloquiality that might reflect what MacLeod was hearing spoken in the Gaelic community (bearing in mind, of course, that MacLeod and the other writers were educated in Gaelic to an unusually-high level for their time). A few examples will serve to illustrate:

> DOMH.—Fàilt' ort a Phàra mhòir. Tha mi 'tuigsinn gu-n robh thu as a' bhaile (CnG 52)

> (DOMH.—Welcome big Pat. I understand you were out of town/ away from home)[3]

Here, the author or editor has tried to evoke colloquiality by eliding the *e* from the end of the word *fàilte*, and has similarly used an apostrophe to indicate the aspect marker that would more formally precede *tuigsinn*. Also notable is the use of the familiar address forms in *ort* and *thu*, in favour of the more formal *oirbh* and *sibh*. Exclamations, exhortations and mild imprecations are common, and are often linked to insults:

SEOR.—Am bumalair truagh! Cha-n 'eil ann ach sgonn gun tuigse (CnG 94)

(SEOR.—The wretched oaf! He's nothing but a blockhead)[4]

[. . .]

FIONN.—Tha thusa 'an sin Iain òig, a' deanamh nan cliabh a thoirt dhachaidh na mòine, obair a tha 'nis a' dol á cleachdadh. C'àit an d'fhuair thu na slatan bòidheach caoil so? (CnG 21)

(FIONN.—There you are young Iain, making the creels to take home the peat, work that is going out of practice now. Where did you get those pretty twigs?)

The second extract here shows what I have described as the 'narratistic' tendency in the conversations (Watson 2010 and forthcoming a), but it also illustrates colloquial features such as the greeting, the use of epithets, the use of the familiar forms, and contractions that are intended to echo speech patterns. The direct address of a simple question in particular brings the dialogue close to speech patterns that must have sounded natural to the contemporary reader.

The *còmhraidhean* or dialogues were not the only contribution made by the Rev. Dr Norman MacLeod to the development of prose writing. He also wrote a number of tales that were undoubtedly influential on the new fiction. In many ways, his tales bridge the gap between the folklore, the sermon and prose fiction, and this was evident even to Archibald Clerk:

Dr Macleod may also be looked upon as the connecting link between the oral and the written literature of the Celt. (CnG xxxii)

MacLeod himself seems to have seen his literary efforts as part and parcel of his role as a Christian minister (CnG 4), but it is also clear that his other political and ideological leanings provided him with motivation to write and publish (see Kidd 2000). Thus, in a tale like 'Long Mhór nan Eilthireach' ('The Great Ship of the Exiles', CnG 263–73), MacLeod makes no effort to disguise his support for the emigrations from the Highlands that were taking place in his own lifetime. Referring to John Stuart Blackie's praise of that story, William Watson agrees that it:

is indeed a fine example of restrained and dignified pathos, and in Dr. MacLeod's hands, Gaelic proved itself a not less effective vehicle of gaiety, of humour, and of orderly exposition. (Watson 1929: v)

'Long Mhór nan Eilthireach' is a highly descriptive account of one ship that
is preparing to leave Mull for the New World, complete with its cargo of
Highlanders and islanders. For the first part of the story, the reader might
be forgiven for thinking MacLeod was not in favour of the emigrations.
His descriptions of Mull, the bay, and especially the trees of the island,
tending at times towards hyperbole, paint a picture of an edenic idyll,
rather than a place one would rush to escape. For three pages, the story
then appears to consider the human cost of a policy that breaks up families
and sends some members to the other side of the world (CnG 264–6). One
speaker even laments the loss of his friends so much that he wants to join
them, despite the fact that he was not due to be on board the ship. Finally,
however, the minister arrives to allay the fears of the doubters and spread
calm and reason. The minister, like the island, is described in terms that
tend towards hyperbole: he is so noble that he 'brings a tear to the eye', and:

> Bha ni éigin ann an coslas an duine bheannaichte so nach faodadh
> gun daoine a thàladh ris. (CnG 268–9)

> (There was something in the appearance of this blessed man that
> could not but attract people to him.)

There follows a three-page sermon from the minister, which puts all of
the listeners' minds at rest, and the story finishes with a long quotation
from the 22nd Psalm. The long sermon reminds us that the prose writing
of this period is still largely an experiment in finding new ways to spread
religious and moral education beyond the range of the pulpit itself. Like
the *còmhraidhean*, 'Long Mhór nan Eilthireach' takes this a stage further
by advocating not only Christianity but also compliance with any policies
of those in authority (see Kidd 2000). It is apparent that MacLeod himself
could see that this policy had the potential to be harmful to the people,
but he would not allow that side of the argument to develop into a full
debate, just as Iain MacCormaic in 1912 would not allow his own minister
character to be challenged by reasoned debate on the other side of the
argument (see Chapter 2).

Although 'Long Mhór nan Eilthireach' is probably MacLeod's best-
known composition, it is by no means unique in terms of style or theme.
Caraid nan Gaidheal includes a two-part story called 'Sgeul air Màiri a'
Ghlinne' ('A Tale of Mary of the Glen', CnG 288–96 and 297–307). The first
part of the story, like 'Long Mhór nan Eilthireach', is told in first-person
narration. The narrator meets a woman who seems to be on her deathbed,
and the timeframe is immediately and unequivocally established. In contrast, the place-setting is vague, being in a 'baile-mor àraidh nach 'eil fad'

o'n àit' am bheil mi 'chòmhnuidh' (288, 'a worthy city not far from where I live'). Despite this vagueness, there are elements of this story which seem more controlled and 'fictional' than 'Long Mhór nan Eilthireach', and a late twentieth-century reader might recognise the influence of 'Sgeul air Màiri a' Ghlinne' in the writing of Cailein T. MacCoinnich or, especially, Eilidh Watt. This is particularly true of the dialogue, which labours as a result of the over-reliance on Christian-influenced hyperbole and didacticism, leading also to a considerable measure of fatalism on the part of most characters. In 'Sgeul air Màiri a' Ghlinne', a great deal of the narrative is also essentially thinly-veiled sermonising (see, for instance, p. 295).

The second part of 'Sgeul air Màiri a' Ghlinne' is told from Màiri's point-of-view, which is a rather innovative technique for the period. It seems improbable that MacLeod would have been influenced by Hogg, but there is always the possibility that he had some awareness of *The Private Memoirs and Confessions of a Justified Sinner* (1824). In any case, the effect and purpose of 'Sgeul air Màiri a' Ghlinne' are diametrically opposed to those of the *Confessions*. Indeed, it was mentioned above that the dialogue is peppered with Christian sermons, but in fact the narrative is no different. The narrative remains in the voice of Màiri throughout the second part of the story, giving an impression of dramatic monologue. The excessive length of the story is entirely due to the inclusion of so many unnecessary details that do nothing to contribute to characterisation or scene-building. The poetic language used tends to make dialogue unrealistic and narrative unengaging (see p. 297, for example). An interesting moment in the story comes when Màiri is explaining that, although she is terminally ill, her blood comes from stock which is usually uncommonly strong (pp. 297 and 303): this is later one of the recurring motifs in MacCormaic's *Dùn-àluinn*. Slightly later in the story, there is a scene that mirrors one in another of the (much later) Gaelic novels, *Gainmheach an Fhàsaich* (discussed in Chapter 4), when Màiri is recounting her gradual realisation that her love no longer returns her feelings (299–300). In general, the plotlines are unnecessarily complex and convoluted, with no sense of movement or development: that is to say, there is a heaping up of details, many of them either mundane or far-fetched, but none of them particularly interesting in the absence of a character who catches the reader's attention. There is also a sense that, due to the flashback structure, the timeframe keeps slipping between a wider and narrower focus within single paragraphs and without explicit signalling. This results in parts of the story (301–2) seeming undefined or undisciplined compared to other parts. In one exchange between Màiri and the character Mànus, their dialogue is describing the action of the story, rather like in a play or in the *còmhraidhean*. This further estranges the reader from them as characters.

The story which follows 'Sgeul air Màiri a' Ghlinne' also has a good many features that can still be found in the later fiction of Iain MacCormaic and Iain MacPhàidein, and indeed in the much-later fiction of Cailein T. MacCoinnich and others. Again, the title, 'Sgeul mu Choire-na-Sìthe' ('A Tale about Coire-na-Sìthe', CnG 307–14) is descriptive, in keeping with the titling convention for the *còmhraidhean*. Like 'Sgeul air Màiri a' Ghlinne', this story suffers from a tendency to prevaricate and avoid plot or character development. The narrative begins with a page-and-a-half of background before the story proper even starts with: 'innsidh sinn sgeul air duine misneachail, tapaidh, a thàinig troimh iomadh cruaidh-chàs 's a' chogadh fa dheireadh, nach d' thug a chùl riamh air nàmhaid' (308, 'we shall tell a tale of a strong, courageous man, who came through many a scrape in the last war, and who never turned his back on an enemy').

The origins of Gaelic prose – the readings

The last quarter of the nineteenth century marked the stage when the urban Gaels began to evolve cultural expressions of their own. As Donald Meek has put it, 'By the last quarter of the nineteenth century [. . .] the ceilidh-house moved into print' (Meek 2007: 260). The writing that was appearing in print was very often being done by the sort of people who had moved to Glasgow or the other cities and large towns, looking for education or work. Many of them tried to retain aspects of their culture in the city they settled in, preserving their songs and using the language whenever they would meet fellow Gaels. They also tried to maintain their ceilidh tradition, where people would take turns to tell stories, sing or otherwise entertain and enlighten the others present. It would be fascinating to explore in detail the perceptions of the urban Gaels in the later part of the nineteenth century and investigate their sense of identity and their motivations. In lieu of a thorough study, I have briefly and tentatively speculated in an article that the ceilidh books collected by Henry Whyte and others might have been inspired by the need to bridge the cultural gap among Highlanders and islanders originating from different communities: that is to say, to provide a specific set of communal artefacts to facilitate their shared desire for these gatherings (Watson 2008). It may be that the 'readings' and other entertainments compiled at this time were intended for use back in the home community as well, but it seems most likely that their primary *raison d'être* was to take the place of the tradition-bearer for the ex-patriated Gaels in Lowland Scotland and elsewhere.

One of the earliest of these collections of readings, and certainly the most influential, was Henry Whyte's *The Celtic Garland*, published by Archibald Sinclair of Glasgow in 1885. The book is a collection of translations of pre-existing Gaelic songs and some English songs, along with original material in the form of some poems, songs and prose works. For the purposes of this present book, only the prose works will be mentioned here, but the other aspects of *The Celtic Garland* deserve further study elsewhere. Henry (1852–1913), known by his *nom de plume*, 'Fionn',[5] was the younger of the prolific Whyte brothers originally hailing from the tiny Argyll island of Easdale, although he spent much of his life on the mainland.[6]

In the introductory remarks to *The Celtic Garland*, Fionn wrote:

> Having been frequently asked to indicate where pieces suitable for public reading at Celtic entertainments could be found, I have added a few such. (CG vi)

Some of these additional 'pieces' were letters and other writings that appeared in the periodicals of his day. Others were original, composed specifically for inclusion in the book. Fionn's use of the term 'Celtic entertainments' is telling, reminding us that he was working during the height of the Celtic Twlight, and his book is thus heavily influenced by Ossianism, Romanticism, and nineteenth century Celticism (see Brown 1996 and Chapman 1978).

The second edition of *The Celtic Garland*, to which I am chiefly referring here, differs slightly from the first, in that a few 'pieces of a puerile nature' (CG vi) were removed, and a few other, of Fionn's own recent composition, were added. Nevertheless, in large part, the two editions are much the same. The revision and re-issue of the book only four years after its initial publication must give some indication of its enduring popularity, as does the appearance of a third edition in 1920.

The third section of the book is what concerns us in our study of prose fiction. This part consists of twenty-five Gaelic 'readings'. Ten of these are translations (most of them by John Whyte, credited to 'I.B.O.').[7] Of the remaining fifteen pieces, eight or nine are by Fionn himself, three are by John, and there are one each by 'Mac-Oidhche', 'N.M.K.' and the Rev. D. MacCalum. One piece is unsigned, and is probably also Fionn's work. Throughout most of these pieces, we can discern features which may be thought to influence the fiction that emerged twenty and thirty years later. If their influence was not direct, then it may at least point towards underlying trends which found their way into the fiction discussed here in Chapters 2 and 3 in particular. Thematically, for instance, Fionn and his contemporaries are highly exercised by the need to define 'Gaelicness' and the 'Gael'. In places, this is depicted in terms of the noble traits and virtues that make up 'Gaelicness', including the place that tradition has in the Gaelic identity. Elsewhere, we see the authors pitting the Gaels against Lowlanders in various kinds of linguistic and moral competition. It is evident that, as islanders who moved to urban Scotland at a young age, Fionn and his brother felt a need to assert themselves and their own identity, but the writing of the period in general suggests that their personal situation was symptomatic of a wider, similar malaise that bedevilled the Gaelic literati of the time. In John Whyte's 'Màiri agus an t-*Admiral*' ('Mary and the Admiral', CG 149–50), for instance, the whole story is a slightly weak joke based on the idea that it is not just the Lowlanders who mock the Gaels for the way they speak: the Gaels themselves do it, too, sometimes. On the other hand, Fionn's 'Am Fear a Ghoid a' Mhuc' ('The Man who Stole the Pig', CG 155–61) is a morality tale, of a type that he would have heard in the oral tradition folklore. Set in Islay, it is a parable about the different kinds of characters to be found in small communities, and how the interconnected nature of the small community means that any meanness of spirit will be found out and dealt with quickly.

An interesting feature in 'Am Fear a Ghoid a' Mhuc' is that it lapses into *còmhradh*-style presentation when there are nine uninterrupted turns of dialogue. This is something that happens from time to time in the prose writing of the period, suggesting that the lines between *còmradh* and early 'fiction' were not altogether sharply drawn as yet. The following story does the same thing. This is 'Alasdair Sgiobalta, Tàillear Lag-an-Droighinn' ('Nimble Alasdair, Tailor of Lag-an-Droighinn', CG 162–4) by John Whyte. This story is typical of the elder Whyte's work: it is clever and engagingly written but ultimately devoid of any real substance. It is the story of a mischievous minister who tricks the local tailor when the pair of them are drunk. The minister bets the tailor that he cannot jump over a chair for half-an-hour, shouting out his name and saying nothing else. The minister then invites people to come and watch the spectacle, without explaining it to them. The tailor, Alasdair, is taken for a madman, is subsequently restrained, and thus loses the bet. The minister takes pity on Alasdair and pays him his stake anyway. It is possible to see in this drunken, mischievous, cunning and forgiving minister a template for Iain MacCormaic's Ministear Mór in his novel *Dùn-àluinn*. The part of the story that lapses into *còmhradh* seems to do so gratuitously, as if the author was in a hurry to get through all the turns of conversation, but perhaps the turns are deliberately sped up like this for ease of reading aloud, and to enhance the effect of quick-fire dialogue when read out to a gathering.

The third section of *The Celtic Garland* contains at least one piece that is entirely in the form of a *còmhradh*, and also has at least one story where characters fence with each other through the medium of song, which is a motif that relates to the oral tradition. The Rev. D. MacCalum's only contribution to the volume is 'Ruairidh Bàn Òg' ('Fair Young Roderick', CG 245–8), which is about the loss of Gaelic. Fear that the Gaelic language may be dying, or that the 'traditional' way of life may be on the wane, underlies a good deal of the writing in this period. It is easy to understand these fears, considering that most of the writers were themselves people who moved to urban Scotland and came to see the Gaelic milieu from the outside, and through the medium of a different language and culture. 'Ruairidh Bàn Òg' at least also reveals the comedy in a situation of language shift and language loss, a comedy which is otherwise so often missing in Gaelic writing, or else so dark as to be downright cynical. The story is told in macaronic fashion, and also includes a letter almost entirely in English (as does the novel *Cailin Sgiathanach*, published forty years later). The few Gaelic expressions in this letter, and the English expressions in the narrative of the story illustrate the process of hybridisation that had overtaken the language by this period.

Imaginative prose evolves into early fiction

Iain MacCormaic (known in English as John MacCormick, 1860–1947) from Mull was one of the most prolific and, in many ways, successful of the early practitioners of prose fiction. Not only is he credited with the first Gaelic novel (*Dùn-àluinn*, dealt with in Chapter 2), but he also published the first novella, three books of short stories, a number of plays, and regularly wrote for the periodicals of his day. His short story collections were published during a particularly productive five-year period which also saw the publication of the aforementioned novel and novella.

The titles of MacCormaic's three collections evoke rural or island life, and they point towards a Gaelic 'tradition': they are *Oiteagan O 'N Iar* (1908), *Seanchaidh na h-Airigh* (1911) and *Seanchaidh na Tràghad* (1911), which translate roughly as 'Breezes from the West', 'the Storyteller of the Sheiling', and 'the Storyteller of the Shore'. The 'West', in MacCormaic's day, as now, would archetypally be associated with Gaelic and the Gaelic community, and so MacCormaic was being both literal and figurative with this title, using 'West' as either a synecdoche or a metonymy, depending on whether he was invoking the place or the people (most likely, both, without being overly conscious of it). The 'Breezes' part of the title is suggestive of an association with the natural world, which is prevalent in Gaelic literature (see Watson 2006b on this). The word *seanchaidh* which appears in the titles of the other two books is one which carries rather more nuances than the rough translation of 'Storyteller' would suggest. The term *seanchaidh* is sometimes translated as 'tradition-bearer'. The tradition-bearer was one of the central figures in Gaelic society while the oral culture still endured. The tradition-bearer was a personal storehouse of knowledge about the history, traditions, genealogy and customs of the area or clan. While the telling of stories was part of the *seanchaidh*'s function, these stories would ordinarily have been the memorised 'lore' of the people. Thus, by using the term *seanchaidh*, MacCormaic was appealing to all of these associations and aligning his new fictions very closely with the traditions they would eventually replace. The sheiling and the shore represent two of the environments that framed the lifestyle of the Gael in MacCormaic's time, and would be especially pertinent to an islander like himself.

Oiteagan O 'N Iar features seven stories and one play. Many of the stories share similarities, both with one another and with MacCormaic's other works, especially *Seanchaidh na h-Airigh*, *Dùn-àluinn* and *Gun D' Thug I Spéis Do 'n Àrmunn*. There are a number of stories about rationalisation of superstition, stories that focus on the well-to-do, stories featuring shipwrecks and men who flee the country, leaving behind women they love. In some cases, almost all of these features appear in a single tale, which is made possible by the extended length of many of the stories. Like *Dùn-àluinn*, there is commonly a focus on social distance, sometimes thrown into relief by the love of the leading man and leading woman, one of whom is beneath the other's station. The woman, for instance, loves the main character despite having an opportunity at a much more lucrative match. In most cases, despite adversity, the two leads are finally reunited after a string of bizarre coincidences in which the male character becomes unexpectedly rich. Often, the leading man has been exiled or has left home because of a misunderstanding or because of conflict caused by his choice of sweetheart; when he returns, he is not recognised at once, sometimes because he is in disguise. It is clear that some of these elements took on formulaic status, echoing the style of the folk tale that MacCormaic was evidently trying to emulate.

The first story in *Oiteagan O 'N Iar*, 'Am Bàillidh Mabach 's Am Muillear Crotach' ('The Confused/Stammering Bailiff and the Hunchbacked Miller'), features two ugly men, a factor and a miller, who both have hunchbacks and who are both married to beautiful women. The factor and miller dislike each other intensely and prosecute a feud against one another. In the end, the beautiful wives have the last laugh by turning the men's own nasty tricks against them. The story relies on mistaken identity, disguise and assumed identities, which are staples of MacCormaic's technical repertoire. Similar devices are used in the book's only play, 'An Réiteachadh Rathail' ('The Prosperous Arrangement/Union': MacCormaic was one of the pioneering playwrights in Gaelic, although the history of Gaelic drama has been under-researched to date; see Macleod and Watson 2007). Disguises and mistaken identity are particular favourite devices of Mac Cormaic's, and they underpin the dénouement of *Dùn-àluinn* (which is discussed in Chapter 2).

MacCormaic was evidently fond of adventure stories and far-fetched plots, as we can see in both 'Driodfhortan Eachainn Sheòladair', which is in

Oiteagan O 'N Iar, and also in 'Spùinneadairean Shìne', which is in his 1911 book *Seanchaidh na h-Airigh*. The former, whose title we may translate as 'The Misadventure of Hector the Sailor', has knife-fights, pursuits, coincidences and a kidnapping. The main character is captured by two hoodlums and strung up in an elaborate manner which, although apparently perilous, affords him the opportunity to escape. Similarly, 'Spùinneadairean Shìne' ('Pirates of China'), has a kidnapping and lucky escape. This fifteen-page story also features piracy, shipwreck, characters hiding in caves, and action-packed escapes with fights and pursuits. Another of the stories in *Seanchaidh na h-Airigh*, 'Eilean Dideil' ('The Island of Dideil'), has a good deal in common with these two. Dideil is the name of a fictitious island, although it is perhaps intended to echo the Gaelic name of Easdale, an Argyll island near Mull, from where MacCormaic's peers, the Whyte brothers, originated. In 'Eilean Dideil', a Frenchman visits the small Argyll island and befriends the natives. For much of the story, the narrative plays it for laughs, by making fun of the Frenchman's semi-fluent Gaelic. Near the end of the story, however, things attempt to become more serious, when the Frenchman reveals his reason for visiting: he has come to the island to show the natives where they can find a pirate hoard that was buried when he was a child living on board a pirate ship. He wants the islanders to benefit from his guilty knowledge, which he can finally reveal now that he is about to die. Like 'Driodfhortan Eachainn Sheòladair' and 'Spùinneadairean Shìne', 'Eilean Dideil' has many sure touches, particularly in descriptive passages, but is let down by the careless plotting and shallow characterisation.

Shallow characterisation besets much of MacCormaic's writing: he tended to rely on archetypes, in which he may well have been influenced by his knowledge of the traditional folk tales from the oral culture. Thus, the main characters in ''S Leam Fhèin an Gleann' ('The Glen is My Own') and 'Oighre 'n Dùin-bhàin' ('The Heir of the White Fort'), both in *Oiteagan O 'N Iar*, are almost indistinguishable from one another, which is exacerbated by the fact that the plots are also rather similar. ''S leam Fhèin an Gleann', is the title of a pipe tune which is central to the plot in the eponymous story. The main character is a piper, who uses the tune as a signal to let his sweetheart know he wants to meet her. Unfortunately, the laird hears the tune and banishes the piper (as a result of various kinds of jealousy). Years pass, the young man makes his fortune and finds himself in a position to buy the glen himself. He returns just in time to stop his beloved from marrying another man. In 'Oighre 'n Dùin-bhàin', piping is again central to the plot, and again an insult is implied by the piping. This time, the main character, Murchadh, believes he has been insulted by a piper, so he strikes the piper. Fearing he has killed the piper, Murchadh flees the country. Many years pass, during which Murchadh has many adventures and travels to the other side of the world. In Australia, he meets a fellow Gael. When this man plays a pipe tune for him, Murchadh realises that this is the piper he thought he had killed. They are glad to be reunited, and Murchadh realises he can go home to his beautiful sweetheart (who, even after his twenty-year absence, is presumably still waiting for him, Penelope-like).

A more serious attempt at story-making in Oiteagan O 'N Iar is 'Troimh Chruadal' ('Through Hardship'), a:

> story of the heroic feats of a young man, Calum, sent as a messenger
> from Mull to Inveraray on behalf of the laird. Calum has to battle
> through terrible weather and conditions. On his way, Calum meets
> various Mull people and thinks he sees a ghost. The story includes
> MacCormick's much-favoured shipwreck motif, as well as buried
> treasure, a deathbed reunion and a series of unlikely coincidences.
> The bulk of the story, though, tracks Calum's difficult journey, as he
> chooses to take perilous short-cuts through the icy glens to save his
> landlord's possessions. (Watson 2008: 580)

There are several weaknesses in the story, but descriptive passages are particularly successful, and the young man, Calum, who bears the burden of the message is one of MacCormaic's better-drawn characters. 'Troimh Chruadal' gives every impression of being influenced by Stevenson's *Kidnapped*, although it may be that it is simply one of the genre of tales inspired by that novel.

The characterisation, structure and narrative style of 'Troimh Chruadal' mark it as what we would recognise as a 'short story', using that term in a more technical sense (while recognising the unanswered questions that pertain to such a usage: see May 1994, throughout). In contrast, there are other kinds of stories in *Oiteagan O 'N Iar*. 'Am Togail nan Creach' is largely distinguished by its long description of the Argyll islands and the setting in Mull. It then turns into an adventure yarn which lacks any real suspense, but which owes a good deal to the oral tales MacCormaic would have heard in his youth. It has a good deal in common with some of the writing of MacCormaic's contemporary and fellow Mull native Iain MacPhàidein (1850–1935). Like MacPhàidein, MacCormaic sometimes tended towards an edenic myth vision of Mull (although 'Troimh Chruadal' shows up the bleak and dangerous side of the island). In particular, he often depicted the people of the island as paragons of various kinds of virtues. 'Troimh Chruadal''s Calum is a young man of both fortitude and honour, for instance. Similarly, another Calum, the hero of 'Calum an Oir' ('Calum of the Gold') in the same book, is portrayed as a good man who is badly treated by his peers until he runs into a fellow Gael, who treats him kindly and punishes the non-Gaels who have abused him.

Seanchaidh na h-Airigh and *Seanchaidh na Tràghad* are similar in many ways to *Oiteagan O 'N Iar*. A motif that takes on additional significance in both of the '*seanchaidh*' books is the sea. While *Oiteagan O 'N Iar* is based mainly in the Argyll island group, with occasional maritime forays elsewhere, the other two books focus much more closely on seafaring adventures and on those influences that come to the islands from the sea. From *Seanchaidh na h-Airigh*, 'Spùinneadairean Shìne' and 'Eilean Dìdeil' have already been mentioned. The story that ends the book is 'Bathadh nan Iasgairean' ('The Drowning of the Fishermen'). 'Bathadh nan Iasgairean' is unusually short and is also unusual in its structure and narrative focus. The story describes the loss of a fishing fleet within sight of home. The grief of the families who witness the deaths of their loved ones – and all possible livelihood at the same time – is the main emotional centre of the story. The description is convincing and evocative and brings to mind Dòmhnall Mac na Ceàrdaich's 'Lughain Lir', discussed later in this chapter. The sea in 'Bathadh nan Iasgairean' is a dangerous and unpredictable force, but one that co-exists with the islanders. In 'Am Briuthas Beag' ('The Little Brewery') and 'B' iad sud na Laithean Sunndach' ('Those Were the Days') from *Seanchaidh na Tràghad*, the sea is the thoroughfare for the authorities; it is the conduit that links the island with the Empire, and the means by which imperial order is imposed on the local culture. Both stories take a negative view of the excise and the regulations governing the manufacture and sale of whisky. In 'Am Briuthas Beag', the people of a small village trick the excise men when they are caught distilling and smuggling whisky. In 'B' iad sud na Laithean Sunndach', the excise are again tricked. This story is slightly more complex, in that it employs the frame-tale structure that was a staple of many of the Gaelic writers of this period. The plot is also more complex, with nautical pursuits and journeys to America and Glasgow taking the action away from Mull. When the main character finally returns to Mull, he finds that things on the island have changed for the worse, and we see that this deterioration is attributable to the increased influence of Britain and British ways of life, supplanting the traditional Gaelic ways.

MacCormaic's collections seem to represent a movement towards the short story and away from the yarns that were popular in the ceilidh-book 'readings' up to the early years of the twentieth century. Donald John MacLeod describes MacCormaic's writing as 'usually dependable if uninspired' (MacLeod 1977: 212), and it would be difficult to argue with that indictment. MacCormaic had many of the skills necessary for writing short stories, but usually failed to apply them with the balance and consistency to produce convincing stories. Where this could be overlooked in a story spanning ten or twenty pages, it is a terminal failing in the more extended fiction and explains the weaknesses in both *Gun D' Thug I Spéis Do 'n Àrmunn* (discussed later in this chapter) and *Dùn-àluinn*.

Another native of Mull, Iain MacPhàidein serves as an interesting contrast with MacCormaic. Like MacCormaic, MacPhàidein was relatively prolific and was regarded as a successful writer in his day. Indeed, MacLeod has described him as the 'most popular of those writers who addressed themselves' to the new market demanding ceilidh 'readings' and entertainments (1977: 209). MacPhàidein produced *Sgeulaiche nan Caol: original Gaelic readings, sketches, poems and songs*, published by Archibald Sinclair of Glasgow in 1902. From the dedication page onwards, the tone of MacPhàidein's book is rather different from MacCormaic's writing, especially the anti-establishment sentiments of *Seanchaidh na h-Airigh*. MacPhàidein dedicates *Sgeulaiche nan Caol* ('The Storyteller of the Narrows') to:

> Colonel Sir Fitzroy MacLean, Bart., of Duart, Morvern, and Brolas, C.B., Chief of the Clan MacLean, as a Token of the Author's Respect and Esteem.

It is evident in much of MacCormaic's writing that he was at best suspicious of the clan chiefs, laying at their door the blame for much of the hardship suffered by Gaels in the nineteenth century. *Sgeulaiche nan Caol's* dedication, in contrast, not only praises one of these very clan chiefs, but also celebrates the Britishness of his identity. MacPhàidein records Fitzroy MacLean's honours as part of the British Empire and collocates all of this with his role as a clan chief, as if that is an imperial, military position.

'Cia mar a chumar a' Ghàidhlig beò?' ('How may Gaelic be kept alive?'), which opens *Sgeulaiche nan Caol*, follows the manner of the 'conversations' discussed earlier, although it is not set out as such. In fact, it is set out as if a story, but quickly develops into dialogue only. There is an introductory passage, in which the author/narrator explains that the Lowlander often thinks all Gaels agree about everything, and so, to illustrate that this is not true, he presents a conversation he claims he has heard between two Gaels. From this point onwards, the story consists of conversation only, albeit still set out with speech marks, as if part of a story; each turn runs into the next, laid out as if narrative. The one character teases the other that the Gael has no idea how to keep Gaelic alive. The other character responds by pontificating at some length about a number of obvious measures that could be taken to help the language. The dialogue is stilted and unconvincing throughout, to the extent that the reader is never likely to accept either of the interlocutors as characters: they serve as a dialectic that allows MacPhàidein to vent his polemic about the inaction of his fellow Gaels.

Dòmhnall Mac na Ceàrdaich (Donald Sinclair, 1885–1932) of Barra was known as a poet and dramatist, but also wrote occasional short stories. His 'Lughain Lir' was considered by Donald John MacLeod to be one of the few jewels in the fiction of the early twentieth century. MacLeod wrote that 'little of lasting literary merit' was produced in the short story at the time, but singled out 'Lughain Lir' as an exception to this (1977: 213). 'Lughain Lir' appeared in the short-lived periodical *An Ròsarnach* in 1921. As MacLeod has stated, it is 'a slow-paced, sensitive account, shot through with religious symbolism, of an old Highland fisherman and his relationship with his godchild' (1977: 213). Equally importantly, the story gives a fictionalised, but convincing insight into the lives of a fishing family at around the end of the nineteenth century. Mac na Ceàrdaich's own father was a fisherman and he spent some time fishing himself before moving to Edinburgh as a young man. This first-hand experience gives credence to his accounts of the family who await news of the fishermen and also of the men themselves and their relationship with both the boat and the sea. The descriptions are full and natural, and the narrative and dialogue articulate with one another more seamlessly than in most other fiction of the period.

The story is based in Barra, although the boat ranges far afield in its search for herring. At one stage in the story, they are sailing around the small isles of Rum and Canna. The boats sail out of Port-nan-Leachd, some time after St Andrew's Day, which means that it is late in the year, a time for storms and bad weather at sea. The main character is one Dòmhnull Mac Eòin, known as 'An t-Eun', who is 72 at the time the story takes place. He has taken responsibility for Calum Bàn, the young son of a widow, and the two of them are shown at the beginning of the story to be inseparable. An t-Eun's wife, Catriona Bheag, and daughter, Mórag, have to wait for the men while they are away, not knowing whether they will return alive, or, if they do, whether or not they will bring a catch with them. The other important character is Eachann Mhicheil, An t-Eun's son-in-law.

There is one further 'character' in the story: An t-Eun's boat, 'An Oigh' ('The Maiden'), is consistently anthropomorphised throughout. Clearly, this begins with the name of the vessel itself, which is undoubtedly a reference to the Virgin Mary. From her first mention, 'An Oigh' is seen by An t-Eun as having human characteristics, although it is worth noting that the other fishermen's boats are also anthropomorphised at times:

> Am broilleach a' bhannail sgothan ud bha 'An Oigh' gu sèamh 'na cadal, is tonnagan beaga a' chaoil a' maoth-leumna ri a broilleach geal mar gum b'ann ag iarraidh a pòige. (51–2)

(In the midst of thon crowd of skiffs 'The Maiden' was sleeping peacefully, with the little ducks of the kyle softly jumping to her white bossom as if seeking her kiss) (Note that the word *bannal* often means a 'crowd of women'.)

Playing on the maidenly connotations of the name rather than the Virgin Mary associations later on in the story, we see the boat springing into action as the men go to find the herring:

Mar mhaighdinn mhaisich air a h-imeachd ri maduinn ghréin á seòmar a sgeadachaidh bha 'An Oigh' 'na h-uidheam agus i mar gu'm b'eadh a' feitheamh ri tighinn fear na bainnse. (59–60)

(Like a beautiful maiden that has gone into a sunny morning out of her dressing room, 'The Maiden' was dressed up as through awaiting the bridegroom.)

It is not just 'An Oigh' and the other boats that are personified, either: Mac na Ceàrdaich uses the device of pathetic fallacy in relation to both the sea and the elements throughout the story.

The opening sequence is more evidently fictional than that of most of 'Lughain Lir''s contemporaries. A brooding atmosphere is immediately established, and this endures throughout the thirty-three pages of text. Terms like 'gart seang', 'néul ciar' and 'gàirdeanan loma cnuadach' (51) all add to the ambience, while at the same time acting as both synecdoche and metonymy for the character of An t-Eun himself. The reader knows, without being told, that the sentient centre of the story is an old man, who is tough and wiry, both physically and mentally. Within the first paragraph, the reader also has a sense of both time and place, and all of it situated in the context of action. The overall impression is of engaging narrative, building layer upon layer of knowledge about the story; this is in sharp contrast with the typical style of the time, which is to state characteristics, descriptions, and events as facts, usually in sequential or chronological order. From the first page, therefore, it is easy to see why MacLeod was drawn to this story in particular. The character of An t-Eun is particularly well-drawn, with Mac na Ceàrdaich perhaps using his memories of his own father or grandfather.

'Lughain Lir' is the only story of note to appear in *An Ròsarnach*. The magazine ran for only four issues between 1917 and 1930. Although fictional stories were rare in the magazine, there was a good deal of prose writing. In many cases, the contributions were 'historical' pieces that were evidently modelled on the fictional paradigms of the time and probably contributed to the development of the fiction as well. Several of the contributions are history or pseudo-history, but there is also some linguistic work. The ubiquitous MacCormaic's 'Bean a' Bhocsa Bhuidhe' ('The Lady of the Yellow Box') appeared in the first number in 1917. While 'Bean a' Bhocsa Bhuidhe' is clearly working towards the short story, it still labours due to clinging to some of the conventions of the traditional tale genre from which it emerges. For instance, there are nearly two pages of introduction before the story gets started, grounding the piece in the emotions associated with New Year customs and local mores. The common motifs of disguise and mistaken identity, and of racing to correct mistakes, are sandwiched between long, unnecessary tracts of dialogue.

Similarly, the second volume of *An Ròsarnach* (1918) contains several tales, but all of them are either folkloristic or anecdotal. None of them are quite what we would call fiction. 'Lughain Lir' appears in the third issue of the magazine, along with D. Mac-a-Phi's 'An Dealachadh mu Dheireadh' ('The Last Parting'). Like 'Lughain Lir', this is much more like a short story.

An Ròsarnach was one of Ruairidh Erskine of Mar's publications, and it followed his *An Sgeulaiche*, which was dedicated to fostering the production of stories. *An Sgeulaiche* ran for eleven issues, from 1909 until 1911. Although Mar might have intended to use the magazine to encourage prose writing and fiction, it also featured songs. Included among the stories were some that also appeared in other collections, such as MacCormaic's 'B' iad Sud na Laithean Sunndach' and 'Sean Chuimhneachan air a' Choire Ghlas'. Other pieces that appeared included opinion columns broadly similar to the kind that were common in *Guth na Bliadhna*: a particular concern was defining and describing Gaels and stating what they should be like. Many of the stories are in the style of the traditional tale: there are archetypal characters, episodic structures, repeated runs, groups of three people and occasional instances of magic and mysticism. Dialogue sometimes stretches for several pages without interruption and can even include stories within the story: sometimes at more than one level.

An Comunn Gaidhealach's National Mòd used to run competitions for writing both drama and stories.[8] *Uirsgeulan Gaidhealach* is a collection of four of the prize-winning stories, edited by Calum MacFarlane. It contains an unusual story by Hector MacFadyen and two stories by Katherine Whyte Grant, who was a cousin of the literary Whyte brothers, Henry ('Fionn') and John ('Iain Bàn Òg'). MacCormaic's 'Oighre 'n Dùin-bhàin', mentioned above, appears in *Uirsgeulan Gaidhealach* ('Highland Tales/ Legends', 1912), although the story's earlier publication is not acknowledged. Other books of collections, such as *Am Feachd Gaidhealach* (1944), were sometimes drawn largely from previously published work.

Katherine Whyte Grant was a poet and the author of *Aig Tigh na Beinne* (1911). In her prose writing, she relied heavily on imagery, especially similes, perhaps revealing the influence of her poetry. In general, her writing is tighter and more controlled than that of many of her contemporaries, and has much in common with Dòmhnall Mac na Ceàrdaich's 'Lughain Lir'. The two stories by Katherine Whyte Grant that are collected in *Uirsgeulan Gaidhealach* are rather similar in style to one another, although the subject matter is strikingly different. The first, which opens the book, is 'Clach na Lànain' ('The Stone of the Couple'). This story relies on a twist in the tale, which is a common device used by later writers such as Eilidh Watt, Cailin T. MacCoinnich and Dòmhnall Alasdair (all of whom are treated in Chapters 3 and 5). In Whyte Grant's case, she uses the device effectively, creating enough texture and tension within the body of the story to conceal the true significance of the foreshadowing until the end, but without leaving the reader feeling cheated. Unlike in much of the work of some of the later writers just mentioned, she also manages to avoid sentimentalising at the end: there is emotional content, but this is embedded throughout the story.

Whyte Grant's other story in the book is 'Mòrag na Làraich-mheadhoin' ('Morag of the Middle Area'), which is about the perennial Gaelic themes of exile and prodigality. Like 'Clach na Lànain', 'Mòrag na Làraich-mheadhoin' benefits from Whyte Grant's ability to build narrative layers, subtly and gradually. Description is handled particularly well in this story, painting a vivid picture of the scenes. Despite this, the style is engaging and pacy, and at times gives the impression of having been influenced by reading in English, possibly within the genre of the Brontë sisters. The dialogue is more convincing than is the norm during this period, although it still has the tendency at times to be explicatory and compliant with the narrative movement, feeling like an extension of the narrative rather than the actual speech of characters. The story features the dream of the returning exile, which underpins much of the Gaelic literary consciousness, and is part of what is called by Michelle Macleod (Macleod 1999) 'the *cianalas* code'. Many other stories in Gaelic also have characters who nurture the same dream: having gone away from the home community for many years (often to the other side of the world), they are either happy or unhappy with their lot, but they continue to retain the sense of duty, love and loyalty for what they left behind. Eventually, in many of these stories, the character returns to find that those left behind have waited for them and are overjoyed to see them coming back. This theme is also dealt with ironically in some of the post-1960 literature of what we might think of as the 'modernist' period in Gaelic fiction, and it is discussed in Chapters 3 to 6. In particular, stories of Iain Mac a' Ghobhainn and Iain Moireach with this same theme link to the fiction of this time, and could almost be said to form a dialectic with Whyte Grant's 'Mòrag na Làraich-mheadhoin'. The following line from

'Mòrag na Làraich-mheadhoin', for instance, would fit into a number of the stories of Mac a' Ghobhainn or Moireach:

> Chaidh a màthair a steach an uair a chunnaic i ban-choigreach a' deanamh air an dorus aice. (56)

(Her mother went in when she saw a stranger approaching her door)

Aside from these two pieces by Whyte Grant and the MacCormaic return-from-exile story, *Uirsgeulan Gaidhealach* also contains one of the more unusual tales from the period: Hector MacFadyen's 'Pòsadh an Dealain-dé' ('The Butterfly's Wedding'). As the title suggests, this is a fable about a butterfly, who decides he wants to marry. He sees a woman in a dream and decides he must marry this woman: this clearly links to the *aisling* (vision) motif in earlier Gaelic literature, but without being an overt attempt to forge a link. The butterfly eventually meets a swan, who tells him (again in a dream) that she will sleep for seven weeks[9] and gain the knowledge of three worlds[10] and give him three signs to help him find his dream woman. The butterfly meanwhile passes the time by teasing a rainbow because it is not as colourful as the butterfly. The butterfly then sees two suns and two moons and:

> Bha gàrradh de chraobhan mu'n cuairt an tighe, is ùbhlan òir a' fàs orra. (63)

(There was a wall of trees around the house, with golden apples growing on them.)

[. . .]

> Bha uinneagan a' bhothain mar sgàthan. (63)

(The windows of the hut were like a mirror.)

All of these kinds of images, and the way dreams and reality keep fading into one another, make this a very unusual story for the period. Indeed, in Gaelic fiction in general, fables are rare, so it is worthy of note to find a story featuring a butterfly and swan as its main characters at this stage in the development of the fiction.

Gun D' Thug I Spéis Do 'n Àrmunn ('She Gave Her Love to the Soldier') is a single, continuous piece of extended fiction. It marketed itself as 'a novelette, the first of its kind in Gaelic', but we might describe it as a novella today. Published by Aonghas MacAoidh of Stirling in 1908, *Gun D' Thug I Spéis Do 'n Àrmunn* presages the short-lived burst of novel-writing activity that took place over the following fifteen years. The title is a slight alteration of the first line of a song, and the book's marketing translates it as 'She gave her love to a soldier'. Although there are 117 pages in the book, the number of words per page is rather small, and the total word count may be estimated at around 14,000, which makes it slightly smaller than Iain Mac a' Ghobhainn's *An t-Aonaran* (1976). Nevertheless, *Gun D' Thug I Spéis Do 'n Àrmunn* must be considered a linguistic achievement, blazing the trail for the other, longer works which soon followed.

In common with many of the short stories of this period, *Gun D' Thug I Spéis Do 'n Àrmunn* is a frame-tale. The book begins with a prologue, which sets the scene with all the family sitting down together at Christmas to hear a story. The story itself is then divided into eleven sections, which are, essentially, chapters. The main plot is based during the Napoleonic wars, switching between Mull and the front in Belgium. The twists in the tale rely on mistaken identity and on there being three significant characters in the book all called Iain. The first of these, and the 'hero' of the novella, is one Iain Bàn na Saor-pheighinn from Mull, who has been on leave from the war. As the book begins, the war is beginning to intensify again, and Iain is recalled to the front. Although reluctant to leave his sweetheart Màiri, daughter of the local shepherd, he bids her farewell and heads back to rejoin the Army. They promise to wait for each other. There follows an extended pathetic fallacy that in many ways resembles the section in *Dùn-àluinn* when Cailean's mother dies (see Chapter 2): not only is Iain reluctant to leave his darling and his island to return to the war, but the land itself is also unhappy because Iain and the cream of the island's youth are going off to war, some of them never to return. This is one of the most effective passages in the novella, and again underlines the fact that MacCormaic is at his best when writing descriptive passages. The second chapter focuses on a gathering at the local *cèilidh*-house, where the people who were left behind assemble to lament the loss of their young men. There is a certain amount of self-reflexivity here, with the layers of fictionality blending into one another (for instance, we hear frame-tales within the frame-tale, and we hear legends reported as fact and clairvoyance mix with ghost stories and genuine worry).

A second character to share the key name in the story is Iain Taibhsear, although his possession of the name is not integral to the plot, unlike with the three others. He and another minor character both have clairvoyant visions which are crucial plot devices as they motivate other characters' decisions and cause the dramatic tension at the heart of the novella: both visions involve mistaken identity, or at least their interpretation does. The following chapter cuts to the muster of the armies in Belgium, and there is an extended description of the cameraderie of the Gaels from different parts of the Highlands and Islands who meet one another there and share news. At this point, Iain Bàn and Màiri are discussed, and the second case of mistaken identity occurs here, when some of the men are convinced that Iain is already married. This wrong understanding makes its way back to Mull, where Màiri gets to hear of it. Although she dismisses this news at first, it evidently plays on her mind; so, when she later believes Iain Bàn has been killed (a third case of mistaken identity), she eventually gives up on him and marries yet another Iain, Iain nan Tòrr. Some time after this, a wounded soldier named Iain returns to Mull and is reunited with his wife and child, and it now becomes clear that he was the one the rumours spoke of and not Iain Bàn. Iain nan Tòrr dies not long after this, leaving Màiri a rich widow and, against all hope, Iain Bàn comes home, limping from old wounds but delighted to see his sweetheart. Throughout the book, Màiri has been compared to Penelope, and it is evident that the Odysseus myth was one of MacCormaic's inspirations for the plot of *Gun D' Thug I Spéis Do 'n Àrmunn*.

As is perhaps clear from this brief description, *Gun D' Thug I Spéis Do 'n Àrmunn* is full of weaknesses. Many of these are derived simply from the attempt to extend the story over a larger number of pages than was conventional at the time. The main plot is much the same as many of MacCormaic's other stories, albeit that the Napoleonic War strand is unusual. Given that there is no more substance to the main plot than in many of his much shorter works, MacCormaic needed to do something else with *Gun D' Thug I Spéis Do 'n Àrmunn*. Instead of seeing this as an opportunity to work on characterisation, he simply added confusing and poorly-executed secondary plots. To some extent, he attempted to fix these problems in his novel, *Dùn-àluinn*, but he was not always successful, as is discussed in the next chapter.

Conclusion

It is clear then that the Gaelic prose fiction that emerged in the twentieth century grew from both organic and synthetic root systems. There was a long history of the making and transmission of imaginative stories, that can be traced back many centuries. Gaelic has an ancient store of both oral and written tales, and they exhibit a rich range of subject matters, plot lines and character types. The advent of the printing press did not initially result in inspiring the creation of novels and magazines. However, following the establishment of numerous periodicals in the nineteenth century – in many cases, motivated by religious zeal – a modern prose writing style gradually began to develop. At first, the fictional writing was didactic or allegorical, another vehicle for ministerial sermons. In time, writing began to move towards a modern fiction. By the end of the nineteenth century, the new audience for 'readings' popularised imaginative writing in the language. It may be that this would have led to writers trying their hand at short stories and novels regardless of any sociolinguistic pressures. However, enthusiastic individuals like Ruairidh Erskine and large groups like An Comunn Gaidhealach made deliberate efforts to foster an environment in which Gaelic prose fiction could germinate. Their efforts were partly rewarded in that a number of writers did begin producing fiction. However, the work that was published in the first half of the twentieth century was generally weak and error-strewn. It was only in the second half of the century that fiction truly began to come into its own.

Chapter 2

The Early Novels

The periodicals mentioned in the previous chapter provided a forum for writers to experiment with various kinds of prose forms and try their hand at fiction. The publication of several books incorporating 'readings', short stories, conversations, playlets and yarns, as discussed in Chapter 1, is further evidence of a burgeoning enthusiasm for fiction in the early part of the twentieth century. Perhaps the strongest sign that authors and publishers wished to develop the literature, though, came in the form of the novels. Novels require a tremendous amount of commitment, from all concerned: the author must spend weeks, months or even longer writing and editing them; the publisher must commit significant resources, and risk financial loss; and the reader must part with a substantial amount of cash for a luxury item and then dedicate many hours to consuming that item. As Donald John MacLeod rightly puts it, the emergence of the novel in Gaelic is 'of some historical interest' (MacLeod 1977: 213), and it would be worthwhile examining that historical interest in further detail elsewhere. Work by Donald Meek (2003, 2007b, 2007c), Sheila Kidd (2000, 2002) and others has already begun to prepare the ground for allowing us to understand the social and literary dynamics that were in place at the early part of this developmental and, clearly, transitional period (see also Macleod 2010). It may be that further work will succeed in giving us a fuller picture of how and why writing and publishing were going on at the time, as well as who was reading the literature and what they thought of it. It may be that there are obvious reasons for the steady increase in publication and the rapid expansion of genre development in the period: the changing demographic reality of the Gaelic speech community, for instance, is one reason that has been suggested (Watson 2007, 2008). Another is the increase in access to literature in English and Scots brought about by the imposition of English-medium education (Kidd 2006). Similarly, the effects of the two world wars and the resultant loss of population in the Gaelic-speaking areas would suggest themselves as obvious reasons for the subsequent reduction in publication of fiction. And yet, it may be that we should look deeper and refuse to accept these obvious solutions. After all, it is a long-held view that times of crisis – especially wars – tend to inspire, enrich and embolden literary efforts. As if to confirm this view, with the First World War looming, several books of short stories, the first novelette and the first two full-length novels all appeared. Then, in the inter-war years, stories continued to appear in periodicals like *Guth na Bliadhna* and *An Ròsarnach*, and a further novel was published. The third and final 'early' novel and the demise of these two periodicals all occurred within a few years of each other, and it may be that an investigation into the factors affecting Gaelic writing in the 1920s would be of particular interest in furthering our understanding of the development of fiction in the language.

A first novel

Two novels vie for the title of the first Gaelic novel, but Iain MacCormaic's *Dùn-àluinn: no an t-Oighre 'na Dhìobarach* (1912) is usually recorded as the first (see Kidd 2006: 202, for a discussion of the rivalries and tensions prevalent at the time, and the underlying hint of competition between MacCormaic and MacDhonnachaidh). Aonghas MacDhonnachaidh's *An t-Ogha Mór: no Am Fear-Sgeòil air Uilinn* (1913) was earlier published in serial form (as was *Dùn-àluinn*), but, at any rate, *Dùn-àluinn* was published in bound form in 1912 by Alexander Gardner of Paisley. Alexander Gardner and the publisher of *An t-Ogha Mór*, Alasdair MacLaren and Sons of Glasgow, were very active producers of Gaelic books at the beginning of the twentieth century (see MacLeod 1977 and MacDonald 2007 for further discussion of the relatively healthy position of Gaelic publishing at the time, and for some hints as to the publishers' relationship with the language and its literature).

Iain MacCormaic's stories were discussed in some detail above in Chapter 1, but it would be fair to say that his most significant contribution to Gaelic fiction – and perhaps Gaelic writing in general – was the novel, *Dùn-àluinn*.[1] *Dùn-àluinn* is not a particularly long book: although there are 267 pages in the 1912 edition, the number of words per page is small, and I have estimated that the total word count for the book is somewhere in the region of 52,000. By nineteenth-century standards, we might almost call that a novella. In any case, it was a first: as Sheila Kidd has put it, the 'forgotten first' (Kidd 2006). Although *Dùn-àluinn* has always been acknowledged as an innovation, it has not attracted a good deal of positive criticism. Prior to Kidd's article, a review by Ronald Black, and an article of my own, the novel was largely either ignored as a literary artefact or else dismissed in unflattering terms. Donald John MacLeod described it as 'a rather anaemic adventure yarn' (MacLeod 1977: 212), and made it clear he felt MacCormaic over-reached the limits of his talents with the book. Similarly, in his

Companion to Gaelic Scotland (1994), Derick Thomson dismissed the novel with the following passage:

> *Dùn-àluinn* is a mixture of sentimentality, tub-thumping and the kind of anecdotage-with-repartee that is popular with Gaelic audiences. The hero, Dùn-àluinn, is the liberal-minded heir to a profligate and oppressive landlord, and the Ministear Mór . . . delivers some rousing diatribes against such oppression, leading to a riot. The plot has a love theme, some murders and scenes in New Zealand goldmines, and coincidences move the plot to its dénouement. (218)

Black's review, however – which was written when a facsimile print of the novel became available in 2003 – was considerably warmer in its praise. In his role as the Gaelic editor for the *Scotsman* newspaper, Black wrote that we are greatly obliged to Llanerch and Clò Charraig for reprinting the book. He also wrote (in Gaelic), 'I am pleased to tell you that *Dùn-àluinn* is good – but it is not as good as the two new books'. The two new books he refers to here are *An Oidhche Mus Do Sheòl Sinn* by Aonghas Pàdraig Caimbeul and *Ath-aithne* by Màrtainn Mac an t-Saoir, both of which are discussed in Chapter 6. Black does admit that the plot would not hold up to scrutiny, and he also admits that the characters are rather one-dimensional, but he insists it is well worth reading, nevertheless.

The novel takes place some time in the nineteenth century. Watson (2008) and Kidd (2006) both discuss the timeframe and the geographical setting and come to similar conclusions. The New Zealand gold rush and the Highland evictions known as the Clearances both point to a mid-century setting. Kidd's useful identification of the Duke of Argyll's factor, John Campbell, as a likely influence on the plot and characterisation, adds weight to this (2006: 206–7). Much of the action takes place on a fictional estate in Argyll, which Kidd has persuasively suggested is probably meant to be in Mull (2006: 206), but MacCormaic's much-favoured device of sending his characters in exile to the other side of the world also appears here (see Chapter 1). The main characters are Cailean Mór of Dùn-àluinn, the landlord of the estate that provides the background; his son, Cailean Òg; Mariette Wolfe, a Frenchwoman who eventually marries Cailean Mór, after the death of his first wife; am Ministear Mór, initially a local minister and then a vagrant; and Perkins, who turns out to be the henchman to Wolfe, who is the villain of the piece.

The novel opens with Cailean Òg's mother dying after warning him to be careful of his self-interested father. Although Cailean Òg dismisses this initially, the warning is later shown to be a good one. With his wife dead, Cailean Mór returns to his womanising ways and soon marries Mariette Wolfe. Wolfe's machinations quickly become clear, when she engineers a quarrel between the landlord and his son and effects Cailean Òg's exile from the estate. Cailean Òg travels, eventually, to New Zealand, where he makes his fortune prospecting for gold. He encounters an unsavoury character, Perkins. Meanwhile, Cailean Mór's policy of clearing people from the land has almost sparked a riot, inflamed by the Ministear Mór's polemic. Cailean Mór dies, apparently in a freak accident (but we are probably supposed to assume he has been murdered), and Cailean Òg returns just in time to prevent Mariette Wolfe taking possession of the estate.

It is evident that the plot suffers somewhat from its initial partly-serialised format and also from MacCormaic's inability to resist his penchant for far-fetched adventure yarns. As a result, the effect is a fragmentary and confused structure, where narrative lines are begun and then abandoned and the significance of events or even characters is, at times, randomly developed. Thus, as Kidd has noted (2006: 206) the Cailean Òg plot as outlined above is almost a carbon copy of some of MacCormaic's other stories, as discussed in Chapter 1, such as ''S Leam Fhìn an Gleann' and 'Oighre an Dùin-bhàin'. However, the Ministear Mór plot and the introduction of a pair of actual villains take the story in a number of different directions at once, and most of them are not complementary. An example of this is the treatment of Cailean Òg's sister, Mór Bheag. When the novel opens and Cailean's mother is cautioning him to be wary of his father, she entreats him to look after his young sister. He duly responds that he will do so. Contrary to this, he very quickly loses track of where his sister is, or even whether she is still alive. In the end, he only finds her again by accident and by the help of a remarkable coincidence: there is no indication that he would have spent any significant efforts on looking for her. A similar coincidence sees Perkins making appearances in Cailean's life both in Argyll and in New Zealand, which gives Cailean the lucky advantage he needs to resolve matters in the end. In another fragment only barely related to the plot, a group of men live in a cave on the estate and meet there regularly to discuss matters. They may be considered to be fulfilling the role of Shakespearean clowns or a Greek chorus, as their main functions are twofold: to facilitate the narrative movement while the action is taking place off-stage; and to provide the moments of levity and humour that are otherwise impossible because of the lack of depth in characterisation and the lack of texture in the main plotlines. The final episode in the novel sees one of these men, Bodach-nan-Duilleag, claim his substantial birthright thanks to the Ministear Mór and Cailean Òg, but this episode has no bearing on the plot itself and appears almost as a weak short story interpolated into the end section of the novel to allow for all of the characters to have happy endings.

As well as the structural weaknesses in the plot (of which there are many more than the few mentioned above), there are problems in the ways in which the plot is developed. The most obvious and ubiquitous of these is in the contrived ways that characters interact with, and react to, one another. For instance, Mariette Wolfe's manipulation of Cailean Òg relies entirely on a compliant narrator and a reader's willingness to suspend disbelief. Similarly, the way Cailean Òg treats Perkins when he is found to be swindling the other prospectors is a device that allows for his escape so that Perkins can be present for the eventual 'reveal' back at the Dùn-àluinn estate. Indeed, Perkins's swindling is itself a poorly conceived plot point, as it quickly becomes clear even to the hopeful prospectors that he has deceived them; but, at the same time, he has no apparent means of profiting from the escapade or even of escaping with his life. Finally, characters comply with the narrative's requirement for them not to recognise each other when in disguise or even simply when fulfilling unfamiliar roles (*cf.* Buchan's Peter Pienaar and his advice to Hannay about this in *The 39 Steps*).

The most evident and egregious flaw in *Dùn-àluinn* is one that it shares with much of the early fiction discussed in Chapter 1 and including the other two novels of the period: the lack of substance or development in characters. In some ways, Cailean Òg's mother is potentially one of the most interesting characters in the whole novel, and yet we learn next to nothing about her. Her death at the end of the opening sequence (she expires after a long narrative digression at the end of the second chapter) effectively marks her exit from the novel. Her influence continues briefly, in that the other characters debate the fate of Mór Bheag, Cailean's young sister, and we also learn that she approved of Cailean's sweetheart Màiri. But, aside from that and a brief mention or two, the mother character disappears almost before the novel has started. This is unfortunate, as she shows signs of being insightful and engaging in her only scene. Her death and those few character details that are recorded are marred by typical MacCormaic hyperbole, although there are aspects of the death that are clearly intended to link to the folklore and literature with which the audience would have been familiar.

Of the three villains, Cailean Mór and Wolfe (almost always referred to as 'the Frenchwoman') get to spend comparatively little time on the page. Their main period of narrative focus comes immediately before and immediately after the Ministear Mór launches his verbal attack on Cailean Mór and the other landlords for their policy of evicting people for economic gain (a scene which compares interestingly with Fionn McColla's *And the Cock Crew* (1945), most especially with regard to the depiction of the minister characters in the two novels). When the narrative comes from Cailean Mór's perspective, he is shown in a very bad light. He is cowardly, mean-spirited and greedy. Just as 'good' characters, such as his first wife, are described in idealised terms, so the 'bad' characters are portrayed as thoroughly despicable (although Cailean Mór appears to achieve a partial, and confusingly temporary, redemption as a result of his wife's death). Cailean Mór is shown to be capable of anger, when he considers a physical attack on the Ministear Mór, but his fear overcomes him. Throughout Chapters 11, 12 and 13, fear, embarrassment, shame, and anger compete for prominence in Cailean Mór's psyche. However, in Chapter 13, his native arrogance and self-satisfaction reassert themselves. This is one of the key moments in the novel and, as with the Ministear Mór's speech (and clearly linked to that), there is a strong sense of an authorial viewpoint underlying Cailean Mór's assertion of his landlordly rights. Mariette Wolfe tries to goad Cailean Mór into taking horrible revenge on the people for rising up against him. Cailean Mór prefers to think the matter through for himself, however, and we are told about some interesting body language, which is only marred by MacCormaic explaining what it means. At this point, Cailean Mór proclaims:

> 'Gabh gu réidh e, a ghaoil. Gheibh sinn rathad; ach cha 'n e sin e. Cha 'n 'eil thusa tuigsinn nàdur a' Ghaidheil. Seall an loch mór ud shìos. Tha cheart cho math dhuit feuchainn ri muir-làn bras an reothairt làidir a chumail air ais le slataig chaoil. Tha cho math dhuit feuchainn ris an loch a thaomadh le slige maorach 's a bhi feuchainn ris a h-uile làn slige thilgeadh thar nam beann gorma ud thall an aghaidh sgairt-ghaoith tuath, is feuchainn ris a' Ghaidheal a chumail fodha no cheannsachadh nuair thogar e.' (DA 129)

> (Take it easy, love. We will find a way; but that isn't it. You don't understand the nature of the Gael. See that big loch down there.
> You would be as well trying to hold back the spring high-tide with a narrow wand. You would be as well trying to decant the loch with a seashell and trying to throw the shell-full over yonder blue mountains against a strong north wind, as trying to keep the Gael under or control him against his will.)

The next two pages continue in similar vein, and it is clear from the tenor of the Ministear Mór's earlier speech, and from many similar sentiments in other stories, that these are largely MacCormaic's own views coming to the fore here. Some of the confusions in the plotting and characterisation, indeed, are caused by the tension between these underlying views and the realities of history. For instance, the narrator takes great pains to explain how Cailean Mór is both a villain and a Gael, but that he is, therefore, an exception and that the 'great tree' of his ancestry sprouted just the one 'rotten branch'. But, even in the novel itself, there is an awareness that Cailean Mór is a synecdoche for his entire social stratum, and that the landlords have abandoned their ancestral roles as clan chiefs. Sheila Kidd discusses this and notes that Cailean Mór is designated throughout the novel as '*uachdaran* rather than *ceann-feadhna*' (2006: 209): that is to say, he is referred to as a 'landlord' rather than as a 'clan chief'. A deft touch in the passage currently being discussed reminds us that Cailean Mór is wearing a kilt, as is his usual custom. He clearly still thinks of himself as both landlord and clan chief, and his further ruminations serve to emphasise this point. He goes on to explain to Wolfe that the only way to control the Gael is by manipulation, by appealing to the emotions, and that only a Gael truly knows how to achieve this. He says:

> 'Tuigidh bean, bean eile, agus tuigidh Gaidheal Gaidheal. Tha iad dìleas d' an cinn-feadhna; 's a dh'aindeoin mar shàraichteadh iad, tha meas aca air euchdan nan sonn o 'n d' thàinig mise' (DA 130–1)

> (A woman understands a woman, and a Gael understands a Gael. They are loyal to their clan chiefs; and no matter how they might be vexed, they respect the feats of those heroes from whom I have come)

Thus, although the narrative does not refer to Cailean Mór as *ceann-feadhna*, he has no hesitation in using the term of himself. This points towards an awareness of what I have elsewhere described as the cultural hybridisation of the Gaelic milieu (Watson 2007 etc., after Bhabha 1990 and 1994). That is, the Gaelic 'nation' was subsumed first by the Scottish state and then by the British Empire. Having become part of the Empire, it took on (and, often, adapted) many of the cultural affectations of Britain and of an imperial power, while retaining some of its own. Some of these ideas were hinted at in Chapter 1, particularly in relation to MacCormaic's shorter stories, and the writings of Iain MacPhàidein and both John and Henry Whyte, but this novel and this character in particular encapsulate the issue most illustratively. In *Dùn-àluinn*, Cailean Mór is a metonym for the process of cultural hybridisation, but he fails to see it: as far as he is concerned, he is the greatest man of his clan; meanwhile, the narrator portrays him as an aberration, too fond of the luxuries associated with London and its Empire. There is a tension within the narrative, however, as the author struggles to excuse Cailean Mór's excesses and his disloyalty to his people; as Kidd has noted, his character flaws are attributed to his being orphaned young (2006: 209). This, however, does not excuse his fellow landlords, and it is clear that they, too, are implicated during the long sequence in which the Ministear Mór debates the land issues with Cailean Mór and his own tame minister: several times, the landlords and their factors are described in unflattering terms, generally compared with little dogs. MacCormaic thus shows that the matter of blame in the Clearances is not clear-cut: in

Dùn-àluinn, Gaels turn on other Gaels, ministers turn on other ministers, and the influences of foreigners can be both positive and negative (the most wicked villains are the Frenchwoman and her English/Lowlander henchman, while Cailean Mór's great ally is an Englishman, and his sister is saved by Londoners).

Mariette Wolfe is rather less complex than Cailean Mór. She is venal and corrupt, but neither the narrative nor her own internal viewpoint offer any explanations or motivations for her actions other than greed and blind ambition. She makes it clear that she wants possession of the estate, and intends that her own son will inherit it rather than Cailean Òg, but this is as much as we learn about her designs. Other than that, we know she is manipulative and ruthless: she apparently attempts to murder her first husband, tricks Cailean Òg and his father into a quarrel that results in the former's exile, is delighted when she thinks he is dead, and expresses no remorse when Cailean Mór later dies in suspicious circumstances. In effect, she is lacking in any redemptive qualities as a character and therefore too bland to be of much interest: she is a trope for wickedness, and thus represents the mirror-image of Cailean Òg's mother, who is kindness personified. Her wickedness is so transparent that it is difficult for the reader to believe that other characters do not see through it: throughout the novel, indeed, both the members of the 'chorus' and Cailean's sweetheart Màiri NicGriogair keep telling people that Wolfe is evil and not to be trusted; and yet, whenever characters get into situations where Wolfe may influence them, they immediately accept her word, no matter how unlikely this seems. The most egregious example of this occurs in Chapter 8. In what is evidently an attempt at dramatic irony, Cailean Òg and Màiri discuss Wolfe, and Màiri tells him her suspicions about Wolfe. Immediately after this, Cailean Òg meets Wolfe and is charmed by her blandishments:

> 'I am in your mother's place. I will not fill her place in your heart; but who will call me evil if I make every right, dutiful effort to spare you and your sister from feeling the loss of your mother.' (84)

Far from being suspicious of her, Cailean at once thinks she is the warmest and most compassionate woman alive. He begins to consider her his best friend (within another half-page). He is thus easily led into the confrontation with his father that brings about his exile.

Earlier critics have regarded the Ministear Mór as the most interesting character in *Dùn-àluinn*, and there is good reason for this. For one thing, he is complex, in that he exhibits a range of character traits that are often in tension with one another: he is intellectual, but physically brave and intimidating, he is compassionate, but quick to anger, he is eloquent, humorous and intelligent, but self-destructive and prone to alcoholism and wastefulness. Moreover, the Ministear Mór is the one character who is not true to type: all of the other characters fit into the archetypes we find throughout the literature of the day and its antecedents (see Chapter 1). The character traits just mentioned would not be found in many ministers in the Gaelic literature of this period; further, we might more readily expect to see the minister on the side of the landlords, and Cailean Mór himself is disappointed that the Ministear Mór is his enemy. One of the most effective passages in the novel comes after their debate about the rights of the people and the duties of the landlord, when Cailean Mór says he would strike his enemy if he were not wearing a minister's coat. Hearing this, the Ministear Mór responds:

> 'My coat' said the minister, taking off his black coat and throwing
> it over the back of a chair. 'My coat! If it's my coat that's coming
> between you and me, there you are! You wait there, minister, until Big
> Donald Stewart gives Dùn-àluinn a thumping.' (112)[2]

To some extent, the Ministear Mór stands in for the absent hero figure in the novel. This is so in two ways: he replaces Cailean Òg as the narrative focus, and the champion of the people, during the long middle section when the latter is exiled in New Zealand; and, secondly, he exhibits many of the qualities and tensions that might have made Cailean Òg a more viable hero. MacCormaic makes every effort to portray Cailean Òg in heroic terms, but this is problematic, as he is so perfect as to lack credibility, and it is also difficult for the novel to achieve any real sense of narrative tension due to his boundless goodwill. In many ways, he is a parallel for Cailein T. MacCoinnich's Daibhidh MacLiuthair character in *A' Leth Eile* (1971; see Chapter 4), except that Cailean Òg does have one flaw which Daibhidh MacLiuthair lacks: naïveté. Unfortunately, if this is his only evident flaw, it is not one which succeeds in eliciting sympathy from the reader, and the result is that scenes with Cailean Òg are stilted and unconvincing. His easy acceptance of Mariette Wolfe's manipulations was discussed above. Similar to this, his misplaced compassion for Perkins allows the latter to escape capture, even though Cailean already knows Perkins is a recidivist murderer, thief and swindler who could never reform. Cailean Òg is, of course, supposed to represent the true spirit of the Gaelic chieftain. If his father, Cailean Mór, is the single 'rotten branch', Cailean Òg shows the true nature of the noble tree of his ancestry. The reality of history (which the author clearly knew), and Cailean Òg's failure to operate as a convincing character, conspire to undermine MacCormaic's efforts to redeem his apparent perception of the traditional relationship between clan chief and people.

Cailean Òg is the most extreme example of poor characterisation, given that he is the main character, but his depiction is in no way unusual: all of the characters are badly drawn in one way or another. One of the reasons why characters are not developed adequately in the novel consists in the failure of the dialogue to sound convincing. Problems in the dialogue stem from the author's repeated attempts to use conversation as a way to tell the story and avoid scenes where any action is really taking place. This is also the main reason for the existence of the odd group of vagrants who live in the cave: their conversation acts as a meta-narrative, telling parts of the story that the actual narrative avoids telling.

A second novel

Sheila Kidd's (2006) article on *Dùn-àluinn* suggests that there was a rivalry between MacCormaic and his contemporary Aonghas MacDhonnachaidh (Angus Robertson), at least in relation to their writing (201–4). As a senior figure in An Comunn Gaidhealach, and a judge at the Mòd's annual writing competitions, MacDhonnachaidh was in a position to influence the reception of MacCormaic's writing. For MacCormaic's part, he 'seems to have preferred to avoid controversy' (202) and apparently did not engage with MacDhonnachaidh's apparent hostility. However, in the matter of the authorship of the 'first' Gaelic novel, it is clear that he was not impressed when some members of the Gaelic literati hailed MacLeòid's *An t-Ogha Mór* (1913) as the first (Kidd 2006: 202).[3]

An t-Ogha Mór has a good deal in common with *Dùn-àluinn*. Both *Dùn-àluinn* and *An t-Ogha Mór* first appeared in serial form. Both are set in the past, making some efforts to latch onto historical events for contextualisation; both focus on the land-owning classes for their heroes and villains; both feature early deathbed scenes of the noble and virtuous mother figure (and in both cases these early scenes turn out to be less significant than they first appear); both take place partly in the Highlands and partly abroad; and both feature intrigue, mistaken identity and adventure.

Another feature *An t-Ogha Mór* has in common with *Dùn-àluinn* is the portrayal of Goiridh Mac Fhraing and Cailean Mór Dùn-àluinn. Goiridh Mac Fhraing is nowhere near as heartless or profligate as Cailean Mór, but he is not a sympathetic character, and Una only marries him out of a sense of duty to her brother. It is unclear whether she ever grows to love him, but she certainly does not trust him to protect her baby when she knows she is about to die. Like Cailean Mór's wife, she entrusts her baby to someone else's care. Goiridh's entrance to the deathbed scene is then highly reminiscent of that of Cailean Mór. However, in Goiridh's case, his distracted nature and elusiveness are justified by the fact that he knows his lands are under attack from an implacable enemy, who is likely to seek him out and kill him.

Significant characters in the novel are An t-Ogha Mór himself ('The Big Grandson'), Iarlom Mac Coinnich, Goiridh Mac Fhraing, Una, Sir Tolmach, Una's daughter Mairearad, Dr Mac Uaraig, and Captain Tolmach. The narrator claims to have heard much of the story from characters who appear in the narrative, including An t-Ogha Mór, who is a great war hero and yet who plays very little part in events considering that his name provides the title of the novel. At the beginning of the book, the plot revolves around the bitter feud between chieftains Iarlom Mac Coinnich and Goiridh Mac Fhraing. Mac Coinnich is in love with Una, sister of another clan chief, Sir Tolmach. Mac Connich's rivalry with Mac Fhraing comes to a head when Sir Tolmach arranges an alliance with Mac Fhraing and seals the deal by giving Una to Mac Fhraing in marriage. Mac Connich flies into a rage and attacks Mac Fhraing's land, burning his properties and chasing him to his castle. Una dies shortly after giving birth to Mac Fhraing's only child, and arranges for her nurse to spirit the child away before Mac Connich can come and destroy Mac Fhraing. The first movement of the novel comes to a close at the end of the third chapter, when Ealasaid the nurse succeeds in finding a good home for Una's baby. At this point, things change radically. Up to the end of Chapter 3, the novel has been about inter-clan warfare. Chapter 4 shifts to the baby's new home in Edinburgh, where she is brought up by Dr Mac Uaraig, a renowned surgeon. As a result of his fame, Dr Mac Uaraig receives a royal command to move to London, which he does. As the baby, Mairearad, grows up, she regularly attends functions in London society. They quickly become caught up in the intrigues and plotting that bedevil the royal court, and guardsman Captain Tolmach learns that there is a plot to assassinate the Queen and implicate the doctor in her death. Iarlom Mac Coinnich disappears entirely from the narrative here, and Goiridh Mac Fhraing is reduced to the status of an incidental character, who really makes no further impact until near the end of the book. The second movement is set in London, and the focus is on Lord Godo's attempts to murder the Queen. Captain Tolmach tries to warn Mairearad that her adoptive father is to be blamed for the plot, and this leads to Tolmach's exile. The narrative begins to refer to him as Iain Ruairidh from here on, and he becomes the main character from this point onwards. In the third movement of the novel, we return to Skye, where Iain Ruairidh has returned to live. Dr Mac Uaraig disappears from the text at this point, after we briefly learn that he was not blamed for the Queen's death, after all. When the action moves to Skye, we discover that Iain Ruairidh and the Ogha Mór are involved in recruiting for the Jacobite cause, and that Iain Ruairidh's father was a fierce Jacobite. Several instances of dramatic irony warn us that Iain Ruairidh is unlikely to survive the coming conflict, or to evade the agents sent to kill him in revenge for his actions. The final part of the book deals with the consequences of those actions, and brings Mairearad back into events.

Much of the novel is set in Skye, and there is, at times, a sense that Skye is as centrally important as any character, just as Mull and Argyll are often so integral in the writing of MacCormaic and MacPhàidein. According to Donald John MacLeod, 'Robertson [MacDhonnachaidh] describes action passably well, but frequently – particularly in descriptive passages – lapses into an absurdly overblown style' (MacLeod 1977: 213). MacLeod then offers an example of this absurdly overblown style, taken from one of the early passages, on the evening of Una's death. He could easily have illustrated the same point by quoting any of the descriptions of Skye and the Broadford Show, which open the novel:

> Is e cuspair nam bàrd a th'ann an Eilean a' Cheò. Cha'n'eil 'san Iar da choimeas; cha'n'eil ann ach aon Eilean—Eilean a' Cheò.
>
> [. . .]
>
>   Eilean a' Cheò: nach fad is cian bho'n a dh'èirich e a tuim an Iar-chuain, mar ailbhinn [a word he glosses in a footnote] fhiaclach air am b'àbhaist do thamhaisg na doimhne bhi cumail cuirm an casgraidh. Ach cha'n ann mar sin a shnuadh an diugh; no mar sid an là anns an d'rinn an t-Ogha Mór luaidh air brìgh nam bàrd. 'S ann aige fhein a bha'n t-alt air sùgan nan rann a shniomh; oir tha bhlàth ri fhaicinn ann an cois bial-aithris. (OM 1)

> (The Isle of Mist is the subject of the bards. There is nothing to compare with it in the West; there is only one Island—the Isle of Mist [a poetic name for Skye].
>
>   The Isle of Mist: wasn't it long and weary since it rose from the waters of the Western ocean, like a great, toothy rock on which the spirits of the deep used to hold their feasts of slaughter. But that is not what it is like today; nor in the day in which the Ogha Mór made a tale of the substance of the bards. He himself had the knack of weaving the strands of the verses; for its effects are seen in the folklore.)

Like MacCormaic, MacDhonnachaidh fell victim to the tendency to explain how his characters were feeling and describe their thoughts from the point of view of the narrator, rather than leaving the reader to understand these things from the description and dialogue. Like MacCormaic, he thus tended to produce writing that was reminiscent of the folktale rather than prose fiction. Again like MacCormaic, MacDhonnachaidh was evidently influenced by the *còmhraidhean* of the early periodicals when it came to writing dialogue:

'Ma 's e naigheachd amharus, tha eagal orm gu'm b' fheàrr lium ann an so e, na far a' bheil e. Ach cha'n 'eil sin ag ràdh nach'eil mathas an Fhreasdail maille ruinn.' (OM 24)

('If suspicion is truth, I fear I would prefer him here than where he is. But that is not to say that the goodness of Providence is not with us.')

This echoes several of the features I have identified as being central characteristics of the early *còmhraidhean* (Watson 2010). This utterance comes from the nurse, Ealasaid, as she tries to comfort Una, who is dying. Their conversation carries on in similar vein, with narratistic turns giving way to didactic turns and all of them in a style that is indistinguishable from the narrator's voice and, thus, unattributable to any individual character (see Watson 2010 for discussion of the terms here). These turns then lead to an extremely long monologue which covers almost two pages. This long monologue introduces the key theme of duty, which is at the heart of the novel.

However, *An t-Ogha Mór* differs not only from *Dùn-àluinn* but also from much of the other fiction of this period by generally favouring narrative over dialogue. The novel's regular structure is likely derived from its initial serialised format. Each chapter begins with a section in which the narrator sets the scene and establishes a tone and a moral (helped along by the inclusion of a proverb or saying or song extract as epigraph). In this opening section, the narrator usually also explains where he[4] has sourced the parts of the plot that form that chapter. This tendency to attribute stories to someone else is a very common feature of Gaelic fiction of this period. It would be reasonable to suggest that it has its origins in the *cèilidh*-house tradition (see Watson 2008 for tentative suggestions as to other features that may originate in that tradition).

The second movement of the book takes place in London, and introduces Mairearad Nic Uaraig, who is apparently Una's swapped child, and Iain Ruairidh Tolmach. Iain Ruairidh is the nephew of Sir Tolmach, and begins the novel as a captain in the King's household guard. He is, however, also a minor clan chieftain, having inherited the island of Scalpay, and apparently Mairearad's natural cousin, although the novel never really explores this point. Mairearad and Iain Ruairidh become aware of the plot to assassinate the Queen, and discover that Prince Frederick and his adviser Lord

Godo are behind it all. Iain Ruairidh also discovers that Godo plans to use Dr Mac Uaraig as the instrument of the Queen's murder, by poisoning his favoured scalpel. When Iain Ruairidh goes to warn Mairearad, he is too late, and Godo and the Prince are already at her residence. Forced to defend himself, Iain Ruairidh draws his blade in anger in the Prince's presence, making him instantly guilty of treason.

From this point (about halfway) to the end of the novel, Iain Ruairidh is clearly the main character. This episode also marks the only real part that the Ogha Mór plays in the action. Godo's spymaster tracks Iain Ruairidh down and attacks him with several of his henchmen. Iain Ruairidh is hard-pressed until the Ogha Mór comes to his assistance. Together, they kill the henchmen and see off the spymaster. They then flee back to the Highlands, knowing that they are condemned men. Iain Ruairidh at this point allows his Jacobite sympathies to win him over to the Stewart cause, and he joins the Ogha Mór in his secret campaign of recruitment, because: 'Chunnaic e buaireas nan Gaidheal a' tighinn' (102–3, 'He saw the tumult of the Gaels coming').

The rest of the novel takes place back in the Highlands, especially in and around Skye, and focuses on Iain Ruairidh's struggle to live long enough to raise a war band to fight for what he now sees as the rightful royal house. The second half of the novel is highly reminiscent of *Kidnapped*, and may well be influenced by that book. In particular, the descriptions of Iain Ruairidh's nobility strike a similar chord to Stevenson's descriptions of Alan Breck, although the two characters do not look alike: the care they take with their appearance, however, is similar, and is seen as part of their heroism. In MacDhonnachaidh's case, it may well be that he is deliberately tapping into aspects of the panegyric code in his constant praise of Iain Ruairidh's virtues and appearance. Two descriptions in particular seem to go beyond the simple exigencies of imagery and stray into the realms of panegyric. These are on pages 150–1 and 153–5. In the former, his physical appearance is described in detail, right down to the flashes in his socks that hold his sgian dubh in place. In the latter, the narrative concentrates on Iain Ruairidh's heroic ability to whistle so loudly and so distinctly that he will be heard and recognised for miles around:

> He was tall from the ground, brawny beyond measure; and his arms muscular in that way. No old woman would think of him without her eyes tearing up, and praying for harm to pass him by. Every maiden wanted him for a husband; because there was no little allure in the strength of his countenance. (150)

[. . .]

Iain gave a whistle with the ends of his fingers that was hard and long. Its sound was as frightful as the shriek of a ghostly apparition. For there are still some alive who would say that it was not entirely worldly; and they would look at you askance if you doubted their opinion. (153)

These heroic attributes are not restricted to Iain Ruairidh. In several places, his friends and companions are described in similarly exaggerated terms. For instance, their nobility is such that, even when they are quarreling and bickering constantly, not a bad word is said between them, and not one of them raises his voice (156). Iain Ruairidh's mother and his sweetheart Eilidh are also portrayed in tragically heroic terms.

At times, the novel seems to seek to define the essence of the Gael, and to distinguish the Gael from either the Lowlander or the English (often seen as more akin to each other than the Lowlander is to the Gael). This becomes much more common in the second half of the novel, when the action begins to pick up pace and there is more killing and betrayal going on. An illustrative example of this comes when Mairearad returns to the action, not long after these passages describing Iain Ruairidh and his men. Mairearad is in the company of a Lowlander, working as an agent on behalf of King George, when she meets a neighbour of Iain Ruairidh's, known as Raitean. Mairearad's companion tries to question Raitean in Scots (described by MacDhonnachaidh as 'Beurl', 'English', by implication in a later passage). Raitean, who is a fiery character in any case, is incensed by both the tone of the stranger and his use of the other language. He mutters that the man sounds like a hound and exclaims in Gaelic: 'No such sound ever came from the mouth of a proper man' (162). When the man persists, Raitean curses his "ablach cànain" (163, 'contemptible/mangled language'). In contrast with this, Mairearad's Gaelic makes a sweet tune (164) when she finally intervenes as they are about to shed one another's blood. She asks Raitean if he does not speak any English, and Raitean responds with disgust at the very notion, stating:

Ever since the Black Watch was raised in Glenelg, I know of nothing but evil that has ever come with English. (164)

At this point, Mairearad and Raitean delight in a verbal joust about their opinions on various matters. From this, they move on to criticise Mairearad's companion for his lack of either Gaelic or manners. Mairearad accepts Raitean's low opinion of the man, but says he is a good servant in spite of being a Lowlander.

MacDhonnachaidh is not guilty of portraying all non-Gaels as wicked and all Gaels as noble[5] and virtuous, which, to some extent, is what

MacCormaic was trying to do with *Dùn-àluinn*, thus resulting in the laboured characterisation of Cailean Mór and the unengaging perfection of Cailean Òg. In fact, much of the conflict, and many of the betrayals, in the novel are precipitated by Gaels. Furthermore, it is made very clear that the Gaels are suspicious of each other, and many of the things that go wrong for them are caused by their distrust of one another and their willingness to betray each other to the Lowlanders and the English. Raitean, in particular, is a seedy and callous figure. Not yet seventeen, he is willing to murder a man in cold blood in revenge for a minor argument and at the instigation of a beautiful woman. He is also willing to betray a man who has looked after him and entertained him for years, knowing he is likely selling him to the executioner. In Raitean's defence, he feels as if he has been bewitched and suspects Mairearad of witchcraft, and he also repents of the betrayal later. However, he commits these acts with wicked intent. Similarly, Iarlom and Goiridh pursue a feud that results in the destruction of the latter's fortune and has horrible echoes down the generations.

On the other hand, it is difficult to identify any decent or good-hearted characters in the novel who are not Gaels. The only one who may fall into this category is Dr Mac Uaraig, the Edinburgh surgeon whose skills are admired even in the royal court in London. It is not entirely clear that Dr Mac Uaraig himself is a non-Gael, though, and he very well could be: he clearly has connections in the Highlands, and his name would suggest a Gaelic heritage. Further, he also manages to raise Mairearad to be a fluent Gaelic speaker who is thought of as a native. Mairearad evidently identifies herself as a Gael, and so do Iain Ruairidh and the clan chiefs she meets when she goes on her mission to Skye. Then again, the Ogha Mór is not convinced: he warns Iain Ruairidh that she is a citified lady and that she would never take a Highlander for a husband.

One of the most notable aspects of the novel is the author's use of language. In the preface, he bullishly proclaims he has written in his own dialect and will make no apology for that (see Watson 2007). The novel does indeed feature some idiosyncratic usages, particularly in spelling, but these do not hamper comprehension, any more than MacCormaic's Argyll Gaelic does in *Dùn-àluinn*. There are several places where MacDhonnachaidh uses English in the novel, and it is worth considering the effects of each. The first time this happens is when a letter has come to Dr Mac Uaraig from an aide of the Queen, asking him to come to London to help her. The letter is very short and would easily have been translated or paraphrased in Gaelic. Presented in English, as it is, it contrasts with the doctor's following dialogue, which is given in Gaelic. The doctor immediately begins to talk about "cùisean nan Gaidheal" (50). These two things together suggest that

Dr Mac Uaraig's usual language of everyday communication in the house is Gaelic, which would explain Mairearad's acquisition of the language.

'English' is used similarly a little later in the novel, when events have moved to the royal court in England. The novel contains a short play (discussed below) that is designed to illustrate the intrigues that beset the court. One of the characters is Fraulain [*sic*] Sgliurach, a German handmaiden of the King's. All of the dialogue (barring a word or two here and there) is given in Gaelic, apart from Fraulain Sgliurach's single turn:

> *Ze Herr Valpool vis block headed; zi King, mein Lord must cut it owf mit a clopper.* (79–80)

This Denglish presents a rather unfortunate parody of a German person speaking English, and it is most marked in the context, considering that all of the other characters would be speaking English and yet their dialogue is in Gaelic (see Storey 2009: 12–13). This is perhaps even more ironic, considering that the royal house was Hanoverian ('céinich Hanobhair', 'foreigners of Hanover', 126). The use of 'vis' and 'owf' in this context may suggest that MacDhonnachaidh's command of German was not strong, and that the parody was not based on real-life knowledge of German speech-patterns.

The other instance of English being used in the text comes during Raitean's heated exchanges with Mairearad's companion. As mentioned above, the Lowland companion's utterances are described as English, but they are rather closer to Scots:

> '*Ken ye they pairts, laddie?*' (162)

[. . .]

> '*I bid ye tell me, gin the Muckle Hoose at Livera be faur frae here?*' (163)

The content of the dialogues is harmless enough, and Raitean's response seems out of proportion, but we are led to believe that many Highlanders have acquired a deep sense of foreboding about the English language by this time. Thus, when Mairearad asks Raitean if he knows any English at all, she has to repeat the question twice more before even receiving an answer, and the vehemence of the answer is again out of all proportion to the question. The English language is equated with the English governing powers and also with Lowland Scots throughout the book. All references to English are negative, and are associated with negative views of both the English and the Lowlanders. Iain Ruairidh, who serves the Hanoverians when he is first introduced, quickly develops a hatred of the English (84–7). The narrator tries to convince him that not *all* English are evil:

'They are like the communities' potatoes—good and bad.' (86)

[. . .]

'Some Lowlanders⁶ are handsome enough,' I said, pulling his leg. (87)

A third novel

The third of the early novels was Seumas MacLeòid's (James MacLeod) *Cailin Sgiathanach: no Faodalach na h-Abaid* ('Skye Girl: or Foundling of the Abbey'), published by Alasdair MacLabhruinn 's a Mhic in 1923, a full decade after MacCormaic and MacDhonnachaidh had tried their hand at the genre. Although there are some far-fetched elements in *Cailin Sgiathanach*, the author clearly tried to avoid the outrageous style of plot that characterised the first two, instead focusing on the efforts of a group of people to get the girl of the novel's title to marry a man of their choosing. As the novel progresses, it becomes clear that their motivations are convoluted and confusing, but, although it may threaten both possibilities, the novel manages to avoid degenerating into a poorly-crafted detective story like the dénouement of *Dùn-Àluinn* or a wasteful and unresolved bloodbath like *An t-Ogha Mór*.

Like the other two early novels, *Cailin Sgiathanach* is set in the author's distant past, more than 'a century ago', suggesting that the timeframe is around the beginning of the nineteenth century, but some of it is even earlier. A letter on page 91 gives the date of 1799 for part of the action. Most of the action takes place in Skye, but the beginning of the novel and a later section take place in and around Lochaber. In what is effectively a prologue, Dòmhnull Ros and his wife Mór arrive at an abbey which fosters orphans. They talk to a young girl orphan before selecting her for adoption. This early episode establishes choice as the major theme of the book. Throughout the novel, people's ability to make choices, and the choices they do make, creates the movement of the plot and reveals the nature of the characters who inhabit the text world.

The novel proper begins twenty years later. The young girl, named Mórag, has grown up in Skye and is in love with Alasdair Caimbeul, who presents her with a ring. The ring is a leaving gift, as Alasdair is about to depart from Skye. The reader soon learns that he is leaving partly because of Mórag's father, Dòmhnull Ros, who has used his influence to make life difficult for him. It later transpires that Ros has done this because he needs Mórag to marry someone else. The novel follows the beginnings of Alasdair's journey. He is heading for North America, where he hopes to find an uncle of his who emigrated earlier, and, as well as renewing his acquaintance, use him as a contact to help him make his fortune. Oddly,

Alasdair is abandoned by the narrative shortly after reaching his destination and takes little part in events again until the very end.

Like both MacCormaic and MacDhonnachaidh, MacLeòid takes every opportunity to use his text to comment on the situation of the Highlanders and on people's perceptions of Gaels and Gaelic culture. For instance, we learn that there were 'three times in the year in which there would be neither feasting nor joy among the Gaels – a fasting-day, the time when an exile ship sails, and the day of a funeral' (20). This effort to establish what kind of people the Gaels are is almost immediately followed by a reminder of how the Gaels have been victimised by their neighbours:

> There is no people on the face of the earth, white, black, brown, or yellow, that has suffered as much as the Gaels on account of creed (a type of faith). (21)

MacLeòid warms to this theme and carries on with it over the page. This eventually leads into a discussion of the Highland dress and the different perceptions of it. There is a measure of irony in this passage, however:

> Although Raasay's Servant was turned out like the rest, he himself and the others believed, if Highland dress was a mark of a good Gael, there was none other so 'Gaelic' as himself. (24)

I have added the inverted commas around 'Gaelic', as it is difficult to translate the term *Gàidhealach*. It is the adjective related to the word *Gaidheal*, 'a Gael'. But, because of the conflation and overlap between the terms 'Gael' and 'Highlander' in English, 'Gaelic' is rarely used as the adjective of 'Gael' in English. Further, *Gàidhealach* tends to be used as much definitively as descriptively, which 'Gaelic' probably does not. In any case, MacLeòid is using *Gàidhealach* definitively in this passage, which continues to establish the characteristics of the Gael and to consider the extent to which common perceptions of Gaelicness genuinely hold. MacLeòid's own ideas of what constitutes Gaelicness are peppered throughout the text by way of contrast: for instance, the Gaels' perception of home (*viz.* where the family is; 31), or the instinct to look after one's family (33). These ponderings in turn give way to a consideration of the Gaels' unfortunate situation, too few to stand up for their rights (34) and betrayed by the clergy, in whom they had placed their trust and belief (35). The minor character who has been the sentient focus of much of these musings finishes off by lamenting the fact that the Highland dress and the bagpipes were ever banned, tangible examples of the abstractions that have just been under consideration.

Throughout all of these thoughts, the theme of choice returns again and again. Although the narrative voice acknowledges that the Gaels were never numerous enough to fight for their rights in pitched battle, there is certainly a suggestion that they still had choices open to them. One of these is the choice to board the exile ships in the first place: is it right, the narrative asks, to leave the land of our birth and upbringing and go to a foreign country (40). The novel stresses that the English were not to blame for the Gaels' predicament, and regards this as a tired and over-simplistic reading of events. Regardless of who governed the Gaels, it was their own choice to give up their language, a choice they made not under duress but through avarice and as a result of aspiration (40–5). Without a language, the narrative seems to suggest, a nation does not truly exist (40–1).[7] But, in spite of protestations to the contrary, the English did not force the Gaels to abandon Gaelic: they made that choice for themselves (41). The novel promulgates the message that language is a birthright that should not be taken lightly.

The motif of birthright is itself important in the context of Morag Ros having been adopted: we later discover that her parents have never told her that she was not their natural daughter, but, unknown to them, she actually remembers her young childhood in the abbey. Notions of birthright, identity, duty and loyalty come to be important as the plot develops further.

The first movement of the novel ends when Alasdair arrives in Nova Scotia. There, he meets an old friend of his uncle's. He learns from him that his uncle has died. The main bulk of the novel then turns to Mòrag's situation in Alasdair's absence. Her father is determined that she must marry a man called Iain Mac Illeathain. What Mòrag does not know is that her father is deeply in debt and needs Mac Illeathain's help to avoid imprisonment. In fact, it is not just Dòmhnull Ros who is relying on Mòrag's marriage to Mac Illeathain: the local landowner, known simply as 'Rasaidh' ('Raasay'), is in a similar position. He and Ros spend a good deal of time plotting together throughout the novel. Rasaidh also plots with his henchmen, MacGrùslaich and Dùghall Gorm. He is concerned about Mòrag's commitment to Alasdair Caimbeul and actually considers murdering Alasdair to free the way for Mòrag to marry Mac Illeathain. In the end, he decides that Alasdair need not actually be dead, so long as Mòrag believes he is. A complex plot is developed that results in Alasdair appearing to have died en route to Nova Scotia. Mòrag never believes it, however, and she returns to the grave after the funeral. She digs up Alasdair's coffin and finds it empty, as she suspected. This gives her the knowledge she needs in order to understand the level of plotting that has been going on behind her back.

Both the reader and a number of the characters wonder if Mórag will turn up for her wedding to Mac Illeathain. She makes various cryptic statements to her father and other people. So, it is a surprise on the day when she does indeed appear. It is even more of a surprise to those present when, after an interruption, she does go ahead and marry Mac Illeathain. However, Mórag has discovered that she is not really the daughter of Dòmhnull and Mór Ros, and so she believes that marrying Mac Illeathain with the name 'Ros' does not morally bind her to him. As soon as the wedding is over, she flees and cannot be found. She has left her father a letter (in English) explaining her decisions: she went through with the wedding to save him from prison, but she cannot live with Mac Illeathain. The theme of choice is to the fore again here, as Mórag explains the difficult choices she had to consider. Perhaps as a result of the stress he has been under, Dòmhnull Ros dies, leaving Rasaidh as the one who must try to hunt down Mórag.

In the final movement of the novel, the narrative voice considers the effect that foreknowledge of life would have on one's choices. The narrative concludes that most people would prefer not to have prescience and allow things to turn out how they might. This leads to the long-awaited return of Alasdair Caimbeul, who has been missing from events since the early pages. Alasdair and Mórag are reunited and ask one another for forgiveness for all they have done since parting. Thanks to Rasaidh's servant, Mórag is reunited with her biological father, too.

MacLeòid's attitude towards England and the English is expressed throughout the novel, and it makes an interesting contrast with the views that appear to be promoted in *Dùn-Àluinn* and *An t-Ogha Mór*. As far as *Cailin Sgiathanach* is concerned, the English are often blamed for the problems of the Highlands and for the suffering of the Gaels, but they are wrongly blamed: the true fault lies with the Gaels themselves. The Gaels have embraced Britishness in an effort to acquire wealth and status for themselves, and, in doing so, have turned their backs on their own language and cultural traditions. The issue of language was discussed above, as was the discussion of the Highland dress and bagpipes, but there are several other instances in which the narrative or a particular character accuses another character of being ignorant of the true nature of the Gael, usually because of being ignorant of traditional customs or manners (see Trevor-Roper's controversial discussions of these issues, 1983, 2009); and, as a good Gael should know:

air feadh nan eileanan, is fearr a bhi dhìth a chinn na a bhi dhìth a'
chleachdaidh. (157)

(throughout the islands, it is better to be without a head than to be ignorant of customs/'out of fashion')

At the same time, however, *Cailin Sgiathanach* is eminently clear (perhaps more so than the other two novels) that England is a different country and English is a 'foreign' language. Oddly, the novel features two letters written by Mórag, both of them in English. Derick Thomson's assessment of *Cailin Sgiathanach* was no more favourable than were his views of the other two early novels. He wrote that *Cailin Sgiathanach*:

> suffers also from overloaded and pretentious language. The fundamental difficulty of finding appropriate registers has not been solved, and this is underlined by the relative felicity of some English letters quoted in the text (Mòrag's letter, pp. 202–3, has clarity and lucidity). (CGS 1994: 218)

In fact, though, the language of the first, longer letter is as 'overloaded and pretentious' as anything else in the novel. The second letter is no more than a short note, and is oddly formal considering that it is written to her sweetheart (albeit in a state of uncertainty and anxiety regarding the future of their relationship). It may be that MacLeòid was attempting to create a sense of the novel's time setting in his use of language, as both the Gaelic and the English seem old-fashioned even for 1923.

Conclusion

As Donald John MacLeod wrote, the advent of the Gaelic novel was of historical interest. And, as he also suggested, the literary merits of the three early novels were variable at best. From the close reading of the three novels offered in this chapter, it should be clear that all three authors had the talent and potential to produce better work. The main errors and failings in the three books were more than likely caused by the lack of precedent in the language, and by a difficulty in understanding who their target audience was: it is all too easy to judge them in the context of what had been done in English and other languages at that point, but we must bear in mind that hardly any written prose fiction had yet been attempted in Gaelic, let alone extended fiction. In MacCormaic's case, he tried to write a novel on a premise similar to that of one of his stories, and the characters were too flat and undeveloped to sustain this. MacDhonnachaidh tried to write a historical novel, perhaps in the style of Scott, but did not have enough flair for vivid detail or compelling language. Both MacCormaic and MacDhonnachaidh wrote better action than dialogue, but neither of them seem to have realised this, and so they failed to capitalise on what could have been a real strength. Both of them also seem to have been confused by conflicting political and ideological sympathies, rendering their novels thematically opaque. While MacLeòid managed to avoid some of these errors, he did so by basing his novel on a plot line that was intrinsically less active and so the drama had to come from an interest in the characters themselves. None of the characters in *An Cailin Sgiathanach* are rich enough to sustain this kind of interest. The attempts to add complexity and texture to the plot were slightly less hackneyed than those in *Dùn-àluinn*, but ultimately led to confusion and the unnecessary cluttering of minor characters carrying out pointless quests. In the light of the end products, it may be that the explanation for the abrupt halt in novel writing was simply due to writers realising that more developmental work needed to be done on fiction in the language before a successful novel could emerge.

Chapter 3

Periodical Fiction – 1952 to the Present Day

Ruaraidh MacThòmais (Derick Thomson), editor of the magazine *Gairm*, wrote in his last editorial in 2002: ''S ann anns na bliadhnachan sin a thàinig an sgeulachd ghoirid gu ìre ann an Gàidhlig' (297, 'It was in those years [i.e. the *Gairm* years] that the short story in Gaelic grew up'). This is entirely true. As MacThòmais also wrote, and as we have seen in previous chapters in this book, there were many stories written prior to 1952. Some of them were very fine in many ways, and some of them stand up to comparison with more contemporary work. However, on the whole, the concept of the short story did not truly make its way into Gaelic until there was a regular, quarterly magazine in place to encourage it to grow and develop. That magazine was *Gairm*, and it was edited by one of the leading lights in the then-new Gaelic literary renaissance. Perhaps MacThòmais's status as a 'modernist' poet, or perhaps his intellectual rigour as Celtic professor at Glasgow University, also helped encourage contributors to experiment with plot and technique and to push the boundaries of short fiction beyond what had previously been the norm. Or perhaps it was the presence of such a long-lasting and regular magazine that was itself the spur to this new level of creativity: the sheer critical mass of short fiction being produced may well have inspired new writers to ever greater efforts. Perhaps the short story 'grew up', to use MacThòmais's metaphor, as an effect of the poetry renaissance, which was in full flow by the 1950s: but then, of the five greatest poets who are most commonly identified with the renaissance, only Iain Mac a' Ghobhainn (Iain Crichton Smith) and MacThòmais himself contributed to the evolution of the short story, and MacThòmais's contribution was small, albeit effective.[1] Or perhaps again the time was simply right for the short story to move on in Gaelic, especially considering the exposure that the language's users would have had to English literature by the middle of the century. In any case, MacThòmais's statement was correct, in essence: the short story did come into its own during the *Gairm* years, and almost certainly directly as a result of the existence of the magazine. It is entirely fitting, therefore, that this chapter concentrates on work that appeared in *Gairm*, and that the chapter is structured according to movements that can be traced within the magazine itself. Before *Gairm*, and throughout the years since it was established, other periodicals also published Gaelic fiction, although none of them can come close to the sheer volume that became public thanks to *Gairm*. Papers like *The Scotsman*, periodicals like *An Gaidheal* and magazines like *Sruth* and *New Writing Scotland* have published occasional Gaelic stories. Some few short stories were appearing in these other outlets and elsewhere during the half-century of *Gairm*'s existence, but these will only receive a brief mention – not least because they were, for the most part, being written by the same people who were contributing to *Gairm* anyway, such as Iain Mac a' Ghobhainn. The great bulk of Gaelic short stories, several hundred in all, appeared in *Gairm*.

After MacThòmais's retirement as editor, and the simultaneous demise of *Gairm*, it was evident that Gaelic literature would be bereft of one of its major cornerstones: as Donald Meek put it, there would be 'a gap in the firmament' (*Gath* 1, 2). Meek himself therefore established a periodical magazine, *Gath*, in order to compensate for the loss of what had been much more than a magazine in many ways. Meek took his place as leading editor of the first four numbers of *Gath*, but wished to stand down once the new magazine had been securely established, having already determined to retire from his academic career. Richard Cox was installed as editor by the fifth issue, but he found himself unable to continue beyond the eighth number. As a result, there was a hiatus of more than two years between the eighth and ninth issues of *Gath*, with some readers coming to believe that *Gath* was no more. In any event, *Gath* has not yet been able to emulate the regularity or reliability of *Gairm* (considering that four issues of *Gairm* were produced almost every year between 1952 and 2002, MacThòmais's remarkable achievement is unlikely ever to be rivalled).[2] Irrespective of the regularity of *Gath* to date, there is no doubt that it was conceived as, in some measure, a replacement for *Gairm*, and therefore this chapter will consider it as such, even though it is important to bear in mind that the two magazines are different in tenor and character and have no formal connection.

This chapter is structured in two ways. The first part of the chapter takes a chronological view of the movement of the short story from the 1950s to the present day. The second part of the chapter focuses on specific writers, with a particular emphasis on those writers who have not produced a published collection in their own right, so as to give them a measure of parity of treatment with the others who are discussed in Chapters 4 and 5. MacThòmais's statement that the short story grew up during the *Gairm* years will be explored, as will my own suggestion of 1960 as a major watershed in the evolution of the genre, and my contention that the short story reached its apogee in Gaelic around the end of the 1980s.

Gairm in the 1950s

The most striking fact about the short story in the 1950s is that it is effectively a continuation of what had gone before. Although a gap had existed between the literary magazines of the early twentieth century and the establishment of *Gairm*, the early years of *Gairm* featured fiction that could almost have appeared in *An Ròsarnach*. The primary concerns in the stories of the 1950s are community, family relationships, what it is like to be a (rural) Gael, the church, the land, Gaelic, love, fishing, the weather and the hierarchies in contemporary or recent past Gaelic society. Many stories follow the formal patterns of either folktales or the *cèilidh* readings that were popular from the end of the nineteenth century. Some contributors perhaps saw *Gairm* in its early days as a new version of the publications of Henry Whyte or Ruairidh Erskine. As was common in the early part of the century, the line between fiction and fact or biography was often blurred in the stories of the 1950s: indeed, this remained the case throughout the years of *Gairm's floruit*.

There are some flashes of humour in the first few numbers of the magazine, but it was in the middle of the '50s that a confident, convincing Highland humour began to be expressed in the fiction for the first time. Calum MacIomhair's 'Latha nan Seachd Sian' ('The Day of Storms'),[3] which appeared in issue 14 in 1955, is a good example of both of these last two points. The style is highly descriptive and humorous, and yet it is not altogether clear that the story is fictitious. Similarly, Tormod MacLeòid's ''S e Tìde a Dh'innseas' ('Time Will Tell', G18, 1956) is pure comedy. The plot is typically rural: Màiri goes out to graze her cow; later, the cow is nowhere to be found; various crofters make suggestions about where to look for the cow; Màiri meets a stranger who owns binoculars; Màiri and the stranger have an adventure involving a tractor; in the end, Màiri gratefully retrieves her cow and marries the stranger. This story in many ways prefigures Iain Moireach's 'An Gamhainn' (for which, see Chapter 5), and yet it fits squarely into the predominant styles of the time. Dòmhnull Loduinn's 'An Cogadh Fuar' ('The Cold War', G24, 1958) is another highly descriptive, comic story, in which a prideful woman has misadventures revolving around her beloved new hat.

Very many of the stories in the 1950s match Ruaraidh MacThòmais's description of the early novels, when he wrote that they were characterised by the 'kind of anecdotage-with-repartee' (CGS 1994, 218) that he felt tended to appeal to a Gaelic audience. Indeed, in many cases, this 'anecdotage with repartee' is not merely a formal feature of the story, but is the entire point of the story. This is even true of a story written by 'Sgioba a' Chabairnich',[4] 'Na Geamachan' ('The Games', G3, 1953). The tale is based on long, gossipy monologues, mainly focusing on the humour in social situations in small, rural communities, and showing women in a poor light. Donnchadh MacDhunlèibhe's 'Domhnall Mòr agus an Luch' ('Big Donald and the Mouse', G9, 1954) is another comic story that pokes fun at the women of a rural Gaelic community. This time, the joke is on a group of predatory widows, who try to woo Domhnall Mòr when they realise he is still single: Domhnall Mòr is lucky enough to be helped by a friendly mouse, who can speak Gaelic! Other humorous stories involve trickery, such as Fearchar Martainn's 'Cù a' Mhinisteir' ('The Minister's Dog', G5, 1953). In this story, the minister sees an advert from a man who claims he can train a dog to talk. He sends his servant to Glasgow with his dog to attend the training. The servant spends all the minister's money on alcohol and sells the dog. He tells the minister that the dog learned to talk and accused the minister of having an affair with the housekeeper and so he killed the dog to maintain propriety. The minister agrees this was for the best.

The folktale is a regular inspiration in the stories that appeared in *Gairm* in the 1950s. In some cases, the themes, motifs or subject-matter come straight from the folk tradition; in other cases, the style of the narrative mimics the storytelling tradition. From time to time, the stories are completely indistinguishable from folktales. Indeed, *Gairm* sometimes published folklore, and the editors were not always careful to mark the original fiction from the oral tradition. Examples include Scarpach's 'Balach Dhòmhnaill Ghuirm' ('Blue Donald's Boy', G9, 1954), Alasdair MacNeacail's 'An Ite Sheunta' ('The Enchanted Feather', G12, 1955), Niall MacGhille Sheathanaich's 'An t-Each Uisge' ('The Water Horse', G18, 1956),[5] and several stories from the thirtieth issue, which was the last number to appear in the 1950s.

Exceptions to all of these observations come, as we might expect, from writers like Iain Mac a' Ghobhainn, Ruaraidh MacThòmais and Fionnlagh I. MacDhòmhnaill (Finlay J. MacDonald),[6] although each of them contributed only sparsely in the 1950s. Mac a' Ghobhainn's 'Am Bodach' ('The Old Man', G6, 1953) weaves together some of the elements common in some of the other fiction of the time along with a complex thematic arrangement and a narrative style that is highly innovative. The overall effect is powerful and moving, which are effects not generally characteristic of Gaelic short fiction in the 1950s. The winter issue of 1957 (G22) saw the publication of Ruaraidh MacThòmais's 'Bean a' Mhinisteir' ('The Minister's Wife'), one of the few short stories MacThòmais has published in his long writing career. MacThòmais's descriptions are definite and keen, and it is immediately clear that small details are important. The plot is weak and unconvincing, but the writing is otherwise some of the finest of the decade. The very next issue (G23, 1958) carried a story by the other editor, Fionnlagh I. MacDhòmhnaill, entitled 'Air Beulaibh an t-Sluaigh' ('In Front of People / In the Public Eye'). This is one of the most poignant of the early *Gairm* stories, even though its plotline ploughs a very familiar furrow in the Gaelic short fiction tradition. The heroine of the story, Seonag, is a minister's daughter, who is due to marry her sweetheart, Pàdruig. In their excitement at their engagement, Seonag and Pàdruig sleep together and she falls pregnant. Not knowing that Seonag is pregnant, Pàdruig calls off their engagement because he wants to go to university and train as a minister, having been inspired by Seonag's own father. The plot itself is thus melodramatic and predictable, relying on the 'twist'-style ending so popular with Gaelic writers in the first half of the century. What lifts this story above the run-of-the-mill is MacDhòmhnaill's skilful handling of emotion. Little details of Seonag's observations and sensations help to make her seem real. The juxtaposition of a pettiness and nobility in her character makes her ring true as a person. This enhances the effectiveness of her emotional development from boredom and frustration, through elation and then arousal and then finally to suicidal despair. No other story of the period conveys emotion so powerfully or convincingly.

Other strong early stories include Calum MacIomhair's 'Bàrdachd Iain Breabadair' ('Iain the Weaver's Poetry', G4, 1953), Calum Ruairidh MacGillemhoire's 'Cha Deach Eadar Clach is Òrd' ('There Did Not Go Between Stone and Hammer', G26, 1958), and Rarlon Seixias's 'An Starsach' ('The Threshold', G30, 1959).[7]

Gairm in the 1960s

The 1960s saw Gaelic fiction truly begin to emerge from its early foundations in the tall tale, the yarn, the anecdote, the conversation and the folktale. This is not to say that, from 1960 onward, all Gaelic short stories were technically accomplished or highly literary or modernist or indeed even successful. However, there is a clear increase in the proportion of stories that can be described by some of these terms from 1960 onward. At the same time, the tall tales, yarns and all the others continued – perhaps not in such numbers as before, but always present.

The humour established in the 1950s continues, but is sometimes accompanied by a stronger or more unpredictable plot in the second decade of *Gairm*. For instance, in Cathair a' Chùl-Chinn's 'Beagan Anns an Onoir' ('A Little in Honour', G34, 1960), the first-person narrator is convinced that 'there are no people on earth as honourable as the Gaels' (359). Shortly after this, he inadvertently mugs an Englishman and steals his wallet. When he tries to make amends, he is unable to convince the legal system that his actions were accidental. This is one of the earliest stories in Gaelic to make good use of irony. At the same time, although it succeeds as a short story, it retains a strongly Gaelic identity. Other humorous tales are not always so formally accomplished, although they can be amusing and entertaining in their own way: an example of which is Iain Dòmhnallach's 'Am Balbhan' ('The Mute', G33, 1960), in which a Gael learns some English from a dictionary, leading to a comical misunderstanding when he tries to converse with an Englishman.

As in 'Am Balbhan', the concern with the language is one of the features that continued into the 1960s and beyond. In some cases, it was intertwined with a newly-emerging interest in science fiction. For instance, Ruairidh MacLeòid's 'Ri Taobh an Teallaich' ('Beside the Hearth', G34, 1960) is set in a future in which Gaelic has revived to such an extent that it has threatened English and resulted in a Fourth World War, partly fought out between 'Goill 's na Gaidheil' ('Lowlanders and the Gaels', 109).[8] Several other science fiction and fantastical stories feature in the earliest issues of the 1960s. This coincides with the end of what is often recognised as the golden age of science fiction and the era in which the space race began to intensify. In a way, however, there is nothing new in fantastical plots or settings in Gaelic fiction: these things were already inherent in some of the fiction of the early part of the century, inherited no doubt from the mythical strain in the oral tradition.

In some cases, the futuristic stories are ironic or designed as parodies of either the science fiction conventions or of conditions that pertain in the Highlands or in the language Tormod MacNèill's 'Mòd Thorgabail' ('Torgabal Mòd', G36, 1961) is an excellent example of this, as is Rob Shirley's 'An Duine Ùr' ('The New Man', G38, 1961), in which surgeons have discovered a way to reanimate corpses and even fuse the best bits of people to create super-achievers. Other science fiction or futuristic stories are more conventional, such as Cailein T. MacCoinnich's 'An Galair' ('The Disease', G42, 1963), or more psychological, such as Iain Mac a' Ghobhainn's 'An Solas Ùr' (discussed in Chapter 5). Another Rob Shirley story, 'Mr Universe' (G46, 1964), has a clear moral underlying the futuristic setting and science fictional premises. Garbhan MacAoidh's 'An t-Eilean Céin' ('The Foreign Island', G32, 1960) is again set in a future in which Gaelic has returned to a position of some prominence. When American and Soviet colonisers arrive on what they believe is an undiscovered planet, they are greeted by Gaels, who want them to live together in peace.

From the outset, *Gairm* published fiction by more female writers than had ever appeared previously, and this continued to increase throughout the 1960s. In the first years, the female writers often contributed the humorous, socially-based stories, a sort of rustic comedy-of-manners that drew on the *cèilidh* tradition and on the 'readings' of the earlier generation. These stories are often preoccupied with the everyday practicalities of food, caring for the animals, and looking after the land, as well as highlighting local mores and parodying the behaviour of small communities. Women writers are responsible for some of the funniest stories that appeared in the 1950s and '60s, and the use of language in particular takes a step forward in their work. It is in the writing of people like Maireid NicCodrum, Ceit NicDhòmnhaill and Màiri Tàillear that the language really approaches the vernacular of their day, especially in the dialogue. Mòrag NicCoinnich's descriptive language is particularly effective in a small number of her stories.

Young writers like Cairistìona Dick also began to emerge in the 1960s, although not necessarily always writing fiction. Dick's early writings were often autobiographical or indeed straightforward reports of holidays and activities: the writing is always sharp and clear, though, prefiguring her later development into a strong proponent of the fictional story. Dick's early work sometimes appeared in a section of the magazine that was set aside for young writers. This innovation surely helped several younger people gain the confidence to submit their contributions, and there is no doubt that the young writers' section contains some excellent writing. Not all of the contributions in this section are fiction: indeed, there is a range of interests, including a regular feature on beauty and fashion tips for young women. Of the fiction, there are signs of a new experimentalism that also began to appear in the main bulk of the magazine around the same time. This book has taken the approach of not dealing with fiction written by or for anyone other than adults, for the simple necessity of keeping the word count under control. There is no doubt, however, that this regular section for young writers, that ran for several years, deserves to be examined in much greater detail at some future stage.

Fiction in *Gairm* in the 1950s was relatively conservative, both in terms of subject matter and in terms of technique. Alongside the new interest in science fiction and far-flung settings in the 1960s, there began a new movement in experimentation with form. The experimentalism is not by any means radical, if we compare it to what had taken place in English-language fiction in the period of literary high modernism or what was to take place throughout the literary postmodernist era. Nevertheless, a proportion of the fiction being published in *Gairm* in the '60s contrasts strongly with all of the Gaelic fiction that had appeared previously. For the first time, writers attempted techniques like stream-of-consciousness, dramatic monologue, dramatic irony and foreshadowing, and there were deliberate narrative shifts introduced to produce effects (rather than merely as a result of careless writing, as might have been the case before). Some stories have second-person narration or narrative that is based in the present tense. Of course, none of these things sound avant-garde in the context of English-language fiction, but the decade of the 1960s was the first time they had been seen with any consistency in Gaelic. They are addressed in further detail later in this chapter, when we discuss the work of individual writers.

Gairm in the 1970s

Everything that was true of the fiction of the first two decades continued in the 1970s: humorous stories were common, especially ones revolving around social situations or the placing of Gaels into urban settings where they were unfamiliar; stories concerned with the state of the language or its future continued to appear; tales that could almost belong to the folk tradition continued to be popular, especially those with a magical or fantastical twist, and most especially ones involving the second sight or ghostly occurences; stories about young women and their desire to be married also continued unabated; stories about the sea and sailing appeared at times; and the new experimentation carried on, with the emergence of other new writers such as Fearghas MacFhionnlaigh. The 1970s were also the beginning of a period in which *Gairm* was almost dominated by the stories of Eilidh Watt and Cailein T. MacCoinnich.

Tormod Dòmhnallach's fine 'Làraich' ('Sites/Traces/Ruins', G72, 1970) is one of the better stories to appear at the beginning of the decade. The structure, symbolism and imagery all echo the subject-matter and the theme of fracture. In contrast, and yet also well written, Donald Meek (Dòmhnall Eachann Meek) published 'Cuairt do'n Launderette' ('A Trip to the Launderette', G73, 1970) in the very next issue. This is a comical account of a young man leaving the islands to go to study in Glasgow and coming to terms with the fact that he must now look after himself (with a strong sense that cooking, cleaning and washing clothes are normally women's work). When he runs out of clean clothes, he realises he will have to do something about this and he takes himself off to the launderette. The account is well-observed – indeed, it is tempting to read the story as autobiographical – and the detail in the young man's perception and discomfort create a successful comic effect. Stories of this nature are not exclusively written by male writers, of course. Maribal NicMhaoilein published 'Dannsa anns an Fhasan Ùr' ('A Dance in the New Fashion') in the same issue of the magazine. Again, this story is from the perspective of a young islander moving to Glasgow to go to university and having to learn urban ways. In both of these stories, there is a simultaneous sense of loss and gain: the young students are losing what may be a wholesome way of life, and losing their part in its tradition, and yet they are gaining access to modern society and the ability to learn and experience new things. Other similar stories include Oighrig NicCorcadail's 'An t-Ionnsachadh Òg' ('Learning Young', G77, 1971). On the other hand, there are stories where the emphasis is not so much on the positivity of the two aspects of the exile's life. Ailean Friseal's 'Gille nan Eun' ('Bird Boy', G85, 1973) has a main character Iain who grows up and moves to the city. The story traces his growth in the city, showing him becoming more and more worldly and losing his boyishness. When he goes home to visit his home community, he meets his childhood sweetheart Màiri. She thinks they can be reunited, but Iain arrogantly feels he has outgrown her, and that she is part of what he now considers his trivial youth.

A series of slightly surreal stories ran for several issues in the early 1970s, written by someone using the pen-name MacOnfhail. These stories feature a secret society, which is evidently based on a perception of organisations like the Masonic Order, and yet also seems to be parodying Gaelic bodies such as An Comunn Gaidhealach (hence, perhaps, the use of the pen-name!). These 'secret society' stories are very much written for comic effect, and some of the dialogue is effective. Another long series in the 1970s is Garbhan MacAoidh's 'Ishah', which initially appears as a story 'to be continued', but is later described as a short novel in serial form. 'Ishah' is a particularly unusual story, drawing together numerous characters and settings, as well as multiple themes and a wide range of symbols. The descriptive writing is strong, although the plot itself is not always easy to follow. The first-person narrator meets an old woman with supernatural knowledge, who tells him both Gaelic and English are doomed to die. The character takes a sea trip, encounters terrorist hijackers, and determines to track down the mysterious Ishah. The other major serial that began in the 1970s was Iain Mac a' Ghobhainn's 'Murchadh', which is discussed as a novel in Chapter 4.

Of the stories published in this decade, some of the most successful are also the ones that are most experimental. Aonghas MacNeacail's 'Seann Sgeulachd, Sgeulachd Nuadh' ('An Old Story, A New Story', G82, 1973) is an instance of this. Like MacNeacail's poetry, the story avoids conventional punctuation (although, unlike some of his other work, it does at least have full-stops and commas). Although the piece is set out as prose, it is highly poetic in many ways. It is also macaronic, which is one of the devices that began to gain ground in the 1970s, as writers became more aware of the rapid pidginisation of Gaelic. 'A' Cheò' ('The Mist', G85, 1973) by Fearghas Mac-an-léigh is a highly impressionistic story. There is an internal monologue, which seems to come from what would ordinarily be thought of as the viewpoint character, but the character has no conventional perception and is completely lost in some kind of symbolic 'mist'. Thus, the story is almost entirely image-based. The character sees odd colours in the mist and 'he' worries that perhaps he no longer even has a head. In some ways similar to this is Aonghas Pàdraig Caimbeul's 'Bho Dhòchas gu Buenos Aires' ('From Hope to Buenos Aires', G108, 1979). This is a highly impressionistic story. Even the dialogue, such as there is of it, is essentially a succession of statements about colours. The effect is of someone looking back quickly over certain key moments in a life, and of colour memory blurring the moments into one another. Alasdair Lippett's 'An Saighdear Dearg' ('The Red Soldier', G104, 1978)[9] is particularly well written. The story focuses on a soldier who has been hunting Highlanders and who has already killed two on this particular day. He is stalking one other Highlander, but he becomes tired and lies down to rest, falling asleep. The point-of-view is handled particularly well in this story. At the beginning, the reader is introduced to the narrative through the perspective of a hawk that is flying around far overhead. The hawk sees the soldier and wonders what he is, dismissing him as nothing edible. At first, it seems as if the hawk is a metaphor for the soldier, but then this becomes less clear as the story progresses.

Gairm in the 1980s

If it was 1960 that marked the arrival of the formally recognisable short story in Gaelic, it was the 1980s that finally saw an expansion and more general uptake of the genre, especially towards the end of the decade. More writers began to come onto the scene who demonstrated an awareness of the technical conventions, while some of the established writers continued to contribute, and even some of the more conservative writers like Eilidh Watt began to experiment and expand their range. For several years, Aonghas Pàdraig Caimbeul contributed stories that amount to some of the best work of his career. Meanwhile, long-term contributors like Iain MacLeòid went from strength to strength, and there were contributions from other accomplished writers like Pòl Mac a' Bhreatannaich, Dòmhnall Iain MacIomhair and Pòl MacAonghais. Iain Mac a' Ghobhainn published more stories in *Gairm* in the 1980s and 1990s than he had before, there being a gap of eighteen years between his penultimate collection and his final collection in Gaelic. At the same time, the more conventional Gaelic tales and yarns continued as before, many of them written by the same people who had been contributing for twenty years and more, such as Eilidh Watt and Cailein T. MacCoinnich.

Perhaps surprisingly, the 'conversation' began to return in the 1980s (with a few instances in earlier decades). Similarly, the folkloristic tall tale continued throughout the 1980s. At the same time, authors experimented with taking some of these elements from the Gaelic tradition and mixing them with modern technique. So, Dòmhnall Iain MacIomhair's 'Duilleag Eachdraidh' ('A Page of History', G137, 1986–7) merges elements of folklore with concerns about insanity, sexual practices and violence, while Magnus Odin Borg's 'An Tiodhlacadh Beò' ('The Live Burial', G114, 1981) is a strange mix of modern and traditional, featuring a dead man who haunts his wife. Other stories in the era demonstrate that fiction writers were at last learning how to build tension and anticipation. Iain MacLeòid's 'Thill Ailean' ('Alan Has Returned', G140, 1987) is a good example of this. The influence of the television soap opera can be seen in some of the tales in the 1980s and 1990s. Eilidh Watt was the chief proponent of this style of writing, but there were several others who also tried their hand. In a sense, this is a natural progression from some of the earlier melodramatic writing that can be found from the end of the nineteenth century, through the periodical publishing and into the novels of the early part of the twentieth century as well. Another form which (with very few exceptions) was new in the 1980s and continued from then onwards was the epistolary tale. Cairstìona NicAmhlaigh's 'Litir bho na h-Eileanan – sa' bhliadhna 2081' ('Letter from the Isles – in the year 2081, G116, 1981) combines the epistolary form with the enduring interest in science fiction that seems to be related to a concern with the future of the Gaelic language. In this story, Gaels are busily involved in exploring distant planets (still, it should be noted, constantly in 'exile'). There are still Gaels who like to cut peat, though. The story is clearly inspired by the themes of exile and exploration of what tradition means in the poetry of Ruaraidh MacThòmais, Iain Mac a' Ghobhainn and Deòrsa Caimbeul Hay: there are even quotations from some of their poetry in the text.

One of the stand-out comic stories at the beginning of the decade reaffirms the importance of humour in the *Gairm* short story. This is Pòl Mac a' Bhreatannaich's 'Donas an Smocaidh' ('The Evil of Smoking', G109, 1979–80). The comedy is focused on the ways that smoking can be bad for a person, outside of the usual, health-based issues. Mac a' Bhreatannaich places his protagonist into various social situations where smoking turns out to be detrimental. Cairistìona Dick is another fine comic writer. Her 'Talamh Bàn' ('Blank Ground', G126, 1984) makes fun of the Gael who tries to fit into the late twentieth century aspirational lifestyle. Like several other stories from this point onwards, 'Talamh Bàn' incorporates a good deal of English: the deployment of English is one of the key comic devices. The same issue of *Gairm* contains two other culture clash stories. The first is 'Tha Smùdan fhèin an Ceann Gach Simileir' ('Each Chimney Has its Own Smoke') by Tormod E. MacDhòmhnaill, and the other is 'An Teine' ('The Fire') by Aonghas nan Gleann. MacDhòmhnaill's story is set in the time of industrial unrest during the Thatcher years. It explores the effect of Thatcherism and of the strikes and other social troubles on one Highland family who live in the Lowlands. It is a highly powerful and effective story, using the focus of the central family to examine the issues at large. 'An Teine' looks at how it is to live in a transitional age and have access to both the old ways and the new. The main characters are Seònaid and Seòras, a couple who were married for many years and appreciated each other greatly. After Seòras dies, Seònaid realises that a particular kind of warmth has gone out of her life (despite all the modern conveniences) and that she will always now be less than she was.

Calum Iain Caimbeul's 'Sneachd an Earraich' ('Spring Snow', G137, 1986–7) is an excellent piece of writing, and it is a real loss to the literature that he did not contribute more. The narrative is second-person, and the subject matter of drowning kittens contrasts with the romantic imagery of the snow descriptions.

The final years of *Gairm*

By the end of the 1980s, Dòmhnall Iain MacIomhair, Iain MacLeòid and Aonghas MacBhàtair were established as some of the best regular contributors of short fiction in *Gairm*, along with major figures like Iain Mac a' Ghobhainn. In the 1990s, they were joined by Màiri NicGumaraid, Sorcha NicFhionghuinn (briefly) and Ali-B. There was still room for comedy, such as Seòras MacLeòid's 'An Sgiobair Mòr' ('The Great Skipper', G162, 1993), but there was a general movement away from the more frivolous tales towards a deeper and more expressive style of fiction as the century drew to a close. In the fifty years of magazines, there were only a tiny number of collaborations, with two of them coming in rapid succession. The first was 'Crìoch Gach Rannsachaidh' ('The End of Each Search', G164, 1993) by Iain and Ruairidh Dòmhnallach, and the second was 'Na Maraichean' ('The Sailors', G166, 1994), by Peigi and Calum MacMhaoilein. 'Crìoch Gach Rannsachaidh' has a very unsual, fragmentary style, and is laid out in a manner that deliberately draws attention to this. It takes the form largely of a kind of dramatic monologue, and it features a good deal of repetition, at times almost hypnotic in effect. The story's main character is a woman who has lost her husband of many years. The structure mirrors the way her thoughts are now fragmented and her feelings are shattered. The writing is very effective. 'Na Maraichean' conveys a sense of adventure and a genuine love of boats and sailing, which also comes across in Dòmhnall Alasdair's 'Ceit' ('Kate', G176, 1996) and in Dòmhnall na Hearadh's 'A' Càradh Eathar Dhòmhnaill' ('Mending Donald's Rowing Boat', G195, 2001). The descriptive writing in 'Na Maraichean' is engaging and convincing. The story continues in a later issue.

Even as *Gairm* was coming into its final years, there were still new writers emerging. Some of them, such as Gregor Addison, have gone on to find outlets elsewhere. 'Solas Madainn a' Gheamhraidh' ('The Light of a Winter Morning', G199, 2002) by Gregor Addison is a powerful and moving story about the hard reality of life and death. The main protagonist finds his dying mother with her neck broken and is confronted with the fact that family members die no matter how fiercely you might wish them not to. This leads to him clinging on to little fragments of the people who have left him behind as they die one by one. It is one of the most emotionally charged stories to appear in *Gairm*. Addison has also published effective stories in *Gath* and in the bilingual *Causeway/Cabhsair*. His 'Eadar Moch is Dubh' ('Between Dawn and Dusk', *Gath* 8, 2007) has a reminiscent, nostalgic tone, as the first-person narrator reaches two milestones in his life: his fortieth year, and the opportunity to leave the country and make a new life elsewhere. He comes to realise that maturation is not a steady process and that there are still aspects of the child within him, which is why he sometimes mourns his past. In 'Là Eile air an t-Saoghal' ('Another Day in the World', *Gath* 9, 2008), the reminiscent tone is still present, this time exploring the childhood relationship of two brothers and the effect of that on the main character's adult persona. Throughout the last years of *Gairm*, a number of stories appeared by Donnchadh MacGillÌosa. These are all loosely related, and they appeared later in the collection *Tocasaid 'Ain Tuirc*, which is discussed in Chapter 6. Similarly, Màrtainn Mac an t-Saoir, who later published *Ath-Aithne*, made his Gaelic fiction debut during this closing era. *Ath-Aithne* is also discussed in Chapter 6. Fionnlagh MacLeòid published only a few stories in *Gairm*, but his more recent work appeared in *Gath*, before being collected, along with many new stories, in his book *Dìomhanas*, which is discussed in Chapter 6.

Iain Mac a' Ghobhainn

Iain Mac a' Ghobhainn receives considerable attention elsewhere in this book, and so this section will take only a brief look at his uncollected stories. I am currently co-editing Mac a' Ghobhainn's collected Gaelic stories, and the volume will include extensive notes on both the stories that appeared in his five books and also in papers and magazines. As a result, there will be no damage done by keeping this discussion brief.

Gaelic stories are among Mac a' Ghobhainn's earliest published work, with 'Am Bodach' appearing in only the sixth issue of *Gairm*. 'Am Bodach' ('The Old Man') introduces a number of motifs that were prevalent throughout Mac a' Ghobhainn's work, some of which surely come from his own life. In particular, the motif of the boy next door dying is one that returns many times in both prose fiction and his poetry. 'Am Bodach' is told in a highly conversational style, which was innovative at the time, and the narrative often addresses 'you'. Several of the stories that would later appear in *Bùrn is Aran* and *An Dubh is An Gorm* were first published in *Gairm*. These include 'An Solas Ùr', ('The New Light'), 'Am Maor' ('The Factor'), 'Is Agus Esan' ('He and She') and 'An Cuan 'S Na Faoileagan' ('The Ocean and the Seagulls'). Stories that were not collected include 'Gammy', which was one of Mac a' Ghobhainn's first published works, 'An t-Iomradh' ('The Mention') and 'An Telegram', all of which appeared in *An Gaidheal* (60, 1965). One of the outstanding stories in Mac a' Ghobhainn's early years is 'Turas Do 'n Fhitheach' ('Journey to the Raven', *Gairm* 45, 1963). The first-person narrator is a doctor, who has a year to come to terms with the fact that he is dying. He finds the experience peculiar for all sorts of reasons, not least because he has dealt with these situations from the other perspective (and this is symbolised in the story by his repeatedly seeing himself in a mirror). A centrepiece of the story is the viewpoint character's manly, professional conversation with a fellow doctor, whom he knows well. The experience leads him to consider how strange the difference between life and death is:

> It wasn't right that people should die – the mind couldn't grasp it. (26)

[. . .]

> One minute he was alive and the next minute he was dead.
> But he was clearly the same person. (30)

The character is also struck by the idea of knowing about death. animals, he is sure, do not fear or dread death, and so they live in a different reality to the one inhabited by humans, who are aware of their own transience. He also finds that the knowledge that death is coming seems to make him want to spread it around, and he wonders if the knowledge of his impending death is changing his outward appearance. He thus gradually disconnects from his life, so that the prognosis is, in itself, a kind of self-fulfilling prophecy, as the warning of death has effectively killed him.

'Granny Anns a' Chornair' ('Granny in the Corner', G54, 1966) is either a series of short stories or a story broken into four parts, each one with a different point of view. The first part is in dramatic monologue style, and it essentially sets the scene for the other three. The other parts are 'Coinneach', 'Iain X + Y = Y + X', and 'Tormod'. The second, third and fourth parts each focus on one character introduced in the first part. Coinneach, Iain and then Tormod recall their personal histories after moving on from the first environment. Much of the focus is on their different interpretations and emphases in the recollections. 'Granny Anns a' Chornair' was anthologised in *Dorcha Tro Ghlainne*.

Considering Mac a' Ghobhainn's prolific output, it is almost surprising that only a handful of his stories appeared in magazines during the 1960s and 1970s. Among them are a few that would be familiar to readers of his English work, such as 'Maighstir Trill agus Vergil' ('Mister Trill and Vergil', G53, 1965), 'Anns a' Chafe' ('In the Cafe', G56, 1966) and 'Bràthair mo Mhàthar' ('My Mother's Brother', G93, 1975–6), which draw on the same pool of characters, motifs and settings as the English-language stories. Sometimes, the cross-over between the English and Gaelic stories is so great that translated versions of the same story are published in different places. Then again, stories like 'An Leanabh' ('The Child', G82, 1973) are unique to Gaelic. 'An Leanabh' is a sad and moving story about a little boy whose parents are divorced. He is swapped back and forth between them. It is not just the boy who is sad, but also his parents, and their guilt is imaged in various ways throughout the brief story.

Two further uncollected stories deserve a mention before we leave Iain Mac a' Ghobhainn. These are 'An Turas' ('The Trip', G140, 1987) and 'An Gunfighter' ('The Gunfighter', G141, 1987–8). These are both poignant stories about the ageing process. In 'An Turas', an old man's family take him to see the last bit of the island that he has never visited before in his life. They expect him to be happy that he has finally seen his whole island, but he becomes angry and uncommunicative. Evidently, the goal of seeing the whole island was one of the few things left to him, and he now understands that there is nothing left but death. His old age and his loss of his one remaining goal leave him upset. 'An Gunfighter' is about the way ageing changes people and, especially, about how someone's perception of another person can become stuck in the past.

Iain Moireach

It is much to be regretted that Iain Moireach's output as a short story writer has been so small. Then again, it may be that he has exercised good judgement by publishing only his best work, where other writers have diluted their reputations by allowing fiction of variable quality to reach the public eye. Moireach's 1965 story 'Dà Mhionad, no Fracas' ('Two Minutes, or Fracas', G53) introduces a theme that is often present in his work: the failure of communication. In this story, the characters theoretically share a language, English, but one of them speaks the Cockney variety and the other finds this exotic and incomprehensible. Moireach tropes this incomprehensibility in the way he writes the Cockney's utterances. In a similar way, 'Dealachadh' ('Split', G56, 1966) deals with friends who fall out because of a failure to communicate adequately. The narrator's friend,

Dòmhnall, is particularly vividly depicted in this story. Moireach has great skill with creating disturbing images and atmospheres. We see this on occasion in his collection, *An Aghaidh Choimheach*, which is discussed in Chapter 5. 'Am Bucas' ('The Box', G85, 1973) is one of the most striking examples. The story centres on two boys who live in a box. One of the boys has a missing leg. The other main character is a soldier whose sergeant has recently been shot by guerrilla fighters. The box, the missing leg, the soldier's sordid attempt to negotiate with a prostitute, and the whole atmosphere of poverty, depravity and underlying menace make this one of the more memorable of the stories to appear in *Gairm*.

Moireach's 'An Tuiteamas' ('The Happening') appeared in *Gath* 1 in 2003. The plot and the narrative style are in striking contrast to one another, although this appears not to be the case at first. For the first few paragraphs, the story seems to be shaping up to match the machismo of the first person narrator's assessment of a man who catches his attention in a coffee shop. Before the end, the reader begins to realise that the plot is a highly imaginative flight of fancy. In the next issue of *Gath* (also 2003), Moireach published 'An Imeachd' ('The Progress'). The style and plot of 'An Imeachd' could scarcely be more different from 'An Tuiteamas'. The third-person focal character is in the last years of his life, and he seems resigned to letting go. Then the story takes an unexpected romantic turn. The imagery in the story is well-worn in some ways – such as the main character's casting off of his old clothes that symbolises his casting off of his old personality – but it is handled well nevertheless. The lack of sentimentality helps to make the imagery seem fresher than it might. Moireach's third story in *Gath*, 'Mo Chrannchur' ('My Lot', *Gath* 3, 2004) is a beautifully written dramatic monologue in the person of an ageing sailor. He is telling his story to a fellow passenger on a ship bound for Bombay, using money he won on the lottery to go in an almost-certainly vain search for a woman he saw once. The descriptive language is economical and evocative, Moireach at his best:

> Ach aon latha, ann am Bombay, choinnich mi ris a' ghruagach a bu bhrèagha a bha coiseachd air talamh Dhè. Chunnaic mi pìos bhuam i, a' coiseachd thugam air sràid ghleadhrach. Bha i a' gluasad mar oiteag gaoithe, mar sgòth de dh'itean mìn, ioma-dhathach, cùbhraidh. Thug mi an aire, ged a bha a falt dubh, gun robh craiceann a gruaidhean na bu shoilleire na an cumantas – agus na sùilean aice eadar a bhith glas agus gorm. Co às a bha i? Carson a bha creutair cho àlainn, le soillse cho sònraichte, a' gluasad mar reul leatha fhèin ann an dòmhlachd sràid ud, far an robh seòladairean buaireasach a' losgadh an cuid airgid? (23)

(But one day, in Bombay, I met the most beautiful brownie ever to walk on God's earth. I saw her a little way away from me, walking towards me on a clamourous street. She moved like a breath of wind, like a cloud of fine, fragrant, multicoloured feathers. I noticed, although her hair was black, that the skin of her cheeks was paler than usual – and her eyes were somewhere between gray and blue. Where was she from? Why was such a gorgeous creature, with such a special sheen, moving like a star in the throng of that street, where wild sailors were burning their money?)

The narrator's pursuit of the woman is reminiscent of Pwyll's attempt to catch up with Rhiannon in the old Celtic story, and it is likely that this is a deliberate, if subtle, allusion.

Iain MacLeòid

Iain MacLeòid, author of the children's novels *Spuirean na h-Iolaire* (1989) and *An Sgàile Dhorcha* (1992), and the fine collection of very short stories *Sràidean is Slèibhtean* (1971), was a very regular contributor to *Gairm* for many years. His stories were often among the best in the magazine, with very few weaker ones among them. The range of subject matters and themes is wide and multifaceted. Some of his less successful stories were among the earliest, such as 'A' Bhreith' ('The Birth', *Gairm* G38, 1961), which is well enough written but suffers from trite, unnecessary dialogue. Similarly, 'Am Ministear Ùr' ('The New Minister', G86, 1974) has some fine touches in the use of language and imagery, but the plot itself is weak, relying as it does on a heavy-handed and predictable twist. MacLeòid's first short story to be comparable with the highest rank in Gaelic fiction is 'An Leabhar Ùr' ('The New Book', G93, 1975–6). This is a fictionalised account of John Carswell, the creator of the first printed book in Gaelic (his 'translation' of the *Book of Common Order*, in 1567). Carswell's achievement is always cited as one of the greatest milestones in Gaelic cultural history. And yet, as MacLeòid suggests in this story, it is also a milestone in the long decline of Gaelic: despite the innovation of a printed book, Gaelic literature did not proceed to flourish either in the sixteenth century or even in the seventeenth or eighteenth centuries. Dramatic irony in the narrative subtly suggests these things even while allowing Carswell to feel relief at finishing his mammoth task (see also his 'An Oidhche a Bhruidhinn Pangur' ['The Night that Pangur Spoke', G184, 1998]).

'Dealbhannan' ('Pictures', G141, 1987–8) demonstrates MacLeòid's ability to convey depth of emotion, as the main character accidentally takes a picture of the woman he loves in the arms of another man. Similarly, 'A' Chathair Fhalamh' ('The Empty Chair', G144, 1988) effectively deals with loneliness and the artificial barriers people erect between one another. MacLeòid is also capable of comedy. His 'Aisling Otis' ('Otis's Dream', G139, 1987) pokes fun at his American main character, who has the uneducated ambition to move to an island and become a Gael. It is only when he gets there and sees the other side of rural life that he realises his dream was foolish. 'Thill Ailean', which was discussed briefly above, is a marked contrast to 'Aisling Otis'. It has one of the most menacing atmospheres in any Gaelic story. It is tightly structured and makes good use of technical devices such as the flashback and foreshadowing to suggest impending violence. 'Ketilsdalr' (G152, 1990) does not stop at the threat of violence: it is one of the most explicitly violent of all Gaelic stories. The main characters are Picts, who have been taken as slaves by some vikings who have taken possession of their island home. One of the slaves is obsessed with the idea of killing one of the viking leaders.

One of MacLeòid's most interesting contributions is a series of stories about a magical creature called the Gruagach. In 'Trioblaidean a' Ghruagaich' ('The Brownie's Difficulties', several issues in the mid-nineties), the Gruagach lives among humans, hiding his true nature from them. He falls in love with the mortal woman Peigi, and gradually realises that this will rob him of his own relative immortality: passion is the thing that separates humans from brownies, and by feeling passion he is speeding up the passing of his life. It is difficult for him to make the choice to commit to a shorter, more exciting life with Peigi or accept his original destiny and remain a brownie for millennia. The folkloric influences are clear here, and this sequence makes for an interesting comparison with the stories of Donnchadh MacGilliosa and Fionnlagh MacLeòid's novel *Gormshuil an Rìgh* (discussed in Chapters 3 and 6): it also compares with MacLeòid's own 'An Leughadair' ('The Reader', G175, 1996), in which the title character does not commit enough of himself to life because he spends too much time reading.

Dòmhnall Iain MacIomhair

Dòmhnall Iain MacIomhair, author of the novel for teenagers *Cò Rinn E?* (1993), contributed many stories to *Gairm* over a period of many years and became especially prolific during the magazine's latter years. An early story in MacIomhair's *ouevre*, 'Am Briseadh' ('The Break', G116, 1981) establishes his quirky sense of irony, which is shown again in the delightful 'An Leabhar Buidhe' ('The Yellow Book', G150, 1990), in which the main character buys a new notebook. Instead of writing in his book, he simply stares at the blank pages and imagines all manner of wonderful stories and pictures. Many of MacIomhair's stories eschew conventions of realism, and some of them are particularly surreal. 'Ceangal is Dealachadh'

('Joining and Separation', G125, 1983–4), 'Duilleag Eachdraidh' ('A Page of History', G137, 1986–7), 'Seònaid' ('Janet', G160, 1992) and 'Blàr na h-Inntinne' ('The Battle of the Mind', G167, 1994) are all examples of stories that are surreal in one way or another. 'Ceangal is Dealachadh' starts off in second-person narration, which has rarely been attempted in Gaelic. Vivid descriptions of the physical landscape contrast with the bizarre visions going on in the focal character's mind. 'Duilleag Eachdraidh', as suggested above, mixes elements of folklore and insanity. 'Seònaid' begins conventionally enough, focusing on a main character who becomes infatuated with a glamorous air hostess. At first, it appears that Seònaid takes the place of the focal character's lost love, and the narrative points towards a romantic development or else a story of unrequited love. Seònaid becomes deified in the main character's mind to the extent that he begins to slip out of reality. Eventually, she gets up from her seat and flies out of the window, taking her deification to its natural and absurd conclusion. MacIomhair's quirky humour shows up once more in 'Seònaid', both in relation to the unexpected development in the plot and also in his use of language, such as in the zeugmatic: ''s i a' toirt na troilidhe agus a casan leatha' (373).[10] 'Blàr na h-Inntinne', in some ways the strangest of all MacIomhair's stories, is connected to 'Duilleag Eachdraidh' by the motif of Culloden. The main character Uilleam is suffering from vivid visions of his dead father, but he also begins to see scenes from the battle at Culloden, which he has studied at school. The people who care for him become concerned, but Uilleam seems to be beyond their reach.

There are other stories in which either the plot or setting are more conventionally real but in which one particular character stands out as strange in one way or another. Among these stories are 'Criosaidh' ('Chrissie', G142, 1988), 'A' Choinneamh-Ùrnaigh' ('The Prayer Meeting', G153, 1990–1) and 'Tuigidh Tu Fhathast' ('You Will Understand Yet', G170, 1995). In 'Tuigidh Tu Fhathast', a normal couple take in a girl who begins to tell them all sorts of unlikely yarns. They find her tales strange and somehow disturbing, until her father arrives and the husband at least begins to understand why the girl is how she is. The girl in 'Tuigidh Tu Fhathast' has a good deal in common with the title character in 'Criosaidh'. People find it difficult to communicate with Criosaidh or understand her, as she seems to inhabit a different reality. When she predicts her own death and then disappears, her family become fearful. 'A' Choinneamh-Ùrnaigh' is a highly symbolic story of a madwoman who enters a prayer meeting armed with a Bible and a gun. She absurdly claims those in attendance have killed her a long time ago. Unexpected events also occur in stories which have more of a sentient focus: in 'Turas na Ceiste' ('The

Journey of the Question', G194, 2001), the main character climbs up to Heaven in order to speak to the poet Uilleam Ros.

One of MacIomhair's concerns is the meeting of two or more cultures. Several of his stories deal with this, with varying levels of success. 'An Dèidh na Sìthe' ('After the Peace', G131, 1985) is a rather obvious and hackneyed story of a young woman, Màiri, bringing home a German boyfriend from university. Màiri's father was in the Second World War and has never recovered from the trauma of his experiences, so he cannot cope with having a German boy in the house. The ending is left ambiguous. Related to this, but more effective, is another culture clash story, 'Hussein Assam' (G154, 1991). This time, the young woman Sìne brings home an Arab boyfriend from university, but the results are not as violent or upsetting as in 'An Dèidh na Sìthe'.

MacIomhair's greatest strength as a writer of fiction is his skill with structure. His best stories, such as 'Mona Lisa' (G126, 1984), 'Facail Sheumais ris an Psychiatrist' ('James's Words to the Psychiatrist', G144, 1988), 'Uinneagan' ('Windows', G180, 1997) and 'Màiri' (G181, 1997–8), are all very carefully and deliberately structured. 'Mona Lisa' is infused with a sense of transition: liminal spaces and mirrors give the focal character cause to consider his own identity and his apparent angst. Unexpectedly, he then meets a woman and their meeting rounds the story off with a sense of possibility and hope. 'Facail Sheumais ris an Psychiatrist' takes the form of a dramatic monologue. The other interlocutor, the psychiatrist, is implied by some of the responses that Seumas gives. Seumas is troubled by rather Socratic questions:

> although you can tell a person what a table is by showing him a table, you can't do that with love. (356)

> [. . .]

> Where is my reason? I don't see it. I don't feel it. (357)

The conversation gradually descends from a normal session to the stage where Seumas realises the psychiatrist is going to have him certified. He is then angry that it is so expensive to be declared insane. 'Uinneagan' does not have a linear narrative or a single sentient focus. Instead, it is a linked sequence of eight fragmentary tales. In each one, a character looks through a window and sees something that is suggestive of something in his or her own life. Some of the characters are fortunate and others are less so. Some of the characters achieve epiphanies as a result of what they see through the windows, and others do not. 'Màiri' only works as a story because of the care with which it is structured. It is only by the gradual revelation of what Màiri has been doing and where she has been that the story gains significance.

Rob Shirley

Rob Shirley has contributed several stories to *Gairm* and *Gath*, although has not been as prolific as Dòmhnall Iain MacIomhair. Shirley exhibits a keen interest in science fiction and in ideas of what alternative futures might be like, particularly in his early work. His 1961 story 'An Duine Ùr' ('The New Man', G38), for instance, is set in a future in which Mary Shelley's vision has become scientific reality and surgeons are capable of reanimating corpses. They have even discovered a way to graft the best parts of different corpses onto each other in order to create superior beings. In another futuristic story from the same era, 'Mr Universe' (G46, 1964), Shirley's main protagonist is a Gael from the Western Isles who is spotted by a talent scout for the Mr Universe contest. In this version of the contest, the winner is appointed to the government. The main character, Dòmhnall Mòr, is a strong contender because of his natural, rural lifestyle, avoiding all the weakening influences of the convenience society. The story pokes fun at our increasing globalisation and reliance on technology, while also raising the alarm about societal tendencies. It is still topical more than forty years after it was published.

After a long hiatus, Shirley returned to publishing in *Gairm* with the risqué 'Obh, Obh Ghranaidh!' ('Oh dear Granny!', G195, 2001), which relies on misunderstandings brought about by the use of Gaelic and imperfect English. Shirley's 'Mo Bhotainn Chlì' ('My Left Boot', G198, 2002) is more of an adventure tale with a slight twist, where 'Dìreadh is Teàrnadh' ('Climbing and Descending', G200, 2002) is based on a single main metaphor. His stories have continued to appear, more regularly, in *Gath*. His 'Seann Amadan' ('Old Fool', *Gath* 3, 2004) features a character who prides himself on retaining his faculties into his seventies and, like 'Seanchaidh an Taoibh Tuath' ('Storyteller of the North', *Gath* 5, 2006), it positions itself within a modernised traditional Gaelic culture. 'Iar-ogha an Fhuadaiche' ('The Exile's Great-Grandchild', *Gath* 8, 2007) does the same, but this position is strongly tempered by an awareness of globalisation. 'Iar-ogha an Fhuadaiche' is so heavily reliant on dialogue that it is almost a 'conversation'.

Rarlon Seixias (Dòmhnall MacDhòmhnaill)

Rarlon Seixias was the pen-name of Dòmhnall MacDhòmhnaill in the 1960s. He contributed several entries to *Gairm*, including a few short stories, and then was silent until 1992. His 'Curstaidh' ('Kirsty', *Gairm* G158, 1992) is a particularly moving tale about someone who is caring for a relative who is bedridden after a stroke. MacDhòmhnaill handles emotion with great sensitivity. As Seixias, he was responsible for two of the highlights of the fiction in the early years of *Gairm*: 'An Starsach' ('The Threshold', G30, 1959) and 'A' Phrosbaig' ('The Telescope', G49, 1964). In 'An Starsach', religion is used as a metonym for the indomitability of the human spirit: it is depicted as a sort of cipher, a device that people use to overcome hardship. The young boy who is the sentient focus of the story learns a lesson about the human spirit by observing the way his family react to a catalogue of disasters that threaten to bring them all to grief. In 'A' Phrosbaig', the main character lives his life vicariously, relying on his telescope to bring him second-hand life from his neighbours. As Donald John MacLeod states: 'The author clearly, if unobtrusively, sympathises with him rather than with the police who take him away and the family he has been watching, who express uncomprehending disgust' (MacLeod 1970: 103). Seixias has also written more light-hearted fare, reminiscent of some of the work of Cailein T. MacCoinnich, such as 'Grian is Grian-Uisg' (G40, 1962).

Eilidh Watt

Eilidh Watt was almost certainly the most prolific of all the writers of short fiction in Gaelic. Her stories for adults appeared in two main collections, which are discussed in Chapter 5, but she also contributed staggering numbers of uncollected stories to *Gairm* over the course of two decades. For several years in the 1970s and 1980s, in particular, scarcely an issue of the magazine appeared without at least one of her stories in it. The quality of Watt's stories is variable, but there is no doubt that much of her best writing appeared in *Gairm* rather than in her published books. One of the earliest is 'A' Bhàs' ('The Vase', G75, 1971), in which the vase is a trope for the main character's youth, her early home and thoughts about her mother. It is a powerful and well-written story. On the other hand, stories like 'Aon Fhacal anns an Dus' ('One Word in the Dust', G78, 1972) and 'Bannan' ('Bonds', G89, 1974–5), which concentrate on personal relationships and love, often tend to descend into melodrama. There are also stories like 'An Comharradh' ('The Mark', G83, 1973) which are doomed to bathos by a misguided attempt to contrive significance. Others still, such as 'Far-ainm' ('Nickname', G96, 1976) lack any *raison d'être*. In 'Ribeanan Dearga' ('Red Ribbons', G103, 1978), Watt demonstrates her considerable skill with imagery. Disturbing juxtapositions serve to make this story of a horrible killing very powerful. 'Pururaich Cait' ('Purring of a Cat', G118, 1982) is another of her more successful stories. Although, like 'Ribeanan Dearga', it has death and suffering at its core, 'Pururaich Cait' is completely different in style and subject matter. A group of boys growing up learn about the harsh necessities of life, and perhaps also about mercy and self-sacrifice, when their father drowns kittens in a bag. The boys begin to understand their own place in the world thereafter, although one of the boys resolves to rescue one kitten. Both 'An Dèidh-Làimh' ('Afterward', G121, 1982–3) and 'Roghainn' ('Choice', G123, 1983) show Watt's interest in the golden age-style science fiction that was so popular among *Gairm*'s contributors in the 1960s and 1970s. The former tells of the aftermath of a global catastrophe such as a nuclear holocaust, while the latter is set in a future in which an authoritarian interplanetary society regards people involved in interpersonal relationships as 'throwbacks'. 'Seumas' ('James', G141, 1987–8) is one of Watt's darker and more complex stories. The interplay between characters is convincing. Seumas, the title character, finds himself covering for his son, who has accidentally killed a neighbour who has been molesting him. The story is rich in psychological texture.

Cailein T. MacCoinnich

Like Eilidh Watt, Cailein T. MacCoinnich was an enormously prolific contributor to *Gairm*, mainly contributing stories that did not appear in his published collections. For the most part, MacCoinnich's stories are plot-driven or moral-based. As in *Nach Neònach Sin* (discussed in Chapter 5), some of them focus on paranormal events or are based in slightly altered realities. Many of them, however, fall into the patterns in *Mar Sgeul a Dh'innseas Neach*, and are either contrived mysteries or rather didactic yarns. A significant bulk of the stories feature a protagonist (usually an associate of the main character) who uses his considerable mental skills to solve a conundrum or to win an argument. In this way, MacCoinnich's stories often owe a great deal to the 'conversation' tradition, as discussed in Chapter 1. As in the conversations, the plot of his stories often hinges on the author's control over the turns and the manipulation of facts to suit the favoured character's argument. MacCoinnich made frequent use of the Agatha Christie-style revelation in which all of the characters/suspects are lined up and then the clever detective explains all. An example of this is 'Lorgan san t-Sneachda' ('Prints in the Snow', G117, 1981–2), which mainly consists of a long-winded trawl through the clues and suspects, along with an unengaging discussion of motives and possibilities. In the end, there is a twist, as the detective reveals that nobody 'dunnit': the victim has been killed by a large icicle falling on him; the icicle subsequently melted and left no trace of what caused the wound.

Aonghas Pàdraig Caimbeul

Despite his much wider fame as a poet and novelist, Aonghas Pàdraig Caimbeul's short stories account for some of the sharpest and freshest writing in his career to date.[11] He exhibits a range of techniques and subject matters, and exercises particular skill with imagery. His 'Madainn an Dealain-dè' ('The Morning of the Butterfly', G111/112, 1980) is almost poetic in some of its structural features. The plot is based on the same kinds of elements that dominated much of the fiction at the beginning of the century (such as lovers separated by the sea), but the technique is innovative and engaging. Similarly, 'Canabhas Uaine agus Ceap an t-Seòladair' ('Green Canvass and the Sailor's Cap', G109, 197–80), about a young woman who strikes up a conversation with a stranger, is highly imagistic and replete with powerful symbolism. It is one of his most successful pieces. In much of Caimbeul's work, the sense of a Gaelic identity – or indeed a more localised version of identity than even that – is of paramount concern. 'Ciontach no Neo-chiontach' ('Guilty or Not Guilty', G110, 1980) is therefore of interest precisely because it is so infused with an Anglo-Lowland cultural sensibility. The sense of identity, the vocabulary, and the interests of the main character are all hybridised. 'Canabhas Uaine agus Ceap an t-Seòladair' similarly focuses on a main character who is culturally Anglo-American.

Màiri NicGumaraid

Màiri NicGumaraid, known as a fine poet, is also perhaps one of the most underrated writers of fiction in the language. Although some of her stories are not as strong as others, the best of her pieces can rank alongside anything by Iain Mac a' Ghobhainn or Iain Moireach. NicGumaraid excels at point-of-view and subtle characterisation. 'A' Dol A-mach gu Cofaidh' ('Going Out for Coffee', G194, 2001) is an example of this. Although the plot is mundane, following the lives and relationships of a group of office workers, the point-of-view is innovative and slightly quirky, moving from character to character during the same scene. Her 'Stiopaill is Rudan Eile' ('Steeples and Other Things', G151, 1990) is even more successful. It takes the form of a dramatic monologue, but it is complex and multi-layered, full of religious, literary and cultural allusions. The viewpoint character makes the observation that it is a 'terribly Celtic thing to take an interest in families and who belongs to whom' (258), which places this story within the long tradition of Gaelic fiction that is concerned with trying to identify the traits of the Gael (bearing in mind the other long tradition of using the term 'Celtic' loosely). NicGumaraid's most impressive story is 'Cinn Sgeul' ('Story Ends', G159, 1992), which is set on a train. The unique first-person voice is most convincing. The viewpoint character describes details of the journey, interspersed with details of thoughts, feelings and observations. These descriptions and observations are interrupted by flashbacks and foreshadowing of other times in her life. The fragmenting effect of this is counteracted by the structure of the journey itself, which holds the story together, in much the same way as Caimbeul attempts to do in his novel *Tilleadh Dhachaigh* (discussed in Chapter 6).

Aonghas MacBhàtair

Aonghas MacBhàtair's 'Am Fòn' ('The Phone', G142, 1988) hinges on the metonym of the phone itself, which acts as a cipher for all of the angst and trauma that the main character is experiencing. This character's husband of fifty years has died, and now she must contemplate breaking the news to their children and then making the formal arrangements. All of it must be done by means of the phone, and so the phone has become the object of her hatred for the time being. The first-person viewpoint character's emotions are portrayed in a convincingly restrained manner, which is enhanced by MacBhàtair's skilful deployment of imagery. MacBhàtair's range encompasses poignant stories like this and 'Bruadaran' ('Dreams', G162, 1993), in which people dream of changing their lives, as well as more light-hearted, entertaining fare: in 'Tilleadh' ('Return', G146, 1989), a band of warriors from the ancient past appears in the present day and prepares to raid a village. 'Còmhradh Samhraidh' ('Summer Conversation', G153, 1990–1) parodies the contemporary Gaelic community, with its Anglophone, non-traditional *cèilidhs* and macaronic conversations. 'Sgeulachd Ruairidh Reamhair' ('Fat Rory's Tale', G168, 1994) is pure comedy.

MacBhàtair's 'Bana-Charaid nan Gàidheal' ('Female Friend of the Gaels, G165, 1993–4) addresses the same issue that is also present in Iain MacLeòid's 'Aisling Otis', as mentioned above, while also clearly alluding to Norman Macleod's status in an ironic fashion. The main character in 'Bana-Charaid nan Gàidheal' looks after an old woman who has romantic illusions about Gaelic, the Gaels and the places usually associated with Gaels. The main character is herself a Gael, and perhaps there is a suggestion that their friendship is partly based on this. She has an urge to disabuse her friend of her romantic notions, but, at the same time, does not want to rob her of her pleasant fancies.

Conclusion

Gairm endured for fifty years, a remarkable feat for a magazine that was driven primarily by one individual for the majority of those years. As I mentioned at the beginning of this chapter, MacThòmais's closing editorial claimed that the short story had grown up in Gaelic during those fifty years. His claim was justified. For the first few years, stories followed familiar models, but then they began to turn into more literary works from about 1960 onward. This chapter is regrettably not long enough to be able to do justice to the great numbers of writers who published only one, two or three stories in their careers, and it is evident from this short review that a large-scale piece of work needs to be dedicated entirely to the short fiction published in the second half of the twentieth century. Writers like Sorcha NicFhionghuin, whose output was small but significant, deserve much closer attention. (NicFhionghuin's work is a high-water mark in a second major development in the story that took place in the late 1980s and during the 1990s.) Where convincing characterisation and the formally realistic techniques of description made their appearance in the 1960s, innovations in other narrative techniques were slow and sporadic in evolution before the middle of the 1980s. Some long-established writers like Dòmhnall Iain MacIomhair, Iain Mac a' Ghobhainn and Iain MacLeòid helped to guide the way with these innovations, but the short story truly began to develop in organic fashion when Aonghas Pàdraig Caimbeul, Ali-B, and Aonghas MacBhàtair joined them. With the addition of Màiri NicGumaraid, Donnchadh MacGillÌosa, Aonghas Mac-a-Phì and Sorcha NicFhionghuin, the short story in Gaelic came close to eclipsing poetry as the premier form of literary expression in the language at the end of the twentieth century.

In some ways, in terms of the fiction published in its pages, *Gath* has effectively been a continuation of *Gairm*, even though the two magazines are different in other substantial ways. Several of the same writers who modernised the short story in the pages of *Gairm* have continued to send their work to the new magazine, including a few of the youngest writers who had just started publishing as *Gairm* came to an end. A small number of anthologies have been published in the period in which the short story came of age. Among these are *Dorcha Tro Ghlainne* (1970), edited by Dòmhnall Iain MacLeòid (Donald John MacLeod), *Eadar Peann is Pàipear* (1985), edited by Dòmhnall Iain MacIomhair, and *Amannan* (1979), edited by Pòl MacAonghais. The more recent anthology set *An Claigeann aig Damien Hirst* (2009) has not been drawn primarily from previously published work. If *Gath* can establish itself on a regular and long-term basis, if Ùr-Sgeul keep encouraging the publication of both collections and anthologies, and if magazines like *New Writing Scotland* and *Causeway / Cabhsair* continue to publish some Gaelic stories along with their other content, there is every reason to expect that the short story will continue to go from strength to strength as a form. If Frank O'Connor (2004) was correct in his view that smaller societies suit the short story, then the short story has perhaps found a suitable home in the Gaelic community.

Chapter 4

The Second Wave of Novels

Following the publication of *Cailin Sgiathanach* (1923), more than forty years passed before novels began appearing in print again. We may consider the second wave of novels as encompassing those that appeared between 1971 and 1996. This quarter-century period saw a gradual adoption of the form, but the sporadic appearance of novels during the period suggests that a lack of enthusiasm persisted for the remainder of the twentieth century. It has only been in the present century that a third wave of novel writing has emerged, nurtured and supported by the Gaelic Books Council. The third wave of novels is discussed in the chapter on contemporary fiction.

Although more than twenty-five novels have been published since 1980,[1] there is still no question that the two most successful novels in Gaelic to date were Iain Mac a' Ghobhainn's *An t-Aonaran* (1976, 'The Hermit') and Tormod Caimbeul's *Deireadh an Fhoghair* (1979, 'The End of Autumn'). As a phenomenon, the novel in Gaelic gave every appearance of having been a short-lived experiment, amounting to no more than the books discussed in Chapter 2. It may be that the three early novels were ill-received by their audience,[2] or that the linguistic exploration involved in developing sustained prose fiction at that time proved too much of a challenge for anyone other than MacCormaic, MacDhonnachaidh and MacLeòid. Or, it may simply be that the inter-war years left the Gaelic literati feeling disillusioned about the prospects of the novel in the language. At any rate, the next novels did not start to appear until the end of the 1960s. The first of them were children's novels, with Pòl MacAonghais's *Teine Ceann Fòid*, a translation of Allan Campbell MacLean's *Ribbon of Fire*, blazing something of a trail in 1967.[3] The number of novels written for children and adolescents has grown steadily since then, and includes several translations as well as original works. One of the earliest, and most notable, was Iain Mac a' Ghobhainn's *Iain a-measg nan Reultan* (1970, 'Iain among the Stars'), which Donald Meek described at a talk in 2001 as a seminal moment in Gaelic fiction. According to Meek, this was the first successful attempt at any kind of sustained science-fiction in Gaelic that managed to come across naturally and yet fire the imagination at the same time. The present book does not consider literature written for children or teenagers, as that would expand the size of the volume enormously and requires a rather different approach. It is work that should be done in future, however.

An t-Aonaran

An t-Aonaran is only questionably a novel at all. At around 18500 words, it is only slightly longer than MacCormaic's *Gun D' Thug I Spéis Do 'n Àrmunn*, which was marketed as a 'novelette'. To many readers, it would be a 'novella'. Indeed, an English version, 'The Hermit', was published as a short story in *The Hermit and other stories* (1977). However, to avoid a potentially fruitless examination of the technical differences between novel and short story (see, among others, various essays in May 1994 for sometimes conflicting views on this), it is best to accept the wishes of the author and publisher and call the book a novel for the time being. For the reader who has an imperfect reading ability in Gaelic, 'The Hermit' makes *An t-Aonaran* accessible, but the style works significantly better in Gaelic. Máire Ní Annracháin rates it highly: 'any literary tradition which has masterpieces like Iain Mac a' Ghobhainn's novels clearly has access to resources which make up for its numerical limits' (Ní Annracháin 2006: 141).

The plot of *An t-Aonaran* is simple enough for a short story: a hermit comes to live just outside a small Gaelic-speaking community; the locals are disturbed by his presence; the retired schoolmaster experiences a peculiar personal reaction to him and arranges for him to be run out of town. Unlike the plotting in the three early novels, or even in *A' Leth Eile* (1971) and *Gainmheach an Fhàsaich* (1971), *An t-Aonaran* is minimalist in the extreme. But, also unlike these other novels, the plot remains entirely credible throughout. As the novel progresses, character-perspective reminiscences, and sparingly used flashbacks, fill in background details that help us to understand why people's lives and relationships are the way they are. (In this way, the structure of *An t-Aonaran* resembles Iain Moireach's story 'Am Partaidh'.) We learn that the retired schoolmaster, Teàrlach, had an unhappy marriage to a wife who was never content with their lifestyle: her unhappiness mainly stemmed from her feeling like an outsider, as she was not a Gaelic-speaker and was more at home in the city than in a rural community. We also learn that Teàrlach's unhappiness and inability to communicate with others may have their origins in his childhood, as he was brought up by a mother who prioritised his education over all other forms of development. We learn that Teàrlach, too, was perhaps happier when he lived in the city, and that he and his wife were contented together before they moved back to his home village. All of these details become significant as the novel progresses, but their significance only becomes clear as the whole picture emerges.

Characterisation in *An t-Aonaran* is far more subtle and effective than in any other Gaelic novel to date. Mac a' Ghobhainn's spare, uncomplicated style lends itself to a highly economical depiction of character traits, foibles and emotions. As an example of this, we may consider the part of the novel when Teàrlach decides that he would like to start taking fresh milk from a neighbour who owns a cow. Through dramatic irony, the reader is already aware that Teàrlach's motivations may not be entirely to do with the milk: the neighbour has an 18-year-old daughter, Seonag, whom Teàrlach has been admiring as she passed his window every day. When Teàrlach goes to ask his neighbour for the milk, the neighbour is honoured and embarrassed to be entering into a transaction with a respected member of the community such as the retired schoolmaster. Seonag, however, shows no interest in the negotiations as Teàrlach and her father engage in small-talk: 'Bha Seonag ag ithe a biadh le a ceann crom' (31, 'Seonag was eating her food with her head down'). When Teàrlach first raises the subject of buying milk from the family, Seonag looks directly at him: 'Thog Seonag a ceann 's sheall i orm airson a' chiad uair' (32, 'Seonag lifted her head and looked at me for the first time'). Still, she makes no contribution to the discussion, and neither her mother nor her father appear to notice her reaction. Teàrlach then suggests that Seonag could deliver the milk, and: 'Sheall Seonag dìreach 'nam aodann' (32, 'Seonag looked me full in the face'). Prior to this, we know next to nothing about Seonag, other than that she is a beautiful young girl and that Teàrlach imagines she is rather vacuous. This exchange, and her interpolated reactions – noticed only by Teàrlach – suggest that there is rather more to her than there first appeared. When Seonag's father then mentions her fiancé, she is suddenly embarrassed, although she has shown no overt emotion up to this point: the novel thus depicts her conflicting feelings and her desire to keep this aspect of herself from Teàrlach. Teàrlach's initial reaction is disappointment that Seonag is already spoken for, and we may infer that her anticipation of this reaction was what caused her embarrassment. However, Teàrlach immediately rationalises that it is perfectly natural and normal for a girl of her age to be intending to marry and he should not have expected anything else. Seonag, meanwhile, remains silent, and the narrative keeps emphasising her silence, which has been broken only once up to this point. For the first time, Teàrlach as first-person narrator drops a stronger hint that his interest is more in Seonag than in the milk, and he makes this hint through his analysis of Seonag's observations of him:

Chunna mi Seonag a' sealltainn rium airson diog le sùil ghéir, mar gum bitheadh i a' tuigsinn nan nithean nach robh mi ag ràdh. Eòlas aosd 'na sùilean. Eòlas aosd nam boireannach. (33)

(I saw Seonag looking at me for a second with a sharp eye, as if she understood the things I was not saying. Old knowledge in her eyes. The old knowledge of women.)

As the chapter closes, Teàrlach begins to work on a painting which has a man in a trap and a wild cat with striking eyes. By saying and doing almost nothing, Seonag has managed to lead him into what he sees as a perilous situation, and he does not know how to escape: all of this is imaged in his painting.

A central theme of *An t-Aonaran*, as I have suggested elsewhere, is that of metaphysical estrangement (Watson 2002). Specifically, this relates to the issue of characters not speaking the same language as one another. For instance, Teàrlach's late wife felt exiled from the community through not being a Gaelic speaker. At the same time, the hermit himself is removed from the community, both physically and metaphysically. His metaphysical exile is the more profound of the two, and it is caused by his refusal to speak to anyone (we know he is capable of speech, as he is overheard mumbling to himself). Teàrlach is also isolated because of conversation, however, but in a more subtle way. In the episode described above, in which Teàrlach arranges for Seonag to visit him, there is more than one level of conversation going on. He is unable to express his true purpose because he cannot risk losing his standing in the community, even though that standing is based on keeping himself aloof from everyone. Throughout the novel, there are many other instances of Teàrlach being unable to communicate fully because of various barriers that he himself has imposed. In many cases, Teàrlach's inability to communicate with his neighbours is caused by his interest in literature and art and his refusal to believe that he thus has anything in common with the other local people. It becomes clear very quickly that even his wife could not communicate with Teàrlach adequately, despite her own background in higher education and their shared experiences of living elsewhere:

I would listen to her as I read my book as if I were listening to a burn running past on a summer day. (6)

Despite this, Teàrlach exhibits a constant awareness that it is not normal or natural to live in isolation from other people. He has a repeated mantra that people must live among other people, and he finds the hermit incomprehensible because he violates what Teàrlach sees as a basic human law.

It is his dogmatic adherence to this tenet that leads Teàrlach to make the reprehensible decision that brings about the novel's climax.

An t-Aonaran is a remarkable book, no less significant for all its brevity. At the beginning of this brief discussion, I noted that it is only questionably a novel at all. This point relates primarily to its length. The movement of the book, in the way it charts Teàrlach's character development, makes it read like a novel despite its length. It is one of the most important Gaelic literary artefacts from the twentieth century and deserves to be studied at much greater length.

A' Leth Eile and Gainmheach an Fhàsaich

An t-Aonaran was not the first of the new novels. The first two novels written for adults after the half-century hiatus were Cailein T. MacCoinnich's *A' Leth Eile* ('The Other Half') and Màiri NicGill-Eain's *Gainmheach an Fhàsaich* ('The Desert Sand'), both published in 1971. Neither of these novels was especially well-received when they were first published, but Donald Meek's 're-assessment' of MacCoinnich included a relatively positive reading of *A' Leth Eile* (Meek 1983).

Unusually among Gaelic novels, *A' Leth Eile* does not have either a clutch of Gaels as its central characters or a Highland setting.[4] Indeed, this fact invited the faint praise of Pòl MacAonghais's review of the novel in *Gairm* in 1972, where he hinted that, although the book was well-written, it was not very *Gàidhealach*. By the standards of the more recent novels, this charge would be much less likely to be applied at all, although there does still seem to be a tendency for authors to cling to Gaels as characters or to typically 'Gaelic' settings.

The main character in *A' Leth Eile* is a young man called Daibhidh MacLiuthair, who, at the beginning of the novel, has recently graduated with an LLD. Thus we know that he is a very scholarly young man. We also learn at once that he lived with his aunt and uncle until they died a short time before, so there is a sense that he is cast adrift, alone in the world: although he has a cousin, it is clear that their relationship is not close. He decides to do some travelling, to get out and find out how the 'other half lives'. As Donald Meek has pointed out, it is never entirely clear just who this 'other half' are, and the concept even seems to shift at times during the course of the novel (Meek 1983). At any rate, he sets off with little in the way of money or provisions, but he has his youth, his health, strength and good brain. In fact, Daibhidh's ability to get by and make his way in the world is the most striking feature of the novel: he is a character unsurpassed in talents and abilities. This is just as well, as he imposes some stringent challenges upon himself: he determines that he will walk at all times, regardless of what transport may be available, and he will refuse all charity unless in dire emergencies. These challenges reveal Daibhidh as a strong-willed, proud and self-reliant man, who feels equal to anything that might come his way. Indeed, an underlying theme of the novel is the idea that people can have hidden depths, and it does not do to judge anyone too hastily. Daibhidh himself is not overly quick to judge, although the narrative sometimes presumes to do so on his behalf, in order to highlight just how shrewd Daibhidh himself is. For instance, he meets a 'tinker' on the road. He gives the tinker some of the last of his good tobacco and the man instantly recognises its quality. They have a good chat and Daibhidh gives him food too. The man is surprisingly well-read and knows his philosophy and other scholarly writing, 'revealing refinement that is not common in his sort' (18), and leading Daibhidh to conclude that 'many a noble man is in rags and many a blackguard in finery' (18). The tinker gives him directions and they part on good terms, promising to look out for each other if they meet again. They do, in fact, meet again, and Daibhidh is determined to use his lawyerly skills to defend his friend when he fears he may face a murder charge.

Daibhidh's abilities are not restricted to scholarship and even-handedness, however. A powerfully built young man launches an unprovoked physical attack against him, but Daibhidh displays considerable prowess in dealing with the larger assailant. Shortly after this, he shows himself to be a good fisherman and a clever negotiator, who knows how to seal a bargain. We soon discover that he can turn his hand to any kind of physical work, and has some skill at working wood and engineering. Indeed, it seems he can best anyone at any skill given just a few days' practice.

If the character of Daibhidh MacLiuthair is, at times, too good to be credible, the contrast with *Gainmheach an Fhàsaich* is stark, as the main character in that contemporaneous novel is only barely able to look after herself at all. She has a strong streak of determination, which serves her well at times, but it also leads her astray when it turns to stubborn refusal to see reality. *Gainmheach an Fhàsaich* has some elements in common with *Dùn-àluinn*, especially at the beginning. The main character, Sìne, has lived alone with her father since her mother died. Although her father, the local landlord, cares for her, their relationship comes under threat when he meets and marries a woman who is sometimes referred to as 'Ban-tighearna' ('Lady'), in almost-conscious echo of *Dùn-àluinn*'s 'Ban-Fhrangach'. Sìne is urged by her father's old servant (whose role echoes that of the nurse in *Dùn-àluinn*) to marry, as this will secure her position, if she feels under threat from her new step-mother. Then the step-mother tries to undermine Sìne's relationship with her father by lying to her about things he has said.

Sìne's father is seen to be weak and slightly foolish, realising quickly that he made a mistake in his second marriage but not wanting to do anything about it, as he does not wish to cause trouble. All of the secondary characters are fascinated with the idea of marrying Sìne off, but she is determined not to settle for anyone other than her sweetheart Ruaraidh, who went off to work in Africa some time before the novel's opening. Even by this stage, however, the reader is ironically aware that Sìne's relationship with Ruaraidh may not be as loving as she maintains – both to herself and to the other characters. Ruaraidh has not been in touch with her for some time, and she has even begun to have doubts herself about whether they are still in love. Sìne's friend tries to convince her that she has no future with Ruaraidh, who has shown himself to be unreliable. However, Sìne's stubbornness comes to the fore and she makes for Africa in spite of all advice. There is some clumsy writing here in Chapters 5 and 6, where the narrator interrupts the flow of the text to admit that some important things had been missed out of Sìne's conversation with her friend. There is no developmental justification for this, and it is simply a mistake that could have benefited from better editing. When Sìne arrives in Africa, she discovers that Ruaraidh is a drunken layabout, who has lost all interest in her, thus living up to the judgements of Sìne's step-mother, who dismissed him as a commoner, beneath Sìne's station. The rest of the novel details Ruaraidh's rapid further decline, Sìne's dutiful care for him, and the development of her relationship with her friend's brother Daibhidh. Over the course of the next few chapters, Ruaraidh tries to fight his alcohol addiction and become worthy of Sìne's care, although it is evident he no longer loves her. He finally achieves redemption by helping to save some of the others from a terrible fire. As a result of his own weakened state, however, he dies shortly after the fire. His death leaves Sìne free to marry Daibhidh without having to feel guilty about abandoning Ruaraidh.

Ideologically, *Gainmheach an Fhàsaich* is oddly poised between pro-imperial Britishness and anti-English Gaelic 'orientalism' (after Said 1978 etc.). Throughout the novel, there is a sense of disdain for the English and their language, at the same time as the English-derived class system is embraced. Main characters in the novel consider themselves superior to the low-born, to servants and, most especially, to foreigners. According to the novel's ideological position, British people have a right and a duty to rule the native people of Africa (and, by implication, elsewhere). Those natives are depicted as ignorant, childlike and cruel, easily cowed and in every way inferior. The hierarchy of superiority, as depicted in *Gainmheach an Fhàsaich*, holds that (wealthy) Gaels are the best people, followed perhaps by other Scots, then other British people, and then other white Europeans. Other white Europeans may, however, be villains, as they are clever and powerful enough to be able to challenge the just and proper British rule. Similarly, within the British establishment, the English are not as trustworthy as fellow Gaels, and their language in particular is subject to the author's contempt. In Watson (2007), I have shown the lengths to which NicGill-Eain goes in order to avoid using English at all in the text (expressing her disdain for the language at the same time), and noted how much of a contrast this is with subsequent novels.

Gainmheach an Fhàsaich is not as well-written as *A' Leth Eile*, giving the impression of having been published in early draft form. Further, it is like *Cleas Sgàthain* (discussed in Chapter 6) in that it wavers between being a book written with an audience of women in mind and being a book more suitable for teenagers. According to Donald John MacLeod:

> Mary MacLean's *Gainmheach an Fhàsaich* . . . is a Romantic novelette, with the exotic locations, creaky plot, far-fetched denouements and one-dimensional characters of that genre. There is an urgent need for this type of popular fiction in Gaelic but *Gainmheach an Fhàsaich* does not represent a very propitious beginning. (MacLeod 1977: 217–18)

In fact, NicGill-Eain's characters are more convincingly developed than those in the three novels that appeared in the first quarter of the century. In *A' Leth Eile*, there is a clear shift from fantastical and action-packed plots that take in many exotic locations but have archetypes instead of characters: MacCoinnich's novel attempts to foreground the character of Daibhidh and promote his goodness as a theme. *Gainmheach an Fhàsaich* also tries to focus on character, but has a surprising amount in common technically with the three early novels. The long passages of uninterrupted dialogue, so reminiscent of the *còmhraidhean*, are still present, for instance. Similarly, the long internal monologues that are used in the early novels to explain characters' thoughts and emotions immediately after any action are also a feature in *Gainmheach an Fhàsaich*. Conveniently timed deaths are favoured plot devices in the three early novels, and are also a feature of both *Gainmheach an Fhàsaich* and *A' Leth Eile*: characters can be seen as obstacles who are in the way of what needs to happen, and so they are simply killed off to allow the plot to move towards its dénouement.

Where *A' Leth Eile* received criticism for not trying harder to be *Gàidhealach*, *Gainmheach an Fhàsaich* marks the point where cultural hybridisation becomes an unavoidable part of the novelist's consciousness. The main characters think of themselves as Gaels, but there is, in fact, nothing that marks them out as different from any other participants in the colonisation of Africa. Significantly, they are members of the landowning classes, which is made very clear from the start, when Sìne and her family debate the possibility of her marrying a commoner. Similarly, when Sìne vists her friend Siùsan in London, the pair conduct themselves like any socialites. It is interesting that Pòl MacAonghais, reviewing *A' Leth Eile*, suggested that the de-Gaelicisation of the Gaelic novel might be inevitable in the modern, culturally-hybridised world (although he did not use these terms). He wrote:

> Now, I felt that there was a Lowland shape and feel to this novel, something which cannot be helped, I am sure, since the story is about Lowlanders. (MacAonghais 1972)

He suggested that, since most of the Gaelic literati were already living in towns and cities by the early 1970s, it would be inevitable that they would end up writing about Lowlanders and Lowland situations. The evidence of the years has not yet seen this prediction come true, partly because there seems to have been an almost conscious effort to avoid exactly what MacAonghais thought might happen. Indeed, where novels have been set outside of Gaelic-speaking areas, or featuring non-Gaels as characters, their success has tended to be mixed at best, to date. Even Iain Mac a' Ghobhainn – in many ways the most cosmopolitan of native-speaking Gaelic writers – produced his best novella when he set it in a Gaelic-speaking community; and his weakest was the one he set in Africa. This is not to say that Gaelic is incapable of producing a novel that works well when set outside of the Gaelic area or featuring characters who are not Gaels: it is simply that the authors have yet to find a convincing way of expressing the relationships between the language, the characters, and the medium, and bringing all of it together in a way that gels naturally. It may be that they have felt constrained by Frank O'Connor's contention that cultures like the Gaelic one are suitable for the short story, but are not grand enough to be vehicles for the novel (O'Connor 2004, and MacLeod's discussion of these views 1977: 218–19). There is no doubt that authors have experimented with all of these things in recent years, and there is also no doubt that there has been some measure of success. However, the strongest of the recent novels have generally been at their best when on home ground. It may be that this will shift in the years to come, but it is possible that it will only happen once the process of cultural hybridisation has reached a stage where there is essentially no difference at all between Gaelic culture and Lowland culture, or between Scottish culture and British culture. If that comes about, then only the language itself will mark the novels as Gaelic (see MacLeod 1977: 220).

Na Speuclairean Dubha

Iain Mac a' Ghobhainn returned to the genre of the Gaelic novel in 1989 with *Na Speuclairean Dubha* ('The Dark Glasses'). This was one of the last major pieces of Gaelic writing that he published, although he carried on writing until his death in 1998, and *Am Miseanaraidh* was discovered and subsequently published in 2005. Like *An t-Aonaran*, and indeed *Am Miseanaraidh* (discussed in Chapter 6), *Na Speuclairean Dubha* is an exploration of the loner or outsider character. *Na Speuclairean Dubha* has a clearer sense of structure and setting than either Mac a' Ghobhainn's own *Murchadh* or Caimbeul's *Deireadh an Fhoghair*, both of which are discussed later. Like so many of the other Gaelic novels, it is very short, almost short enough to be described as a short story and certainly within normal novella parameters. However, the several movements in the story do tend to give it a novelistic flavour. There is also a fairly clear sense of plot, although the plot we believe we are following at the beginning gives way to an entirely different one from about the halfway point: in essence, the beginning of the novel seems to derive a good deal of inspiration from Mac a' Ghobhainn's love of detective fiction, with the main character trying to find out why a local man has killed himself; from the halfway point onwards, we realise that the main character's true investigation is into the nature of his own identity and purpose in life.

The main character is called Trevor Bailey, Mac a' Ghobhainn again demonstrating his propensity for using middle-class-sounding, Anglophone names in favour of Highland or even Scottish names. This is all the more striking because the story is set in what appears to be a cipher for Oban, and the setting is otherwise Highland in its depiction: some other characters have Gaelic-derived names, although Bailey's wife is Carol, essentially another imported name. The reader must wonder at the importance attached to Bailey's name, as it does not even appear until halfway through the novel, when it is mentioned by another character.

At the beginning of the book, Trevor Bailey is alone, his wife having left him some time earlier. He is fascinated with understanding why a local man, Lachaidh, has killed himself. The reader later discovers that Lachaidh probably killed himself because he had the ambition to be a writer and could not aspire to be as successful as Bailey, who is a well-known author. One of the central themes of the book is that small, apparently unimportant details of people's lives and behaviour can have inadvertent and unwitting effects on other people. This is perhaps a manifestation of a type of Oedipus Effect, in that there is unconscious overlap between characters' lives in a number of ways, and the idea of a thing may eventually lead that very thing to happen. In a chapter surveying Mac a' Ghobhainn's fiction, published in

1992, Richard Cox also saw Oedipal overtones in the novel. In fact, he felt that there were signs of the Oedipus Complex. At any rate, Bailey himself is aware of his connection with Oedipus, as he likens himself to the tragic hero, in that Oedipus was also involved with tracking down evidence and solving puzzles. In the second half of the book, Bailey takes to wearing dark glasses regularly, which also links him to Oedipus, once the latter has been blinded; the other reasons for the glasses are discussed below.

Trevor's method of working out why Lachaidh died involves interviewing people who knew him. He gradually pieces together an impression of Lachaidh which leads him to realise that he knows less about the people of his village than he thought. By locking himself away in the world of his writing and in the worlds of texts, Bailey has failed to be truly alive in what he now starts to consider 'the real world'. This is itself a self-reflexive irony, because Bailey's 'real world' is, to us, still a text world. Mac a' Ghobhainn uses this kind of irony often in both English and Gaelic. It links Bailey with Teàrlach, too, in that they are both outsiders for the same reason: they are what Mark in Mac a' Ghobhainn's English novel *My Last Duchess* (1971) calls 'Homo textual': they live most of their lives only in books.

As Trevor becomes more involved with the life of the village (largely through interrogating people), he is given a chance for a greater degree of acceptance: he is invited to join the local drama group and write their plays for them. He immediately recognises that this is a test of his new-found, tentative self-awareness. His natural reaction is to refuse, but he knows that that will lead to continuing isolation. He also realises that his wife Carol left him partly because of his anti-social tendencies, and he wonders if this gives him an opportunity to prove her wrong, perhaps even to win her back. He reluctantly decides to accept the invitation, to try to prove to himself at least that he is capable of having relationships with people.

In trying to work out why Lachaidh killed himself, Trevor's only useful clue is that Lachaidh always wore dark glasses. He learns that this was Lachaidh's reaction to a bad experience earlier in his life, where he was accused of molesting a girl in England. The glasses were his way of hiding his shame and inner turmoil. We may imagine that this incident is meant to allude to *An t-Aonaran*, in which Teàrlach brings about the hermit's flight from the village by seeing to it that he is wrongfully accused of molesting Seonag. In *Na Speuclairean Dubha*, Mac a' Ghobhainn explores the possible effects of this kind of accusation on someone: but, instead of exploring it directly by focusing on Lachaidh, he takes one step further back and sees how it then impinges on yet another life, by examining Trevor's struggle with the threat of despair. The dark glasses become a trope for deception, including self-deception, which are the two main themes of the novel. Throughout the novel, characters try to hide things from other people or from themselves. We gradually discover that Trevor Bailey's quest is not so much about learning why Lachaidh died as it is about learning how he deceives himself about his own existence every day. Bailey has the lead actor in the play wear dark glasses, in order to mask his deceitfulness. Finally, when Bailey begins to understand that he can never truly undo the harm he has done his marriage, he himself takes to wearing dark glasses. He is thus the third person in the novel to use the device, and he is the second writer in the novel who is undone by relying on the power of texts to protect him from the harsh reality of the world.

When Trevor sets out to write a play for his new drama group, he decides to base it on the old Gaelic story of Deirdre and Naoise.[5] This story is an archetype for betrayed trust and duplicity, and it links to the novel's central themes of masking and deception, as well as, indeed, the counter-theme of the quest for truth. The use of the Deirdre and Naoise story anchors the novel within a far-reaching Gaelic tradition, despite the main character being an outsider in the Highland community (signalled so clearly by his name) and despite the many allusions and influences from elsewhere. In a review published in 1990, Richard Cox expressed the opinion that this link to the Gaelic tradition was one of the strongest aspects of *Na Speuclairean Dubha*. Certainly, the contrast between Bailey's apparent non-Highland origin and his knowledge and use of the Gaelic story make for an intriguing extra dimension to his character.

A further surge in novel writing

If the 1970s saw the second wave of production of Gaelic novels, then *Na Speuclairean Dubha* heralded a second surge in this revival of the form. After *An t-Aonaran* and *Deireadh an Fhoghair*, there was another hiatus, despite the success of these two novels. *Na Speuclairean Dubha* appeared ten years after *Deireadh an Fhoghair*, with no other novels in the 1980s (other than the section of *Murchadh* that was still to come in *Gairm*). Following *Na Speuclairean Dubha*, there was a small burst of activity that was unprecedented and probably unexpected. Depending on how we choose to classify the novel, around eight appeared in the 1990s, with 1993 alone accounting for four novels for the first time in the history of the language. In comparison with the most recent decade, this achievement loses some impact, but it was, at the time, a seismic shift in Gaelic literature. By the 1990s, the production of vernacular poetry was considerably on the wane in most communities, and the tradition-bearer was almost entirely a thing of the past. Thus, the songs and stories that fired the Gaelic imagination in previous generations were finally supplanted for most members of the Gaelic-speaking community. Further, urbanisation had reached the stage where most Gaelic speakers no longer lived in what might be described as the 'heartland' communities (see

MacKinnon 2010). Thus, Gaelic speakers were, in the main, now growing up culturally similar to the non-Gaels of Scotland, albeit with another language and some awareness of a different tradition. A generation was also growing up in the context of Gaelic Medium Education, an initiative enjoying some level of governmental support for the first time in the language's history. This generation was reading (and thus encouraging the writing of) Gaelic in greater volumes and diversity than ever before. Taking all of this into consideration, it is perhaps no surprise that the novel started to attract more interest. Writers of Gaelic in the 1990s also had access to the literary evolutions and experimentation that had taken place since, especially, the 1950s, in the form of the short story collections and the great store of uncollected material in *Gairm* and other magazines. For the first time, perhaps, the language had reached a stage where authors could employ it with confidence to try their hand at non-literary novels without the same kind of self-consciousness that plagued MacCormaic, MacDhonnachaidh, MacLeòid and NicGill-Eain. They could also perhaps anticipate a less-suspicious reception than that which awaited some of the earlier novels, such as Pòl MacAonghais's surprise at the setting of *A' Leth Eile*, or the controversy that arose between the supporters of MacCormaic and MacDhonnachaidh. If some of the early novels were experimental or extensions of the kinds of things being produced in shorter form, and *An t-Aonaran*, *Deireadh an Fhoghair* and *Na Speuclairean Dubha* were literary works of significant merit, a number of novels appeared in the 1990s which deliberately set out to be entertaining above all other considerations: the 1990s saw the genesis of genre-type fiction in the Gaelic novel, although no one has yet attempted crime or spy thrillers, true science-fiction, western, horror, or any of the more popular genres (Dòmhnall Iain MacIomhair did write a whodunnit, but his *Cò Rinn E?* [1993] reads as if written for the teenage market and so is not discussed here, even though it was counted above among the four published in 1993). At the same time, literary novels continued to appear, and there was no lack of experimentation, either.

This productivity, and especially that of the past decade, might suggest that the opinions expressed by Derick Thomson and Iain Mac a' Ghobhainn in the 1970s are no longer valid. Both Thomson and Mac a' Ghobhainn considered that the novel was unnecessary in Gaelic literature. Thomson suggested that it was possible for Gaelic literature to achieve a status without ever taking to the novel as a form. When asked about this statement in an interview for *Books in Scotland* in 1979, Mac a' Ghobhainn (as Iain Crichton Smith) responded:

> Well, first, if you look at how the novel has developed in other
> cultures you find that it tends to be an expression of a middle-class

stratum of society, and it tends to develop at a particular moment in time. It may well be that the novel is not suited to the Highlands as such. It may be that there's not enough cohesion or even class differentiation, to have the kind of conflicts that are necessary in a novel—you know, to get the tremendous variety of characters that you need to force against each other to get the situations required to make a novel. (BiS 5: 11)

Mac a' Ghobhainn was probably correct in all of his analysis if it were based on sound premises, but he failed to recognise that his perception of the Highlands, and of Gaelic as a medium of communication, was already out of date. Even by 1979, a middle-class stratum was developing in the Highlands, with increasing levels of aspiration, increasing numbers of professionals being located in the area, and increasing awareness of a wider Anglo-American culture. Since the interview – and probably even at the time he gave it, to a large extent – Gaelic has ceased to be the language of the *cèilidh*-house tradition, and has become even more an expression of a sociolinguistic intention, to do with identity and personal politics. Since the time he gave the interview, for instance, Gaelic has ceased to be anyone's sole (or probably even main, except in a very few cases) language of everyday communication. Furthermore, emigration and immigration have become two of the biggest issues facing the kinds of communities he was undoubtedly imagining when he spoke about 'the Highlands' and 'the situations' (although it is noteworthy that he himself was an emigrant). From being a place of homogeneity, the Highland area has become almost as culturally diverse as any other part of Scotland, and there are areas which have been particularly vulnerable to in-migration of certain types of people, who, as characters, are well capable of providing the fuel for exactly the kinds of differentiation and conflict Mac a' Ghobhainn was envisaging. Furthermore, there is, of course, no reason for the Gaelic novel to be set in the Highlands, although some of the discussion above has suggested that experiments with settings outside of the Gaelic area have not yet been altogether successful.

Of the eight books that we may identify as novels from the 1990s, it is not altogether clear that some of them are, indeed, either novels or entirely intended for adult, fluent-readers. Calum MacMhaoilein's *A' Sireadh an Sgadain* (1990, 'Seeking the Herring'), for instance, is only partially fiction-alised, at most. His *Seonaidh Mòr* (1993, 'Big Johnnie'), on the other hand, is possibly aimed at a younger audience. So, too, may be Dòmhnall Iain Maclomhair's *Cò Rinn E?* (1993, 'Who Did It?'), which is a murder mystery that gives the impression it was either written for teenagers or perhaps the advanced adult learner (brief discussion of the adult learner market takes place in Chapter 6). At the same time, Tormod Calum Dòmhnallach's *An Sgàineadh* (1993) is one of the most experimental works of Gaelic fiction thus far attempted, and is, like *A' Sireadh an Sgadain*, only partially fictitious.

Am Fear Meadhanach

Alasdair Caimbeul, brother of Tormod Caimbeul (author of *Deireadh an Fhoghair*), has written poetry and short stories.[6] He is best-known within the Gaelic community for his drama, in which he attempts to bring a dash of modernism into what is otherwise-recognisably community drama. He reuses the same themes and images in poetry, drama and short story writing. He shows a strong interest in the effect incomers have on the Gaelic community. Some of his other work is discussed in Chapter 5.

Like his brother, Alasdair Caimbeul probably produced his best work so far in his only novel to date. *Am Fear Meadhanach* (1992)[7] deals with several of these existentialist ideas, especially free will, choice, responsibility and the nature of individuality. The novel begins by establishing that the main character is the middle brother of three and we quickly realise that a major theme of the novel consists in exploring why three brothers turn out so differently, which places the work in the context of existentialist concerns, which have interested a number of Gaelic writers since the 1960s (most notably Iain Mac a' Ghobhainn and Fionnlagh MacLeòid).

Am Fear Meadhanach is presented from the perspective of a first-person narrator, Murchadh MacLeòid, who has returned home to Lewis to die after being a teacher in Glasgow. The fact that he is dying has led him to reassess the choices he has made in his life and try to come to terms with how his relationships over the years have evolved as they have. This leads him also to consider the ways his brothers' lives have turned out.

What Murchadh realises is that he is as isolated in his Ness home as he was when he lived in Glasgow: his isolation is nothing to do with the place he inhabits or with his illness or impending death. His isolation must be something that comes from his own character. Although he is lonely and has always been lonely, his isolation is something that he has imposed upon himself. Even though he feels like this, there is a strong sense that he is much better or more comfortable interacting with his neighbours than Teàrlach is in *An t-Aonaran* or Trevor Bailey in *Na Speuclairean Dubha*. His sense of isolation seems to stem mainly from his feelings about religion, philosophy, society and the way he regards his own identity and his life. Murchadh shows no real desire to change his isolation or alleviate his loneliness, which is in direct contrast to Teàrlach and Trevor in the novels discussed earlier, who both feel compelled to act because of their realisation that they have exiled themselves from their communities.

Murchadh's two brothers are well-qualified and in respectable positions: his younger brother Uilleam is an eminent psychologist, and his elder brother Dòmhnall is a minister, a former Moderator of the Free Church and a prime candidate to become the professor at the Free Church's college. Murchadh also has a sister, Mairead, but her role is much less important, suggesting that she played less of a part in his definition of his identity. This is signalled by the fact that he does not mention her when he is explaining how he is the middle brother – *am fear meadhanach*. The existence of the two brothers gives the narrator a source of comparison so that he can analyse the effects of his upbringing and consider to what extent his childhood influenced the kind of man he became. Interestingly, his memories of his childhood do not square with the way his brothers remember it, especially Dòmhnall.

The title is very important in establishing Murchadh's sense of his own character. By referring to himself as the *'fear meadhanach'*, he is telling us what age he is in relation to his brothers, but he is also telling us that he is the mediocre one of the three. He is *meadhanach* in every sense, in that the word can mean 'middle' or 'average' or 'mediocre' or 'ill'. All his life, he has been in the shadow of his more brilliant brothers. While Dòmhnall never tried to convert him to Christianity, Uilleam always tried to persuade him to believe in his atheist humanism. Uilleam's beliefs are very heavily influenced by French Existentialism, particularly his belief that religion takes away people's freedom of choice (Uilleam does not refer at all to the Christian Existentialism based on the work of Kierkegaard). There is a sense that Murchadh envies his brothers the passion of their convictions, even though he cannot share either of them and wonders where such great faith comes from. He feels as if he can appreciate aspects of the beliefs of both brothers without really embracing the full implications of either. This is another manifestation of his being the *'fear meadhanach'*, this time meaning that he is the one in the middle ideologically or spiritually.

Another area of commonality between *Am Fear Meadhanach* and the novels by Mac a' Ghobhainn is that marriages are doomed to be unhappy. Murchadh's marriage has not necessarily been miserable, but it has not been satisfying either (rather like Trevor Bailey's, up to the point where Carol leaves him). In fact, his wife has had an affair with his brother Uilleam. Murchadh's failure to be inwardly upset by this suggests that he has never really loved his wife. More tellingly, he is more upset by Uilleam's betrayal.

During the course of the novel, Murchadh examines all of his relationships, his upbringing and his lack of satisfaction with his marriage and career in an attempt to work out whether he has existed authentically. Having been told he is dying, he is actually able to live authentically, in existentialist terms, for the first time, even if it is only a short time. The novel ends with a slightly ambiguous passage which seems to suggest that he dies. The ending very closely echoes the beginning and gives the novel what a poet might call *dùnadh*.[8] Note also the use of the *sloinneadh*, so common in the work of writers from Ness, in particular:[9]

> Bha 'n càr a' dol na bu luaithe a-rithist; 's a' dìreadh gu Loch Bharabhat, bha latha geal air gach taobh, 's coltas fìor latha math; grianach, le adhar gorm, 's sgòthan beaga geal a' seòladh ann; latha son a dhol a thogail na mònach, ged nach b' urrainn dhaibh, son a dhol a-mach air an eathar, ged nach fhaodadh iad a dhol ann, an latha bha Murchadh, mac Dhòmhnaill, mac Mhurchaidh, mac Mhurchaidh Òig, a' tilleadh dhachaigh.

> (The car was going faster again; and climbing to Loch Bharabhat,[10] the day was bright on each side, looking like being a really nice day; sunny, with a blue sky, and little white clouds sailing by; a day for going to lift the peats, although they couldn't, [a day] for going out on the boat, although they couldn't, the day Murchadh, son of Donald, son of Murchadh, son of Young Murchadh, was returning home.)[11]

In a review of *Am Fear Meadhanach* that appeared in *Gairm* in 1993, Ruaraidh MacThòmais[12] was enthusiastic about a lot of aspects of the book, but critical of what he called Caimbeul's '*gamhlasan*', which could perhaps translate as 'pet hates' or 'prejudices'. MacThòmais was sure that Caimbeul deliberately based some of his characters on real people from the Ness community, including other writers and teachers, and showed these in an unfavourable light. It would be difficult for anyone from outside the community to verify whether MacThòmais was correct in his identification of real local people or to guess where Caimbeul's inspiration for characters came from, but MacThòmais is right in suggesting that the characters are rounded, lifelike, and interesting. *Am Fear Meadhanach* is a positive step in the development of the Gaelic novel, and is anything but '*meadhanach*'.

An Sgàineadh

The foregrounding of consideration of psychological states and effects is even more evident in Tormod Calum Dòmhnallach's *An Sgàineadh* (1993, 'The Schism'). Another Lewis man, although actually born in Canada, he published his Gaelic work under the name 'Tormod Calum Dòmhnallach', but also wrote successfully in English. Dòmhnallach wrote in various literary modes throughout his career, and also published some non-fiction, including the 1987 book *Clann-nighean an Sgadain* about the herring fishing industry. As 'Norman Malcolm MacDonald', he published *Calum*

Tod (1976), a novel in English, followed by a second English novel in 2000, *Portrona*.[13] He was a particularly accomplished Gaelic playwright.[14] Dòmhnallach had a varied life, which included a good deal of international travel as a merchant seaman. *An Sgàineadh* draws on his experiences, featuring a Lewisman in New Zealand, a country where the author himself spent time during his own travels.

An Sgàineadh is probably the most experimental of all the Gaelic novels so far, even counting the novels that have been published by CLÀR in the past decade (there is a good discussion of the novel in Macleod 1999). The structure makes it difficult to follow and the style of writing is uncompromising (structurally, it is slightly reminiscent of *Lanark*, although it has nothing else in common with that novel). The book is broken down into four sections, which, at times, are only barely related to each other. The title itself is a reference to the split narrative. The split or *sgàineadh* seems to be related to Jungian 'collective unconscious'. In Jungian psychology, each individual has an 'unconscious' which is made up of certain images, stories and archetypes. In *An Sgàineadh*, these archetypes may include things like elements of a racial or cultural awareness that link the modern Gael to his ancestors: elements heard in story and song from an early age, for instance. When an individual struggles to reconcile these different aspects of the collective unconscious, metaphysical angst can result. This angst is manifested in a splitness of consciousness or a *sgàineadh*. The structure of the book reflects the splitness of consciousness. The four parts are very loosely connected and it is not absolutely clear that the first-person narrator is the same in all four parts.

After struggling with alcoholism in New Zealand in the first part of the book, the narrator – if it is indeed the same narrator – makes his way to London. While he is there, he tries his hand at writing and discovers a talent for it. In part three, he writes a play and in part four he writes a screenplay. So little information is provided about the narrator as character that the reader has to try to piece together any little details in the text and work out what is happening and who it is happening to. The narrator is more interested in discussing his emotional responses to particular events than in recounting the events themselves in any detail.

Like *An t-Aonaran*, *Na Speuclairean Dubha*, and *Am Fear Meadhanach*, *An Sgàineadh* is particularly concerned with the theme of exile. Unlike in the other three books, in this case the exile starts off in a manifestly physical sense, because the main character is in New Zealand, feeling homesick, and especially missing the Gaelic music of his island. And yet, in spite of this homesickness, he admits that he has gained a lot from his time in New Zealand and he values the experiences he has had there. However, because of his alcoholism, he is also an exile in a social sense.

The narrator has a small group of friends, some of whom are also far from home and missing their home culture. The nicknames give away their place of origin and also demonstrate the extent to which these men are associated with their own cultures. Scouser misses Liverpool and is desperate to get home. His homesickness is so great that it eventually drives him mad. The narrator later wonders if he ever did actually manage to get home to Liverpool. Padaidh, on the other hand, manages to devise a plan that lets him leave New Zealand and head home to Ireland. The narrator, by contrast, is left clinging to the most tenuous of connections to his own culture. He manages to meet some other Gaelic speakers and he notices the names of whiskies that are derived from Gaelic words.[15]

The novel explores the ideas of nostalgia and homesickness and also considers the cultural perceptions and customs of the Gael. At some points in the novel, the narrator seems to wonder if nostalgia is a particular predilection of Gaels and whether this is why his homesickness is so acute. Whatever the reason for the sense of homesickness and regret for the loss of the past, the narrator reacts to it by drinking heavily. The more he drinks, the worse his exile becomes. Although being drunk lets him forget about his misery for a while, he feels even worse as the effects of the alcohol wear off. This theme of considering predilections of the Gaels is a common one in the book, as it is elsewhere in Gaelic fiction. The narrator continually thinks about racial stereotyping and about archetypes. He is particularly interested in the portrayal of Scottish culture, Gaelic culture and Celtic culture. He often falls into the trap of using stereotypes himself. For instance, he wonders 'who writes like the Celts[?]' (42).

When he gets back to Britain, the narrator decides that writing might give him a medium for exorcising some of his personal demons. His writing does help him with his alcoholism, as it gives him another way of seeing the world, and gives him a way of keeping the world at arms'-length. As he says:

> Instead of tasting a drink with your mouth, won't you taste with your tongue white paper like a shroud. (43)

An Sgàineadh is a difficult novel. Its close relationship with Dòmhnallach's own life story gives it an emotional realism that many of the Gaelic novels fail to achieve. Although the major themes of exile and identity are the familiar existentialist-derived themes that drive other novels such as *An t-Aonaran*, *Na Speuclairean Dubha* and *Am Fear Meadhanach*, the completely different treatment they receive in this novel makes *An Sgàineadh* a particularly important contribution to the development of the Gaelic novel.

Deireadh an Fhoghair

Tormod Caimbeul is a member of what can be described as a literary dynasty in Gaelic. His uncle was the song-poet Aonghas Caimbeul, known as Am Puilean, who also wrote one of the most significant prose works in Gaelic, his autobiography *A' Suathadh ri Iomadh Ruadh* (1973). His father was the other famous song-poet called Aonghas Caimbeul, known as Am Bocsair. Tormod is therefore known as Tormod a' Bhocsair and his brother, also a novelist, is known as Alasdair a' Bhocsair. The Caimbeuls are from the Ness area of Lewis, which is one of the strongest remaining Gaelic communities. Ness writers, in particular, have had a major impact on recent Gaelic writing, to the extent that much of their work almost assumes a universal knowledge and understanding of Ness frames of reference. This sometimes leads to confusion and definitely skews the picture of the wider Gaelic culture as presented in the literature. There are signs that this may be shifting once more in the Ùr-Sgeul-dominated contemporary period.

Tormod Caimbeul is a poet and short-story writer as well as being a novelist. His short stories have been published in two collections, *Hostail* (1992) and *An Naidheachd bhon Taigh* (1994), which are discussed in Chapter 5. The stories in these books rely heavily on Caimbeul's memories of his own upbringing and most of them are partly autobiographical. The most notable innovation that Caimbeul brings to Gaelic prose is a freshness of humour and irony that comes directly from inspiration and avoids the contrived devices of some of his contemporaries. As a result, his work is among the funniest in Gaelic prose.

Deireadh an Fhoghair is still Tormod Caimbeul's most important contribution to Gaelic literature. It is not an easy read: in a review of the novel, MacAulay (1983) admits to having been confused in places and having to read the novel at least twice before he felt he had a strong grasp of what was going on. This does not undermine Caimbeul's achievement, however. *Deireadh an Fhoghair* is not as formidable as many of the texts that appeared during or since the modernist wave in English literature. Indeed, *Deireadh an Fhoghair* has a number of modernist features, which are, nonetheless, also in keeping with the Gaelic tradition. Most notably, almost nothing happens throughout the course of the book. There are only three characters, all of them old and growing infirm – and it soon becomes clear that their old age is a metonym for the ageing nature of their community and of the wider Gaelic community and its language. Most of the action involves the three characters interacting and discussing the coming winter. The winter is another clear metonym for the end of life and the waning of Gaelic culture.

The three characters are an old man called Coinneach and an old couple called Ailean and Nellie. The entire action of the novel takes place in a single day and night (compare this with Màrtainn Mac an t-Saoir's *An Latha as Fhaide*, discussed in Chapter 6). The slowness of pace is echoed in the style of writing and in the long, rambling conversations between the trio of friends. From the start, the sense of oldness and slowness is emphasised. The book opens with the words:

> Bha esan leis fhéin, mar a b'àbhaist, aig an tocasaid. Tocasaid a bha ann bho linn crochadh nan con; a shiubhail cuantan uair dha robh i, 's a bhuail cladach aig Geodh'-na-Muic. Sin far an d'fhuair a shean-shean-shean-sheanair i, tràth 'sa mhadainn. (1)

> (He was by himself, as usual, at the hogshead. A hogshead that was there from the time of the hanging of the dogs; that travelled oceans once and struck land at Geodh'-na-Muic. That was where his great-great-great-grandfather got it, early in the morning.)

So, the semantic fields of oldness and time are brought right to the forefront in the novel's opening. Another theme of the book, namely isolation, is also established immediately in that opening sentence. And, to continue the quotation into the next sentence, we can see another important theme in the book, which is the theme of *seanchas*, dealt with here as in many other instances with Caimbeul's characteristic ironic humour:

> Thuirt athair ris gun duirt a sheanair gun duirt athair gur e athair-san a thuirt gur e athair-fhéin a fhuair i . . . (1)

> (His father said to him that his grandfather said that his father said that it was *his* father who said that it was his own father who got it . . .)

This description of the hogshead continues to the level of hyperbole as Caimbeul deliberately invokes bathos to illustrate the triviality of the thoughts and concerns of a character who is as isolated as Coinneach. This technique is used again and again throughout the novel to create a sense of world-building. Caimbeul also uses the Gaelic concept of *saoghal*, which usually translates into English as 'world', but also means 'life'. The lives of these characters, especially Coinneach and Ailean, very much encompass their worlds. Or, at least, this is the case if we include what Norman M. MacDonald[16] calls their 'race-memory', which is at least as important to them as anything that takes place in their own lives. In a 1979 review of *Deireadh an Fhoghair*, published in *Books in Scotland*, MacDonald wrote:

> Almost as enduring as the land itself are the memories of those who live and die upon it . . . But as they have no offspring, these three, it is

evident that their memories will die with them and that only the land will remain. (BiS 5: 29–30)

The association between the Gaelic language and a sort of race-memory is a common theme in the work of both Caimbeul brothers and it is absolutely central to *Deireadh an Fhoghair*. Norman M. MacDonald's review hints at a kind of pagan significance to the ritual of naming that is such a feature of the *Gàidhealtachd* and, perhaps, especially Lewis. At any rate, it receives the most coverage in the work of Lewis writers, and again especially in the work of the Caimbeul brothers: on the other hand, naming is of central importance in the novels of Aonghas Pàdraig Caimbeul. Throughout *Deireadh an Fhoghair*, the motif of *sloinneadh* or folk genealogy, and the delight and sometimes obsession with naming are at the forefront. It is through the reciting, sometimes in dialogue and often in internal monologue, of *sloinnidhean*, that we learn most of the back-story of the characters. This is how Coinneach is introduced in the story:

> An còmhnaidh ann an tighinn a' latha cha robh beò ach esan –
> Coinneach Meadhonach, mac Choinnich Mhóir, mac Alasdair, mac
> Choinnich, mac Choinnich, mac Alasdair. 'Se Alasdair a b'ainm
> dha fear treun na tocasaid – Alasdair Caol na Tocasaid. Coinneach
> Meadhonach a chanadh 'ad rise-san, Coinneach Mór ri athair, agus
> Coinneach Beag ri bhràthair beag. (2)

> (Always in the coming of the day there were none alive but himself
> – Middle Coinneach, son of Big Coinneach, son of Alasdair, son of
> Coinneach, son of Coinneach, son of Alasdair. Alasdair was the name
> of the doughty man of the hogshead – Slim Alasdair of the Hogshead.
> Middle Coinneach they would call him, Big Coinneach his father, and
> Little Coinneach his little brother.)

Caimbeul takes this straight out of the cultural heritage of his community and establishes it as one of the fundamental techniques of fleshing out character in Gaelic fiction. Partly due to these techniques, partly due to the nature of the characters, and partly due to the themes and motifs that are important in the novel, *Deireadh an Fhoghair* is possibly the first of the modern novels that feels truly 'Gàidhealach'. This is in spite of the fact that the only female character Nellie is actually an incomer from Glasgow. The death of the Gaelic community is symbolised by the fact that all of the people that Coinneach and Ailean talk about are either dead or have emigrated, and also by the fact that one-third of the number of the remaining survivors is comprised of a Lowland incomer.

Murchadh

If *Deireadh an Fhoghair* introduced humour into the Gaelic novel, Iain Mac a' Ghobhainn's second novel took that humour and mixed it up with surrealism and psychosis and a liberal measure of slapstick and stirred it until it set in the form of the bizarre and brilliant *Murchadh*. So far, *Murchadh* has never been printed in book form. It was serialised in *Gairm* (numbers 106–9), beginning in 1979. The title character Murchadh MacRath is another gifted loner, not all that far removed from Teàrlach in *An t-Aonaran* or Trevor Bailey in *Na Speuclairean Dubha*. Murchadh is a writer, who is clearly going insane, or else he always was insane and people have not paid that much attention. Murchadh's inceasing insanity and the effect it has on his relationship with his wife Seònaid are sad, but this sadness is in direct contrast to the crazy comedy of the situations created by his psychosis: for example, he goes to the shops wearing a red rubber clown nose, he writes a serious letter to the poet Dante, and he has completely bemused the teacher who tried to give him some career guidance.

> 'So what are you going to do when you leave the school?' the teacher said to him.

> '27 x 67 = 1675' said Murchadh.

> The teacher looked at him with horror and his specs almost fell off his nose.

> 'Do you have any idea what you are going to do?' he said again.

> '259 x 43 = 11137' said Murchadh. (G 107: 256–7)

Similarly, he confuses his local librarian by asking for the novel *War and Peace*, by the author Uisdean MacLeòid. When the librarian questions him, he says 'But if you don't have *War and Peace* I'll take anything by the same author, say *The Brothers Karamazov*' (G 108: 377).

All the while, Murchadh keeps trying to write his story that has been inspired by the sight of a big mountain covered in snow that he thinks he can see from his window. The blank sheet of paper in front of him and the virgin snow are repeatedly contrasted as he wrestles with the juxtaposition of the futility of great art and deeds and the triviality of the ordinary. The far-off, snow-covered mountain symbolises the quest motif, and the purity of the snow on the mountain is a synecdoche of the purity of experience that Murchadh seeks.

There is no real plot in *Murchadh*. Instead, the novel is almost a random collection of musings about the crazy character. Chapters start with questions or with vague adverbs of time, such as 'An dràsda 's a-rithist'('now and then'), 'Aon turas' ('one time') or 'aon oidhche' ('one night'). This anecdotal narrative style is a deliberate attempt to avoid the techniques of formal realism which allow the author to anchor the characters and events of a novel in a particular time and place and which lend the narrative a sense of authority. Murchadh MacRath is deliberately portrayed as a kind of cartoon character whose adventures are episodic rather than linear. This deliberate postmodern avoidance of structure emphasises the quest for meaning which underlies the crazy comedy of the book. Like Teàrlach in *An t-Aonaran*, Murchadh desperately wants to understand. He inhabits a consciousness in which Calvin and Dante and Hitler are potentially still alive, because the usual constraints of death, time and realism are meaningless to Murchadh. On writing his will, he offers a reward to anyone who can tell him why we exist. According to Murchadh, we inhabit a world without meaning or substance.

In the end, the quest overcomes Murchadh and he resolves that he can never be at peace until he goes out to climb the big snowy mountain. His wife Seònaid watches him getting ready to go and she can see from the expression on his face that he is being consumed by a terrible, interminable question.

Murchadh has often been considered to be an alter ego of Mac a' Ghobhainn himself, and there is some evidence to suggest that this was Mac a' Ghobhainn's own view of the character. In later years, Murchadh turned into 'Murdo' in some of Mac a' Ghobhainn's English writing; notably, *Thoughts of Murdo* (1993) and *Murdo: the Life and Works* (2001). However, although Murdo is evidently the same character (and some of his adventures are merely translations of portions of *Murchadh*), a zany humour has replaced the genuine pathos of Murchadh's tentative awareness of his fragmented consciousness. In other words, the later Mac a' Ghobhainn chose to focus on the comedy and move away from the tragic side of *Murchadh* that makes it such an under-rated masterpiece.

Clann Iseabail

Only the second novel to be written by a woman, *Clann Iseabail* ('Isobel's Children') by Màiri NicGumaraid, was published in 1993. NicGumaraid is best-known as a poet,[17] having published two collections so far: *Eadar Mi 's a' Bhreug* in 1988, and *Ruithmean 's Neo-Rannan* in 1997. The first-person heroine in *Clann Iseabail* is Ciorstaidh, an islander who is now living in Glasgow. Ciorstaidh has taken up writing as a way to explore her beliefs and her sense of herself. To some degree, the novel is about the confrontation between her writing and her origin place, which treats her work with a degree of suspicion. She overhears characters describing her as overly romantic and implying that she has never grown up or learnt common sense. In one particular area, she is divided from her first world community: she is completely against the British Army's occupation of Northern Ireland. She holds very strongly anti-Imperialist views and she considers the Army's presence in Northern Ireland to be a colonialist aberration. Unfortunately for Ciorstaidh, a young man from her home has been killed while serving a tour of duty in Northern Ireland. This has the result of turning most of the locals against her. They simplistically interpret her views as an attack on the young man, Scotty, and they cannot come to terms with the fact that her politics are ideological rather than personal.

The theme of ideology is central to the novel. Ciorstaidh's views are not based on Ireland alone. In fact, she is anti-Imperialist in general terms and she believes the Gaels have been treated badly by the British establishment over the centuries even to the present day. This is a minority view in her *Gàidhealtachd* home, which is strongly loyal to the crown and adheres to the rule of law set down by the British Government. Several locals come into conflict with Ciorstaidh over this, including Scotty's grandfather Gilleasbaig. In fact, Gilleasbaig is such a royalist that he called his daughter Ealasaid ('Elizabeth') in honour of the Queen. This depiction of a Gaelic community loyal to the Windsor-Westminster establishment makes an interesting contrast with novels like *Cailin Sgiathanach* and some of the other early prose fiction, where England is seen as a different country, and where the suggestion is that the Gaelic nation is perhaps a different country from Lowland Scotland, too.

The action in *Clann Iseabail* is split between Glasgow and Ciorstaidh's island home. This allows NicGumaraid to show the different aspects of Ciorstaidh's character, as she appears in relation to different situations and different characters. Some of the other islanders also have connections with Glasgow, either through studying or visiting friends who live there. This gives the novel a strong feeling of the biculturalism that pervades the renaissance and post-renaissance Gaelic poetry of the past eighty years.

Another aspect of *Clann Iseabail* that gives it a strong sense of biculturalism is NicGumaraid's use of English. This is the first Gaelic novel to use a lot of English. This gives it a sense of realism, in that islanders naturally switch between Gaelic and English, and also tend to pepper their Gaelic speech with English words and phrases. Even the narrative uses English words from time to time, signalling the author's intention to imbue the novel with a feeling of realism throughout. This is in direct contrast to the early novels, which were composed in an era in which the authors and their readers had a richer Gaelic vocabulary and would be used to using Gaelic for a wider range of purposes. It is also in direct contrast to *An t-Aonaran*, where Teàrlach starts to recount some conversation in English and then tells us it is best just to use Gaelic for the rest of the conversation. He does not explain why he considers it best to use Gaelic to report a conversation that took place in English, but we may infer that the statement really comes from Mac a' Ghobhainn, pushing in on Teàrlach metafictionally and suggesting that a Gaelic novel should be in Gaelic. Some of the more recent novels have challenged this assumption: see, in particular, discussions of *Na Klondykers, Am Bounty, Samhraidhean Dìomhair* and *Shrapnel* in Chapter 6 (see Storey 2009).

There is no doubt that *Clann Iseabail* is an interesting step forward in the development of the Gaelic novel. NicGumaraid is the first author to make such a strong link between the Gaels and modern politics. She works hard at achieving realism of character and dialogue and the story holds up fairly well. It is also interesting in being only the second novel to be written from a woman's point of view. It may not be stereotyping to suggest that this is why themes such as love and friendship are more important in this novel than they are in most of the earlier novels, with the possible exception of *A' Leth Eile*, but even that novel has a fairly two-dimensional approach to these themes (*Dìleas Donn, Taingeil Toilichte* and *Samhraidhean Dìomhair* all develop these themes to a high level and are all written by female authors). NicGumaraid has an engaging prose style and writes Gaelic that is natural and readable.

Cùmhnantan and *Keino*

Shortly after the flurry of novel-writing that resulted in an unprecedented four novels appearing in 1993, the well-known television personality Tormod MacGill-Eain entered the scene. He has published four short novels to date, two of which are discussed in Chapter 6. MacGill-Eain's first two novels were *Cùmhnantan* (1996) and *Keino*[18] (1998). *Cùmhnantan* ('Contracts') has a good deal in common with his later novels, *Slaightearan* (2008) and, to a lesser extent, *Dacha Mo Ghaoil* (2005), but, at the time, it marked an entirely new style in extended fiction in Gaelic. *Keino* is significantly different again in terms of style and technique and, especially, atmosphere. MacGill-Eain's four books modernise Gaelic novel-writing in many ways. In particular, MacGill-Eain (for many years famous as the Gaelic entertainer *par excellence*) brought to bear a new focus on the novel's role as a tool for entertainment. Thus, humour, intrigue, (occasionally) action, sex, violence and the threat of violence, and power politics play a prominent part in his novels, and there are many references to music, fashion and the modern trappings of wealth. While all four of the novels lack a classic hero figure, their antihero main characters tend to have down-to-earth flaws that are in contrast with the intellectual hubris that marks out some of the principal characters in other Gaelic novels.

Angst then tends to be on a more practical and everyday level, again in contrast with the metaphysical angst that affects many of the characters in the novels discussed above and in Chapter 6. Then again, *Keino* is, to some extent, an exception to much of this, as will be detailed below.

Cùmhnantan was published by Clò Loch Abair in Glasgow, the city where MacGill-Eain spent most of his youth. He is a Glasgow Gael, with Uist and Tiree connections, who made a name for himself as a musician and comedian, and who has been one of the more recognised faces on Gaelic television for decades. The world of *Cùmhnantan* draws directly on all of these experiences, and the main character, Dòmhnall Caimbeul, is clearly partly autobiographical.

Cùmhnantan is set in the early 1990s, shortly after the real-world UK Government announced a new funding package to support Gaelic broadcasting (initially television broadcasting, but subsequently expanded). In the novel, the figure that is often quoted is £10m, which is slightly more than was made available in reality. The novel's world slightly fictionalises some of the institutions that were associated with the new funding, so *Cùmhnantan*'s STG (Sgioba Telebhisean Gàidhlig) is a cipher for the real-world CTG (Comataidh Telebhisean Gàidhlig) or its other incarnations. Similarly, fictional small, medium and larger broadcasting companies are also created, but it is not difficult to match them up to cognates in the real world. Before the novel begins, there is a disclamatory 'Facal bhon Ùghdar' ('a Word from the Author'), in which he claims that most people involved in Gaelic television are not really like the characters depicted in the novel. The reader is free to choose whether to accept this literally or to interpret it ironically.

The title refers to 'contracts', although the word also has connotations that go beyond the legalistic formal paper contract thus implied: indeed, the issue of trust and faith in other people is paramount throughout the book. This is emphasised immediately, when Dòmhnall Caimbeul and an old acquaintance of his, Murchadh, are wrangling about the contract for a gig Caimbeul will play. Murchadh uses the English word, no doubt to emphasise its legal implications, and this results in the conversation taking a totally different turn:

'An do chuir thu d' ainm ris a' chontract?' thuirt am fear beag.

'Chan eil sìon agam mu dheidhinn 'contracts',' thuirt an duine liath. (8)

('Did you sign the contract?' the little man said.

'I have nothing to do with 'contracts',' the grey-haired man said.)

[. . .]

'Sin a chuala mi,' thuirt am fear beag. 'Chuala mi sin gun teagamh.
'Cha chaomh leis a' Chaimbeulach contract idir. Cha bhi Don
Campbell ag obair le contract.' Tha latha eile agad a-nis, a
Dhòmhnaill.' (8)

('That's what I heard,' the little man said. 'I heard that right enough.
'Campbell doesn't like a contract at all. Don Campbell doesn't work
with a contract.' It's changed days, Donald.')

Among the things to note here are a number of small lexical items which
are used to locate the two characters' origins, such as '*sion*' for Caimbeul,
which suggests he has Uist connections, and '*cha chaomh*' for Murchadh,
which mark him as very likely a Lewis man (which he is). Also of note here
linguistically are Murchadh's use of a traditional way of referring to someone by surname, which is to use the adjectival form ('*a' Chaimbeulach*')[19]
and his codeswitching to 'Don Campbell' when triggered by the proximity
of the English word (and concept). This early exchange allows the author
to foreshadow the main source of tension in the novel for Caimbeul, which
is his current large debt that has been caused by something that happened
on a recent trip to Venezuela. We also find out immediately that Caimbeul
has had a serious alcohol problem and that he is trying to stay sober.

Several lesser characters serve to underline the poisonous and com-
petitive nature of what the novel describes as the 'new world' of Gaelic
broadcasting (and business in general). Caimbeul's friend, Calum Iain
MacAsgaill, who plays accordion (or melodeon) with him, is badly treated
due to contracts and money, as is the young girl Gretta, albeit in entirely
different ways. Throughout the novel, it is clear that one of the main
themes is that a world of legally binding contracts is no substitute for a
community in which people can trust each other and look out for one
another. Aligned with this, there are suggestions that the 'new world' of
Gaelic television is only superficially Gaelic, at best. Behind the scenes, all
the real power is retained by non-Gaelic speakers or by Gaels who wish to
join what they see as the elite ranks of the business and thus they aspire to
be regarded as non-Gaels (see p. 97). These issues come to the fore especially near the end of the novel, when several of the lesser characters are
discussing 'in'-groups, but it has been a clear theme throughout the novel
as exemplified by the character Seòras Kerr (especially pp. 85–7). When
he is introduced, Kerr is the epitome of superficiality, and he thus stands
for the superficiality that is being portrayed as a central element in this
new world of Gaelic television. Kerr's attitude towards Gaelic is entirely

pragmatic: he is evidently not a confident speaker of the language, and he has no particular affection for it either, but he appreciates that he has to be seen to make some sort of effort to use it in his current role. Similarly, other lesser characters represent the seamy side of television: among these is Iain Ailig MacIlleathain, the head of the small production company that is seeking to employ Caimbeul. MacIlleathain is an academic who has been attracted to television production by the allure of the cash and the possibility of picking up lots of women. As he puts it himself:

> 'Fortunately, in the particular area of enterprise in which I now find myself, the brave new world of Gaelic television production, nubile and eligible ladies abound.' (29)

The English-language dialogue as recorded here is not atypical in the novel: characters switch freely between the two languages. Sometimes the switching is caused by the presence of non-Gaelic speakers, but it is often simply a depiction of the kind of codeswitching typical in the Gaelic community. In general, however, the English dialogue is rather stilted and unconvincing in comparison with the Gaelic dialogue, and this is a failing that pervades most of the Gaelic novels that include switching of this kind. As in many of the Gaelic novels, this one relies very heavily on dialogue: there are entire chapters that consist almost exclusively of dialogue (Ní Annracháin also notes this, 2006: 142). There are times when this is appropriate, but sometimes the reader is left wondering why the book has been packaged as a novel and not a play or script.

As well as meaning 'contracts', *cùmhnantan* is also used in the novel to suggest 'promises'. In particular, there are many broken promises, both those made to others and to oneself. This is related in turn to the addiction that seems rife within the society being depicted: various characters are addicted either to alcohol, sexual conquest, money, power, tobacco or other vices. Several of them appear to try to give up their addictions, but no one convincingly succeeds. There is, as a result, constantly a sense that no one can be trusted, in spite of other qualities that they may possess (Caimbeul himself is the most obvious case in point: he has many talents, and is also shown to have some very positive character traits, and yet almost no one trusts him, including, usually, the reader).

Keino has a thoroughly different style and aims at entirely different effects. Where *Cùmhnantan* is primarily entertaining, a cheeky parody of the world of Gaelic television, *Keino* is disturbing and depressing. The main character, Eachann MacPhàil, has some serious psychological problems, which he is forced to confront as a result of the violent events of the novel. Indeed, although *Keino* is 126 pages long, it reads more like a short story. Apart from some early and late framing and a large number of flashbacks, there is really only one main scene in the whole book. The main character is also the first-person narrator; first-person narration is not yet common in Gaelic novels and has, to date, almost invariably signalled that the interest in the novel is on more of a psychological level.[20] As a result of the first-person point-of-view, and the issues Eachann must try to resolve in his psyche, the book has a much more rambling style than *Cùmhnantan*. Where *Cùmhnantan* was punchy and eventful, *Keino* is slow and ponderous, with most actions pausing mid-description so that Eachann can think through the implications or be reminded of a past event that has some associated significance. In places, the internal monologue is almost stream-of-consciousness.

Through a brief conversation and some introspection, we quickly learn that Eachann MacPhàil is, like Dòmhnall Caimbeul in *Cùmhnantan*, a guitar-playing, pipe-playing, singing, Gaelic-speaking womaniser. We also quickly learn that there are rumours he is having an affair with a married woman and that her husband is likely to react violently if he finds out, which thus ironically foreshadows the crucial central scene of the book. The woman in question is Ealasaid Beckett, wife of Ailidh Beckett, both of whom are from travelling families. This adds an interesting extra cultural and linguistic dimension to the book once Ailidh and his son Stephen enter the action. Ealasaid and Ailidh are both Gaelic-speakers, but Stephen does not seem to know Gaelic. All three resort to using English interspersed with a form of Cant, although most of their Cant utterances are repeated in English.

Ealasaid has a tremendous power of attraction over Eachann, who is several years younger than her. As the novel progresses, we discover that their relationship became sexual within minutes of their meeting each other, and that they have often risked being caught. In several flashbacks, Eachann explores his attitudes to sex and relationships with women, and he understands that many of his problems stem from his seeing his father having intercourse with a very young woman (see p. 114). Both here and elsewhere, sex is described graphically, for the first time in extended Gaelic fiction. Eachann remembers seeing his father with the young woman and being caught and accused of deriving a thrill from watching them. He was then tormented by having to try to keep the secret from his suspicious mother, and further tormented by guilt at her reaction when he did confess to her. The latter stages of the novel toy with the idea of whether his father loved him, as Eachann's emotional associations of his father have become buried beneath the burdens of guilt and the anger, shame and disgust he came to feel. He seems to find a resolution of sorts in the end, remembering and accepting that his father did indeed love him deeply, but this realisation leaves him with still another burden of guilt as he realises how badly he treated his father.

While Eachann is disturbingly self-destructive, Ealasaid is also a highly troubled character. She, too, is self-destructive, but is much more willing than Eachann to damage anyone else around her, too. When Stephen catches her with Eachann, Ealasaid has no hesitation about trying to seduce him, and she clearly believes her attractiveness gives her power over the men around her. She also urges Eachann to hurt Stephen more than is necessary, and she has no apparent remorse for any suffering caused by any of her actions. She is not surprised to see Stephen when he catches them, and their initial exchange of dialogue hints that there is something unusual in their relationship. The dialogue is given in English, interspersed with Cant:

'That you, Stephen?' tha Ealasaid a' cantail ri deugaire de bhalach a tha na sheasamh an taobh a-staigh dhen doras.

'Yeah. It's me, whore,' tha an gille ag ràdh, is e a' coiseachd gu stràiceil seachad air an dithis againn gus e fhèin a sgorrachadh air cathair an tidseir.

'Stephen, *nash-a-bree*, beat it, you sneaky little shite!' tha Ealasaid ag èigheachd. 'What the hell do you think you're doing spying on your . . . your mother?'

'*Keck-a-rocka*, shut up, you slag [. . .]' (38)

He then demands that she get onto her hands and knees. This exchange, and the rest of the scene as it unfolds, hints that Stephen has spied on Ealasaid before, perhaps with Eachann or even with other lovers, and that she knew about it. It also hints that Ealasaid believes Stephen desires her sexually or that there has been some kind of sexual history between them already. After Eachann overpowers Stephen and sends him away, Ealasaid is keen for them to carry on with their sexual rendezvous, despite Stephen's threat to come back with his father, whom we already know to be a dangerous man.

The other main character to appear is Ailidh, who shows up with Stephen and four henchmen some time later. While Eachann gives a good account of himself, the five armed men quickly overcome both him and Ealasaid and proceed to beat Eachann up very badly. Most of the rest of the novel (nearly half the text) consists of Ailidh's attempt to torture Eachann (and Ealasaid) psychologically. From this point onwards, we see the first signs that Ealasaid has any kind of feeling for anyone other than herself, as she pleads with Ailidh not to hurt Eachann. Ailidh challenges Eachann to a game of what he calls '*keino*', which is a proposition-bet more commonly known as *nim*. Ailidh claims to be an expert at this game and Eachann seems not to engage with it at first. However, Eachann eventually uses his aptitude at maths to work out the solution and then distracts Ailidh into making a mistake that results in Eachann winning. As a result, Ailidh takes away 'the prize', Ealasaid, but leaves Eachann with only one more physical blow. Ailidh spends most of the time during the game talking, and the game is essentially a device to allow him to talk to Eachann (and Ealasaid and himself) for several chapters almost uninterrupted. Like the other two main characters, Ailidh has had a troubled history, culminating in a prison term. However, he has emerged from this with considerable strength, and he seems to want to use the episode as a way to teach Eachann how to do the same.

Conclusion

The novel from the 1970s until the late 1990s, then, was undoubtedly a much greater success than that produced in the earlier period. There were high points and low points, as there are in any wave of literary production. Authors experimented with a range of different subject matters, techniques, plots and settings. There were literary novels and novels written for entertainment and amusement, and others that are difficult to categorise. Some of the novels drew heavily on a sense of a Gaelic literary or cultural tradition, while others did not. Still others pointed towards the emerging Gaelic cultural milieux and the new situations in which modern Gaels find themselves. For the most part, the authors were already established writers in other media, many of them having published many stories in *Gairm* and elsewhere. This may be part of the reason why all of the novels in that period were so short. In general, they were all around a hundred pages. In some of the novels, this short length lends them the impression of being short story-like. Others, however, do read like novels despite their length and the limitations that are associated with it. This was a positive period in the development of Gaelic literature, despite the many flaws in some of the books.

Chapter 5

Collected Stories

This chapter surveys the collected short fiction that appeared in the period 1960–99. The period is self-selecting, in a sense, as there were no single-author collections between the early writing of the century and 1960. The cut-off point for the chapter has been chosen because the year 2000 is an important watershed in Gaelic writing. Collections that have appeared since 2000 are addressed in Chapter 6, which deals with contemporary fiction. The work before 1960 was already addressed in Chapter 1.

Iain Mac a' Ghobhainn (Iain Crichton Smith) was one of the most prolific of all Gaelic writers, and he almost uniquely contributed in every major genre of twentieth century writing in both English and Gaelic. As a writer of English, he is perhaps most famous as a poet, although some of his prose fiction in English deserves significantly more attention than it has thus-far received. In Gaelic, which was his first language, Mac a' Ghobhainn is also more widely respected for his poetry than for his other writing, but this is largely due to the privileged position that poetry still occupies within the Gaelic literary consciousness (Watson 2010, Gillies 2006, Kidd 2000). In fact, the best of Mac a' Ghobhainn's prose writing in Gaelic is at least as accomplished as his poetry, and we will consider some of that writing in this chapter. Although we have seen in previous chapters in this book that there were earlier collections published in Gaelic that included stories, it would not be unreasonable to consider Mac a' Ghobhainn's *Bùrn is Aran* (1960; 'Water and Bread') to be the first true collection of 'short stories' (see NicFhionghuin 1961 for an endorsement of this view). A fuller discussion of *Bùrn is Aran* appears later in this chapter.

Mac a' Ghobhainn went on to publish four other collections of Gaelic short stories in his career: *An Dubh is An Gorm* (1963), *Maighstirean is Ministearan* (1970), *An t-Adhar Ameireaganach* (1973), and *Na Guthan* (1991). Although all five collections have a good deal in common stylistically, and, at times, imagistically, the tone and underlying themes vary considerably from one to another.

Apart from Mac a' Ghobhainn, the most significant writers who published collections in the period 1960–99 were all also familiar as

contributors to *Gairm*. Iain Moireach has published only one collection
to date, *An Aghaidh Choimheach* ('The Mask' / 'The Strange Face'), but his
reputation as a short story writer at least matches Mac a' Ghobhainn's (see
Marner 2000). Pòl MacAonghais was another writer capable of a deft touch
and keen observations. His book, *An Guth Aoibhneach* (1993), was published posthumously, and contains many well-written stories, although the
quality of the writing is variable. Two other prolific writers were Cailein T.
MacCoinnich and Eilidh Watt, who was the first woman to publish a collection of short stories in Gaelic. MacCoinnich's collections, *Nach Neònach
Sin* (1973) and *Oirthir Tìm* (1969) display a fascination with science-fiction
plots, muddled up with folkloric elements and heavy-handed Christian
didacticism. Watt's books *A' Bhratach Dheàlrach* (1972) and *Gun Fhois*
(1987) substitute the science-fiction for the supernatural, and *Gun Fhois*,
in particular, concentrates on the motif of the second sight. Watt seems to
have considered herself to have the second sight, and so it is not always
clear which of her stories are meant to be entirely fictional and which are
partly or wholly autobiographical. Similarly, with MacCoinnich, some of
his stories depend heavily on folklore and others may derive directly from
folk tales he heard: it is not always clear where the lines of fictionality may
be drawn. His *Mar Sgeul a Dh'innseas Neach* (1971) is less folkloric than
Nach Neònach Sin, but displays a love of the conundrum, especially the
legal or crime mystery.

Of the more recent writers, prior to the Ùr-Sgeul publishing project that
is discussed in Chapter 6, the Caimbeul brothers deserve a mention here.
Tormod and Alasdair Caimbeul are the sons of the village poet Aonghas
Caimbeul (known as 'Am Bocsair').[1] Both of the Caimbeul brothers have
already been discussed in relation to the modern novels in the previous
chapter. Tormod Caimbeul has published two collections, both of which
draw heavily on his own life: *Hostail* (1992), which is highly autobiographical, and *An naidheachd bhon taigh* (1994), which has many highlights and
sometimes approaches the level of excellence of his novel *Deireadh an
Fhoghair*. Alasdair Caimbeul has only published a single collection to date,
Lìontan Sgaoilte (1999), and even that book is not exclusively a short story
collection. *Lìontan Sgaoilte* ('Spread Nets'), as its title suggests, is wide-
ranging and eclectic. Among other kinds of writing, the book includes
short stories, but some of these are so clearly drawn from Caimbeul's own
background that it is impossible to determine whether they are autobiographical 'stories' or simply autobiography.

Another writer who published a collection demonstrates that the kinds
of stories that were discussed in Chapter 1 continued to hold some appeal
for Gaelic audiences even up to the most recent times. Dòmhnall Alasdair
Dòmhnallach[2] was a well-known and popular poet of the so-called 'village'

variety, but he also expressed himself in prose, with his stories being collected in *Sgeulachdan Dhòmhnaill Alasdair* (2001, 'Donald Alasdair's Stories'). *Sgeulachdan Dhòmhnaill Alasdair* has a slightly reminiscent feel, as if drawing on a sense of cultural consciousness that may no longer be current. Dòmhnall Alasdair's stories are driven by plot, humour or other entertaining devices. They are very well written and satisfying.

Iain Mac a' Ghobhainn's *Bùrn is Aran* was, in 1960, the first book of short stories to appear in Gaelic in many years. If we disregard the work of writers like Iain MacCormaic and Iain MacPhàidein from the 'short story' genre, and choose to describe their writings as 'tales' or 'yarns', then we might even suggest that *Bùrn is Aran* was the first-ever book of Gaelic short stories. There is no doubt that the stories in *Bùrn is Aran* represent a considerable departure from what had gone before. Where the emphasis in the earlier writing was on plotting, locus and morals, the emphasis in Mac a' Ghobhainn's work was immediately and centrally on character. Mac a' Ghobhainn's minimalist writing style leaves the reader in no doubt that his interest was in what goes on in characters' minds rather than what happens all around them. This style continued throughout his fiction writing career, and was particularly successful in his short novel, *An t-Aonaran*, discussed in the previous chapter.

When *Bùrn is Aran* was first published in 1960, it included twenty poems in addition to the nine stories. A second edition of the book published in 1974 appeared without the poems, with no explanation for their omission. The third edition, in 1987, again appeared without the poems. The 1987 edition updated some of the spelling, but also inserted a number of errors which were not present in the original text. A volume of Mac a' Ghobhainn's complete collected stories in Gaelic currently in preparation will seek to eradicate some of these errors.

Compared with Mac a' Ghobhainn's later collections, *Bùrn is Aran* has a stronger sense of internal unity, although it is not a short story cycle, by any means. Many of the stories are about people who have left their homes. The people in question tend to be young men, who can be identified with the author in many respects. The homes they have left are usually similar to Mac a' Ghobhainn's own island home. In more than one story, the setting is implied as being Lewis, although Lewis is almost never explicitly referred to. In these ways, *Bùrn is Aran* almost seems to nod to the work of MacCormaic and MacPhàidein: they, too, wrote about exile and about returning home, and they, too, often set their work on the island of their own early memories, sometimes implicitly. Where MacCormaic might have concentrated on the account of how the exile got home, Mac a' Ghobhainn's focus is on the effect that the time away has had on both the exile and those left behind.

These points are illustrated clearly in stories like 'Turus Dhachaidh – I' ('Journey Home – I'), 'An Coigreach' ('The Stranger'), and 'Turus Dhachaidh – II' ('Journey Home – II'). Apart from their similar titles and themes, there is no clear link between 'Turus Dhachaidh – I' and 'Turus Dhachaidh – II', but we must wonder if the author intended for us to make a link between them: perhaps the main character is the same person in both stories, but this is certainly not clear. In both cases, there is a certain irony involved in the titles: both imply significance in a *journey*, but the journey itself is, in both cases, downplayed by the narrative. In 'Turus Dhachaidh – I', the main character's journey home is confined to the last page-and-a-half of the story and is anticlimactic in many ways. In 'Turus Dhachaidh – II', the only part of the journey (all the way from New Zealand) directly recounted is the bus trip on the island itself. The focus of the story is on the anonymity that time away from a small community can purchase for the returning exile. In 'An Coigreach', there is a similar play on words with the title. The young man who is the main character is evidently not a stranger, but that is how he feels when he comes home, and that is how he comes across at first to his mother, who has become blind in his absence. In a sense, the young man has become a stranger by absenting himself for so long: he no longer recognises the life he left behind as his own. Like the main characters in both 'Turus Dhachaidh' stories, he is not entirely able to leave behind all of the aspects of his past, and this is why he has returned. But, also like these other characters, his return does not promise to offer him the kind of reconciliation with himself that he perhaps sought. Even his mother's acceptance of him at the end of the story is rife with ambiguities, especially when we realise that it is never entirely clear at which point she first recognised him and saw through his attempt to deceive her about his identity.

Exile from the home environment, loneliness, and difficulties in communication are central themes in much of Mac a' Ghobhainn's writing. All of them are important in the stories just mentioned, but, in some ways, the archetypal story based around these themes is 'An Duine Dubh' ('The Black Man', BA). The main character in this story is an old woman who lives alone, now that her family have either died or moved away. She encounters a travelling salesman, who happens to be a coloured man, apparently Asian. He, too, is alone and lonely; in his case, because of having come far from home to make money to support his family. In the course of the story, they keep failing to communicate and yet, in spite of this, they somehow achieve a kind of understanding, which is largely conveyed to the audience by means of dramatic irony, one of Mac a' Ghobhainn's best-developed devices.

The exile theme can be found throughout modern Gaelic literature. The reason for this can be traced to the demographic realities of the Gaelic community in the wake of the devastating nineteenth century. Where the eighteenth century marked the end of Highland power, the nineteenth century effectively saw the end of what we might call a 'Gaelic nation'. Famine, vast, long-lasting migration patterns (both emigration of Gaels and then immigration of non-Gaels), disease, and economics contributed to a situation that led to an inexorable Anglicisation of the former Gaelic areas. By the twentieth century, a majority of Gaelic-speakers were also English-speakers (see Macleod 2010 on the social history of the language). By the end of the twentieth century, most Gaelic-speakers were English-dominant bilinguals, and there were almost no remaining monoglot Gaelic speakers. With this linguistic shift, there was also a cultural shift. Throughout the twentieth century, many Gaels felt the need to leave the Gaelic community for one reason or another: often, to avail themselves of a university education or to improve their financial standing in other ways. Significant numbers of these educated Gaels became the literati of their generation, thus resulting in a published literature that has been largely composed by people living outside of the community where the language is spoken on a day-to-day basis. As well as the theme of exile itself, many of these exigencies have found their way into the writing. Thus, Gaelic literature of the twentieth century is a literature riddled with ironies and self-awareness.

In the work of Iain Moireach, for instance, we find returning exiles who discover that return is, in fact, impossible. In the writing of both Tormod and Alasdair Caimbeul, we see the damage and hurt that can be caused both to individuals and to communities by these hybridising processes: characters strive to hold onto a sense of identity, relationships suffer and wither, and everywhere there is a lack of self-confidence or self-belief. Tormod Caimbeul's story 'An naidheachd bhon taigh' ('The news from home', NT) encapsulates all of these ideas (see Watson forthcoming b). The story is set in a small Gaelic community that is depicted as suffering from a colonial malaise: characters speak a kind of pidgin Gaelic that is utterly suffused with English vocabulary, and attention is drawn to this ironically by the device of having them list and discuss ailments, always largely in English. The story lacks movement or development, which emphasises the stagnation of the community. The only dynamism present is owned by the recent non-Gael incomers to the area. Their enthusiasm and energy do not buoy up the local natives; instead, they serve as a point of sharp contrast and, if anything, further stifle the locals' sense of self. Further illustrating the fact that hybridisation is a process and not a state, the only young local person in the story has gone much further than his elders in embracing the new language and culture. He is losing his Gaelicness more quickly and more thoroughly than the other characters, and his solitude pushes him towards the incomers. Similarly, a number of the stories in Alasdair Caimbeul's *Lìontan Sgaoilte* touch on these themes and motifs, albeit often at an earlier stage in the process. Where Tormod Caimbeul's stories are often set at an advanced stage in the de-Gaelicisation process, his brother's work looks for the roots of the developments by exploring the writer's own youth. The story 'Dealbhan' ('Pictures', LS) is set in a little village shop in the 1940s. As the title suggests, it is less a story and more a collection of images that almost certainly are drawn from personal recollections. As the hub of the community, the shop is an economic centre and is the main transition zone between what the author may wish to see as the previously homogeneous Gaelic culture and the advancing Anglicising culture. In 'Dealbhan', Anglicisation is achieved through products, supply-and-demand, and through the ever-increasing global communications network. Isolation is no longer possible, thanks to the radio and newspapers: the Gaelic community is more than ever a part of the world community, and it appears that English must act as intermediary.

Exile is dealt with rather differently as a theme in some of the stories of Pòl MacAonghais. For MacAonghais, it is about the effects on the individual. In 'An Gille Gallta' ('The Lowland/Foreign Boy', GA), the main character is a boy who has been orphaned and relocated during the Second World War. He has gone to live with relatives he barely knew in a Gaelic-speaking area without knowing any Gaelic himself. The story charts his movement from depression and rebellion, through resignation and towards resolution. As he starts to come to terms with his new situation, he begins to develop a relationship with his kind and patient grandfather, who has himself also suffered loss. This story is slightly unusual in that it focuses on a non-Gael who comes into the Gaelic community; and it is also unusual in that the language barrier is shown to be surmountable: as the story progresses, the boy's command of Gaelic improves and, as it does so, he begins to fit in better. Although the focus throughout the story is on the effects of wartime, exile and isolation on the individual, an awareness of the wider implications is retained throughout. The boy and his grandfather encounter a dead sheep on their travels, the sheep being a trope for the community around them, which is being torn apart by the war. Then, shortly after this, they are surprised and frightened when a Spitfire suddenly overflies at a low altitude, catching them unawares because it comes around a hillside. At this point, the lonely hillside is no longer home to either of them: it has become part of the war and part of the ever-encroaching outside world. The boy's foreignness is no longer the issue that it once was, because the barriers of the local and the foreign have been broken down. Despite this, their shared moment of panic helps them to achieve a fellow feeling that had previously escaped them.

Iain Moireach's 'Am Partaidh' ('The Party', AC) explores another different side to the exile theme. The story is set in Glasgow or Edinburgh (there are small hints that point to either), most of it taking place during a party. The main character Ailean also experiences a number of flashbacks, which punctuate the party and provide the structure for understanding his current frame of mind. At first, it appears that his angst is entirely due to his inability to feel at home either in the city or back in the small Gaelic community that he left when he was in his teens. Later, it transpires that his state of mind is also due to the death of his father some time previously and his failure to mend the cracks in their relationship when he still had the chance. Evidently, that failure was also due to Ailean's sense of alienation. In his case, the alienation stems partly from his father's adherence to a Calvinistic faith that Ailean cannot comprehend and certainly cannot share.

Although important, exile is only one of many themes that can be found within the corpus of the modern Gaelic short story. If we turn now to a brief discussion of some of the main collections of short stories that have been published since *Bùrn is Aran*, we will encounter many of these other themes and see how they develop and interact over the course of forty years or so.

Iain Mac a' Ghobhainn

Iain Mac a' Ghobhainn's second collection, *An Dubh is An Gorm* ('The Black and the Blue'), is one of his best. Thanks to the focus of a few of the better known stories in the book, it also contributes to Mac a' Ghobhainn's unjustified reputation for being obsessed with criticising Christianity. Seven of the twenty stories in the book originally appeared in the magazine *Gairm*, which suggests perhaps that they were not initially conceived as part of a collection. As the title of the book would tend to suggest, though, there is a sense of unity in that most of the stories feature some kind of diametric tension: characters are pulled in two opposing directions by different kinds of motivations, or events precipitate difficult choices and decisions.[3] The title story itself, which appears last in the book, is a good illustration of these kinds of tensions and choices that lead to a character being torn between two positions. Similarly, the opening story, 'An Solus Ùr' ('The New Light') – which is itself such an ironic title, considering that it seems suggestive of hope and regeneration and yet turns out to be about nuclear annihilation – has a focal character who is torn between his duty and his humanity. Both 'Abraham is Isaac' ('Abraham and Isaac') and 'An Taghadh' ('The Choice') have characters who must agonise over a decision to kill a loved one. In 'An Còmhradh', fear of death and the unknown pushes an ill boy towards another kind of fear and, perhaps, pushes his mother away from the religion she has embraced. Like 'Jenkins is Marlowe' ('Jenkins and Marlowe'), 'Anns an Uaimh' ('In the Cave') is all about the contrasts between light and dark, black and white and other kinds of oppositions. In 'Na h-Iùdhaich' ('The Jews'), the tension is between the repeated emphasis on the cleanliness of the Nazi guards and the horror of their actions.

Mac a' Ghobhainn's minimalist writing style is highly effective in the short story mode. This is highlighted in 'Am Maor' ('The Factor'), a story about the Highland Clearances. It is not clear whether 'Am Maor' was written before or after Mac a' Ghobhainn's seminal novel *Consider the Lilies*, but it is essentially the same story as the opening episode of that novel. Indeed, it even has much of the same imagery and some similar exchanges of dialogue. Further, Mac a' Ghobhainn's play, *A' Chùirt* (1966), published by An Comunn Gaidhealach, again takes the same story as its basis, although the focus is rather different (see Watson 2004). *A' Chùirt* serves as a dramatic epilogue to both 'Am Maor' and *Consider the Lilies*.

At the beginning of 'Am Maor', Mac a' Ghobhainn's sparse writing style emphasises the fact that the landscape is bare, which echoes the beginning of 'An Coigreach' from *Bùrn is Aran*. In this story, it is implied that there used to be more houses and people and that some kind of community atrophy is in progress. Symbols in the story are often ambiguous or multivalent. For instance, the factor who arrives to evict the old woman from her home carries a whip. At times, it is clear that this whip is a metonym for authority and control. At other times, it becomes a symbol of cruelty and represents the factor's anger and frustration. Again, later, it links the factor with the Duke he serves, showing how he strives to emulate his greater master. The old woman asks if the factor has come to deliver the war widow's pension she believes she is due, and this pension is a symbol for the power relationships between the people and their colonial leaders. Not only is the Duke not intending to pay a pension that had perhaps been hinted at in the past, but he is now intending to put her out of the home she shared with her husband and family, a home she identifies with her own sense of self. Soot, lime and the other realities of everyday life in the old woman's house become symbols of the distance that the factor has worked to place between himself and this lifestyle. He knows that this is the kind of life that he himself has come from and so he is afraid to touch anything in case he sullies himself with the symbols of that old life and is then somehow symbolically returned to it. At the same time, the reader is aware of these things as being the essential by-products of the old woman's everyday life, and they are thus also symbols of how she lives.

In *An Dubh is An Gorm*, knives are among the most prominent motifs. Knives represent different things in the various stories, but they always seem to be associated with menace. Throughout the story 'Abraham is Isaac', the reader is aware, through dramatic irony and allusion to the Biblical story, that Abraham intends to use the knife to kill his son. Abraham tries to objectify the planned murder by imagining that it is the knife that will do the deed and not his own hand: we are told that he spent a whole week sharpening the knife, which represents the premeditated nature of the act, but also hints at procrastination. When Isaac sees the knife, Abraham's guilt comes to the fore, because it is as if Isaac has seen his intention. In 'A' Bhan-Shoisgeulaiche' ('The [Female] Missionary'), the missionary has a knife, which emphasises her distance from the natives, as we see in the phrase 'sgian airgid fhuar' (p. 46, 'a cold silver knife'). Although a knife does not actually play a prominent part in 'An Lèine' ('The Shirt'), the focal character does recognise a knife cut in an old piece of furniture that reminds him of his childhood: that is to say, the impression the knife has left represents the impression on his memory.

Important as knife images are in *An Dubh is An Gorm*, they are not as prominent as they were in *Bùrn is Aran*, most particularly in stories like 'Clachan Chalanais' ('The Callanish Stones').[4] Indeed, the imagery throughout 'Clachan Chalanais' is both unusual and menacing. Early in the story, yellow lights are described as being as bitter as a lemon (*Bùrn is Aran* p. 39), but then the mother character's face is also yellow. Many things shine and flash in this bitter yellow light. Throughout the story, knives are seen in people's hands or in front of people, and they are juxtaposed with images of the standing stones. We might suppose that the stones are being used as a metonym for the kinds of human sacrifice that active imaginations attribute to the druids, and that the focal character is feeling very menaced where he need not be. He seems to imagine himself as a human sacrifice ('mar fhaochaig air creig', p. 43, 'like a winkle on a rock'), and he blames himself for his father leaving the family: in fact, his father has not left, and the boy has been deceived by his own flights of fancy. 'Clachan Chalanais' is an unusual story for Mac a' Ghobhainn in many ways, not least because the ominous foreshadowing turns out to be unfounded.

An Dubh is An Gorm, too, has a standing stone, of sorts, in the story 'Aig a' Chloich-Chuimhne' ('At the Memorial Stone'). This story is about war teaching an artist how to use red. Red does not symbolise merely blood and death, however: it becomes his symbol for his own cowardice, having run away and left his friend to die. The word *dearg* ('red') is also important in the story 'An Taghadh' ('The Choice'). In 'An Taghadh', a family is confronted by the commander of a Hanoverian military unit who wants to exact revenge for the death of his brother at Culloden. He wants not just to kill someone, but to inflict a level of mental torture that will somehow offset his own pain at the loss of his brother. So, he finds a woman with three sons and tells her she must select one of the three to be killed. Her strongest son, Tormod, is prepared to resist the soldiers or even to sacrifice himself for the sake of his brothers and to spare his mother the decision. His hands are 'dearg': it may be that this is to imply he had blood on his hands at Culloden, but it may also be that the redness is associated with the stress of the situation or the hard physical work he undertakes each day. In the end, the mother makes what must be the most practical decision, but it must surely also destroy the family, just as the commander had intended.

It was hinted above that Mac a' Ghobhainn has an unjustified reputation as being an obsessively anti-Christian writer. In fact, only a relatively small proportion of his writing deals with Christianity in any form. Further, there are some indications that he admired aspects of religions, including Christianity. Similarly, he also has a reputation as being a writer obsessed with the figure of the mother or the lonely old woman. Again, while these images are certainly memorable and are clearly important in the work where they appear, mothers and old women are not nearly as prominent throughout the body of his writing as one might imagine. There are two stories in *An Dubh is An Gorm*, however, which do engage with the mother archetype and her relationship with a son: 'An Còmhradh' ('The Conversation') and 'An Lèine' ('The Shirt').[5] The former also deals with the Christianity motif, and not in a positive way. The structure of 'An Còmhradh' is rather experimental for this stage in the development of Gaelic fiction, but it succeeds well: the story is actually a monologue, which is addressed to an unnamed second-person. The second-person implied character, who is the friend of the woman's son who has died, never makes a reply that is reported, although we can infer from the woman's speech pattern that he does indeed reply to some of the things she says. For instance, it seems he has asked if the boy, Tormod, suffered much, when the mother character responds: 'Pian?' (p. 56, 'Pain?'). In 'An Còmhradh', the tension consists in the contrast between Tormod's early, fun-loving ways and his death-bed persona. Tormod has been an easy-going boy, full of tricks and mischief. Along with his friend, he has played pranks on many of the members of the community, but always in good humour. In contrast, his relationship with his God-fearing mother has been more serious and apparently strained. When he became ill, Tormod remained cheerful at first, but his mother and the minister worked hard to persuade him to be fearful and serious. The minister mistakes the fear of death for a love of life or for life-affirming behaviour, and the mother simply follows his lead. Tormod, consequently, gradually recedes from life, retreating into himself. He no longer wants to see anyone other than the minister and he becomes quiet, pale and still. The Bible in the story is cold (58), even though it has been lying in the warmth of the sun: thus, the story contrasts Christianity and life. Christianity, the story seems to suggest, is derived from a fear of death; but, fear of death is itself life-denying; thus, Christianity is in danger of destroying the thing it seeks to preserve.[6] In the end, perhaps, the mother character comes to doubt her role in converting Tormod to Christianity, as she begins to understand that it resulted in making his last days miserable and it changed his character completely.

'An Lèine' has much in common with 'An Còmhradh', but even more so with 'An Coigreach', which was discussed in the section on *Bùrn is Aran*. Again, the story has (apparently) a mother and son whose relationship has become strained. As in 'An Coigreach', the son in 'An Lèine' has been away for many years and has now returned to see how his mother is faring. As in the other story, too, the son does not announce himself, but presents himself as a stranger. 'An Lèine' is, in some ways, then, a reworking of the 'An Coigreach' story, but with a greater level of subtlety. Although the mother in this story is not blind, she fails or chooses not to recognise her son: 'cha mhór gu faiceadh i aodann' (p. 59, 'she could scarcely see his face'). This is a trope for their failure to 'recognise' one another's viewpoints. The opening of the story is full of typical Mac a' Ghobhainn quickfire characterisation, of the sort that marked him as a true master of the short story form. Indeed, there is never any direct textual evidence that these are a mother and her son, but the story makes most sense if that is the assumption that the reader makes, based on the little clues and cues that appear throughout: by giving their respective ages, Mac a' Ghobhainn lets us see that they could be mother and son; by showing us the picture of the man, he lets us know the man is likely dead; by having the younger man look at that picture with spite, he lets us know they may have known each other, and, in the context, that means he must have known both the older man and the woman. When he notices the cut in the furniture that was alluded to above, the focal character shows us that he has been there as a child.

If we do make the assumption that the two characters in 'An Lèine' are mother and son, then the story is heartbreakingly sad. The son does not know how to bridge the gap between him and his mother, when neither one acknowledges the other. He asks her to repair a torn shirt, which she does without comment. Only after she returns it to him does he realise that the shirt has his name on it. Since she has obviously noticed this and not said anything, he chooses to go on his way, neither of them having made an effort to mend their relationship. The predominant theme in the story is the passing of time, and the damage it can do. Throughout the story, there are references to time, to people ageing and changing, and to things growing old and past their best. Finally, the chief protagonist is: 'back in another world (or 'life') . . . as if time had broken through' (61).

Ephemerality – especially of beauty – is a common theme in Mac a' Ghobhainn's poetry, but much less so in his fiction. It appears in 'An Lèine' and also in 'Na Facail air a' Bhalla' ('The Words on the Wall'). 'Na Facail air a' Bhalla' and the story that precedes it, 'Am Prìosanach' ('The Prisoner'), are both, to varying degrees, about the little details that constitute a person's identity. In 'Am Prìosanach', freedom, individuality and isolation are explored, and especially in the ways in which they related to the individual's perception and sense of himself. The story studies how easy it is for the mind to become unhinged when there is nothing for it to cling to. In 'Na Facail air a' Bhalla', the main character sees little traces of people who have lived in the house before and wonders who they were and what they were like (compare Fionnlagh MacLeòid's story 'An Dachaigh', discussed in Chapter 6).

It would be unfortunate to conclude a discussion of *An Dubh is An Gorm* without further mention of the title story. 'An Dubh is An Gorm' is unusual for Mac a' Ghobhainn, in that it is an epistolary story: indeed, there are very few stories in this form in Gaelic at all (Chapter 3 mentions some of the others). The focal character is a young man in Mac a' Ghobhainn's own image, one of many characters in his fiction who have left rural or island backgrounds to go to a university city, normally to pursue their education. The letters from the young man to his mother gradually trace the changes in his attitudes and character as he grows into himself and leaves behind the boy who was dominated by a strictly religious mother. The young man, Coinneach, responds in his letters to what his mother must have said in reply, and we see how he learns to deal with her criticisms. He also gradually becomes more anglicised and less obviously 'Gaelic' in his attitudes and perceptions. The black and blue of the title seem to refer to the contrast in perceptions of the world: Coinneach feels his mother has only seen the black, which may be taken to refer to the Free Church tradition of wearing sombre tones on the Sabbath, but at any rate it depicts her as being monochromatic in her outlook. Coinneach feels there should be room for the black, but that we should also make room for the blue: the blue is perhaps a reference to the blue of the sky or the green of grass (*gorm* means both 'blue' and also 'lush green'). Coinneach comes to see inertia as a kind of sickness, and he equates this sickness with fear. In this way, 'An Dubh is An Gorm' links back to 'An Còmhradh'.

Reviewing *An Dubh is An Gorm*, Fionnlagh MacLeòid noted that Mac a' Ghobhainn's work was blazing something of a trail at the time: that there were no short stories in Gaelic until shortly before and that now a single author had produced two collections in only a few years

(MacLeòid 1963: 431). MacLeòid went on to theorise briefly about what short stories are for, how they differ from the older written and oral tales, and what their place might be in Gaelic literature. Mac a' Ghobhainn's stories, as evidenced in *An Dubh is An Gorm*, were much more contemporary and more topical: they were about how the world of the islands was changing (434). MacLeòid saw a danger in Mac a' Ghobhainn's success, however, if it failed to inspire others to follow on soon: he felt that if Mac a' Ghobhainn carried on publishing his brand of stories, other writers might eventually come to imagine that his was the only way of writing Gaelic stories and that the genre might become formulaic (435). While this fear was undoubtedly justified, matters did not turn out like that. Iain Mac a' Ghobhainn continued writing his minimalist stories, full of emotional and psychological interest and vivid imagery, but they did not inspire a generation of copies. In fact, it is difficult to see much of Mac a' Ghobhainn's influence in any of the short story collections that appeared over the forty year period between the appearance of *Bùrn is Aran* and the turn of the century.

Mac a' Ghobhainn's next two collections, *Maighsteirean is Ministearan* ('Teachers and Ministers', 1970) and *An t-Adhar Ameireaganach* ('The American Sky', 1973) were not so well admired as his first two. Dòmhnall Iain MacLeòid's (Donald John MacLeod) review of *Maighsteirean is Ministearan* ranked the book as Mac a' Ghobhainn's weakest to date. In terms of individual stories, he stated that there were none in the book to compare with the author's best (MacLeòid 1970: 96). In particular, he was of the opinion that the title story was not compelling enough to sustain fifty-four pages, and he compared it unfavourably with a Joyce novel. Richard Cox implied that he, too, was less convinced by 'Maighsteirean is Ministearan' in the chapter on Mac a' Ghobhainn's fiction that he contributed to Colin Nicholson's 1992 book of critical essays. He considered that the story relied on a method that differed from Mac a' Ghobhainn's usual style in order to concentrate on the 'progression of plot', and that this resulted in 'a lengthy, drawn-out affair' (Cox 1992: 197). Although MacLeòid was less negative in his review of *An t-Adhar Ameireaganach* than he was when he reviewed *Maighsteirean is Ministearan*, he clearly considered that collection as also less successful than either *Bùrn is Aran* or *An Dubh is An Gorm*. *Maighsteirean is Ministearan* has a good deal in common with Mac a' Ghobhainn's English-language collections (published under the name 'Iain Crichton Smith') *Survival Without Error and Other Stories* (1970) and *The Black and the Red and Other Stories* (1973). In particular, 'Pickering' (as it should be titled) is aligned with the title story of the former of the English collections, 'Survival Without Error'.[7]

In *An t-Adhar Ameireaganach*, the title story is perhaps the most interesting and unusual. The first-person narrator is a Gael in exile, as in so many of the stories in Mac a' Ghobhainn's *oeuvre*. In this case, he was in New York, but the story is told in flashback mode, and we learn that he left that city a week ago. He began to remember the smell of crabs and became unbearably homesick. Without thinking, he immediately left what he was doing and headed for home. During the course of the story, the narrator realises that there is no way home. In this way, 'An t-Adhar Ameireaganach' relates to the much longer and similarly titled English story by the same author, 'An American Sky'. However, there is an element of the surreal to the Gaelic story. Sensations are of paramount importance in 'An t-Adhar Ameireaganach': not only is it the memory of a smell that compels the narrator to travel across the world, but he is also fascinated by the sound of singing he hears when he is on board the ship. This kind of emphasis on the physical senses is one of the features that marks Mac a' Ghobhainn's writing out as being some of the most vivid and convincing in Gaelic.

Mac a' Ghobhainn's final Gaelic collection, *Na Guthan* ('The Voices', 1991), saw a further development in his narrative style. Stories like 'An Guth' ('The Voice') and 'An Fhìrinn' ('The Truth') epitomise this style, which is characterised by a greater sense of distance between the focal character and the reader. This sense of distance is signalled by the avoidance of conventional speech marks throughout the book, for instance. At the same time, there is a further emphasis on Mac a' Ghobhainn's use of the anecdotal technique in some of the other stories, where the emphasis is on a conversational, personable narrator. An example of this is 'A' Chluas' ('The Ear'), which makes humour out of a horrific incident. At the same time, though, the sense of being removed is still present, as the narrator explains that his story has come to us second-hand. It is possible that the key to understanding this sense of distance is provided in the opening line of the book, in the story 'An Guth', where the focal character insists that he must keep his world 'closed' (1). This character is a poet, who may therefore be a trope for Mac a' Ghobhainn himself. The poet writes:

> I don't have enough time and for that reason I sit at my desk and keep the world away from me. (1)

Na Guthan is a stronger collection than either *Maighsteirean is Ministeirean* or *An t-Adhar Ameireaganach*, although perhaps it is not as engaging as *Bùrn is Aran* or *An Dubh is An Gorm*. This is partly due to the different writing style, which, although it retains Mac a' Ghobhainn's minimalist characterisation and vivid imagery, conveys less immediacy than his early stories did. All five of Mac a' Ghobhainn's collections, and his uncollected work, will be discussed in more detail in a book of his stories that I am currently co-editing.

Iain Moireach

Along with Iain Mac a' Ghobhainn, Iain Moireach is generally considered to be the finest practitioner of the short story in Gaelic: in fact, some critics, including Mac a' Ghobhainn himself, regard him to be the unrivalled leader of the form (Mac a' Ghobhainn 1983). It may be that this status will come to be re-evaluated in the light of the current renaissance in prose writing. Donnchadh MacGillÌosa and Fionnlagh MacLeòid, in particular, do not suffer in comparison with either Mac a' Ghobhainn or Moireach. Moireach's reputation is based on a single collection of stories, *An Aghaidh Choimheach* (1973), and a small output of uncollected stories, mainly published in the magazines *Gairm* and *Gath*. It has long been seen as a loss to the literature that Moireach has not yet produced a second collection, or even a more significant number of uncollected stories. Ironically, one of the reviewers of *An Aghaidh Choimheach* was so impressed with the book that he urged Moireach to pick up his pen and write another book as soon as possible (Moireasdan 1973). Moireach has been more prolific as a playwright: it is no surprise, then, that his use of dialogue is particularly accomplished. Moireasdan's review effectively warns the reader that this book is not a book of yarns like the collections they might have seen before in Gaelic, and that not every story has much in the way of plot, as is normal in stories by Chekhov, Maupassant, Lawrence and other greats.

Not all of the stories in *An Aghaidh Choimheach* are of the same stellar quality, but there are few, if any, that are dispensable. As Mac a' Ghobhainn noted in his study of Moireach's work in 1983, Moireach's ability with third-person stories is generally better than his ability with first-person or stream-of-consciousness (Mac a' Ghobhainn 1983: 170). In the same article, however, Mac a' Ghobhainn acknowledges that one of Moireach's great strengths is his versatility (a point which Moireasdan also makes in his review):

> Without any doubt, Iain Moireach's stories are the best we have
> in Gaelic, and this is because they are diverse but simultaneously
> homogeneous, rising from the same imagination. (170)

The title of the collection means 'The Mask', but could also mean 'The Strange Face', and the word *coimheach* has connotations of alienness as well as shyness and outlandishness. All of these concepts are motifs that appear in various of the stories. The idea of the mask itself is perhaps relevant only in the title story and 'Am Partaidh', although deception and hidden feelings are present in some of the other stories. Sometimes, the motifs of strangeness and alienness are present in ordinary and everyday situations, and the ability to create this kind of tension is one of Moireach's strongest assets. For instance, shyness is partly what holds back Mairi-Anna from trying harder to pursue a relationship in 'Am Partaidh', but the concept is much more important in 'An Gamhainn' and, to some extent, 'Seòras'.

Most of the stories in *An Aghaidh Choimheach* are about the same length, a little over two thousand words or so. The title story is close to double the length of almost any other story in the book. This is a consequence of the different structure, with the story taking place over a more extended time and involving a wider range of characters. It also has changes of viewpoint, giving it a more expansive atmosphere than almost any of the other stories in the book. The other story that is most experimental from a technical point of view is 'A' Chaora Chonadail' ('The Black/Wandering Sheep'). Even after nearly four decades, this is still one of very few stories in Gaelic that come close to producing a sustained sense of stream-of-consciousness. 'A' Chaora Chonadail' is not an unmitigated success, but it does demonstrate Moireach's talents well, most especially his ability to get into characters' heads and express their thoughts and feelings credibly. Indeed, his ability to create character sympathy is one of Moireach's surest gifts as a writer.

In many ways, 'Am Partaidh' ('The Party') is the stand-out story in the collection. Its main character Ailean is one of the most memorable characters in the Gaelic short story. Ailean's angst is almost tangible, and yet there is plenty in the story to suggest he also has the capacity for joy, if only circumstances would allow it. In the story's main timeframe, Ailean is attending a party at a student flat in a city.[8] There are also a number of significant flashbacks, which allow the reader to understand why Ailean is experiencing such troubled emotions. Only Ailean, and then the reader, are aware of all of the significant incidents, so no other character can fully empathise with him, even though Mairi-Anna clearly wishes to.

Ailean is evidently a talented and intelligent young man, who suffers first and foremost because of his difficulty with his sense of identity. He is painfully aware of a split in his cultural identity; as a Gael, he thinks he should relate to the songs of Uilleam Ros (William Ross), but he also identifies with Shelley: his first reported thoughts in the story are a quote from Shelley's 'Music, when soft voices die'. These lines become important again at the end of the story when we realise that much of Ailean's unhappiness is caused by thoughts of his late father. He clings to the Shelley lines as if to affirm that his love for his father lives on. He is, however, undoubtedly aware of the ambiguity of the last line of the Shelley lyric (not quoted in the story): 'Love itself shall slumber on'. Indeed, rather like Eachann in *Keino* (discussed in Chapter 4), Ailean is primarily disturbed because he still does not understand the depth of his relationship with his father and now knows he never will. Like Eachann, Ailean grew up in awe of an intimidating father, whom he then came to disdain. Like Eachann, Ailean then treated his father badly when he was older. Finally, like Eachann,

Ailean only came to regret this treatment and re-evaluate his father's love for him after his father died.

'Am Partaidh' is one of several stories in *An Aghaidh Choimheach* that address the notion of Gaelic cultural identity. Ailean in particular is aware of the splitness and hybridity that is an inherent part of being a contemporary Gael. He attributes his own uncertainties to this split identity:

> sin a dh'fhàg esan cho teagmhach, *Gall-Ghaidhealach*, 'na choigreach anns a h-uile h-àite ach air an trèana no air a' bhàta. (22)

> (that was what left him so doubtful, *Gall-Ghaidhealach*, a stranger everywhere except on the train or the boat.)

Gall-Ghaidhealach is difficult to translate with a neat, two-word phrase. *Gall* is the Gaelic word for a Lowland Scot, although it more literally means a 'foreigner'. *Gaidhealach* is the adjective that describes the Gael, Gaelic or the Highlands. Someone who is *Gall-Ghaidhealach*, therefore, could be described as a Lowland Gael or an urban Gael, but these English phrases do not encapsulate the sense of liminality that is evoked by Moireach's phrase. This liminality is also summed up in the image of the Gael being at home only when on a train or a boat (meaning, almost certainly, a ferry). For Gaels of Moireach's background (and indeed, most pertinently, Ailean's), the only way to access Higher Education was to leave the island. Like Aonghas Iain in 'An Aghaidh Choimheach', Ailean has learnt the hard truth of the matter: once you have left the island, you can never really go back. This is a theme that has pervaded Gaelic literature throughout the contemporary period, as the past three generations of Gaelic writers have had to come to terms with a sense of exile from their home community and yet a sense of not really belonging in the second environment. Ailean is the only character in the story who seems to be aware of the predicament of the Gael as 'other', and it effectively hobbles him socially. He considers Mairi-Anna, for instance, to be ignorant of her difference (22) and Murchadh to be too self-assured to notice (27).

Ailean suffers from an internal ambiguity. He is never sure whether to embrace his 'otherness' and be proud of it, even arrogant about it, or to try to distance himself from it and become anonymous. The dichotomy is illustrated by the following translated quotes:

> That was the polite sound the Lowlander would make to the Gael when he would be saying to himself, 'Oh good grief! How did I end up among Gaels? Them and their Clearances and Great Ship of the Exiles coming down from the mountains with bags full of woe and selling them for a pint or two each week.' (21–2)

[. . .]

There were now eight Gaels at the party and they stood out among the others like trees among grass or bottles of spirits among cans of beer. (22)

[. . .]

That's your uncomplicated, certain Gaelic Gael for you now. The dejected Gael. (27)

[. . .]

When the proud waiter came with pen and paper, it was English he spoke to his father. English. And the old man had no idea what he would have, and he looked to his son for help. He smiled at the waiter, a smile that said, *terrible, these folk up from the country*. (28–9; the italicised portion is in italics and in English in the text)

Although we never really experience narrative from Mairi-Anna's perspective, her character radiates a credibility that is rare in any but the central characters in much Gaelic fiction. Where Ailean's pain is the pivotal emotion in the story, Mairi-Anna's feelings also come through strongly and convincingly.

The same tight focus on characterisation transforms 'An Gamhainn' ('The Heifer') from a mild-mannered comical story into a minor gem. The main character Cailean is dominated by two powerful women in the story, and the reader has a strong sense of the personalities, hopes and aspirations of these two women, even though the entire story is told from Cailean's point of view, and neither woman spends all that much time on the page. The wonderful image of the bull near the end of the story sums up the relationships within Cailean's world, in that it is Cailean who is likened to the heifer and the women who are the 'bulls' of their community. Similarly, although with much less humour, the character of Catriona is brilliantly portrayed in 'Briseadh na Cloiche' ('Breaking the Stone'), even though she barely appears on the page. The focal character spends the entire story labouring on her behalf, even though he has long come to resent and even hate her for her part in letting him see his own inadequacies. Small details show the reader not only what Catriona is like, but also what the main character has turned into, at least partly under her influence.

'Briseadh na Cloiche' is, along with 'Feòil a' Gheamhraidh' ('Winter Meat'), one of the most-admired of Gaelic short stories, and with good reason. These two stories are among the most perfectly constructed of all Gaelic stories. They are economical and yet vivid, emotional and yet open to interpretation, and they both stand up to frequent re-reading. 'Briseadh na Cloiche' and 'Feòil a' Gheamhraidh' mark pivotal moments at either end of the lives of rural men – indeed, there is no reason to suggest that the characters in the two stories are the same person, but it is perfectly possible that they could be, in that the settings are similar and the concerns of the one translate neatly to the other. 'Briseadh na Cloiche' follows the final minutes of the life of a downtrodden man, dominated by his wife as Cailean is dominated by the women in his life in 'An Gamhainn'. 'Feòil a' Gheamhraidh' is a rite-of-passage story about a boy who is just about to transition to manhood, and it focuses on a close-up lesson he receives about the realities of life and death in a rural community. In 'Feòil a' Gheamhraidh', the father figure is strong but remote, offering no comfort and little support to his son, and yet teaching him the lessons he realises his son must learn and doing so in a way that is suggestive of the same kind of gruff paternal love that Eachann in *Keino* and Ailean in 'Am Partaidh' failed to understand until they were too late. The boy in 'Feòil a' Gheamhraidh' takes his first steps towards understanding that the love of his father is at least partly to do with teaching him to cope with violence, death and survival, and that there is a tremendous ambiguity in the crossover of all of these things. Similarly, Eachann's and Ailean's fathers were trying to teach them how to be men, in their own way and according to their own understanding, even though they may have understood that this doomed them to be denied the reciprocal love of their sons. What makes 'Feòil a' Gheamhraidh' so successful is that all of this is implied but never emphasised. The only indication that the father figure is anything but mocking of his son comes at the end, where he finally offers him support, once he sees that the boy has absorbed whatever he can of the lesson:

> He did not move until he saw that his father was ready to go, when the corpse was headless, without wool, without legs and without innards, hung by the heels. His father put his jacket on, and he rolled another cigarette, speckled red.
>
> The boy glanced once at the corner where the head was on the floor. There was a hazy shadow on the eyes, but they were moist, quiet.
>
> 'Come on, pal. That's that past.'
>
> He put his arm around his son's shoulders. The boy looked at the hand. And they walked out to the evening, now growing cold. (106–7)

The boy's feelings are implied but not stated by Moireach, which allows for them to be ambiguous or even downright confused. To an even greater extent, the father's feelings are left to the reader to interpret. The effect is powerful. Feelings are more overtly stated in 'Briseadh na Cloiche', but the reader's understanding of events is mediated through what seems to be an unreliable narrator. This story has a third-person narrative, but it is firmly fixed within the perspective of the leading character. This character, who is not named, is a middle-aged man who is married to a woman called Catriona. The story homes in on his despair as he reaches a crisis point where he can no longer cope with the pressue he feels Catriona has applied to him. What becomes clear to the reader, through the author's subtle use of ironic devices, is that the main character has, himself, not been entirely blameless. In fact, Catriona may have nagged him mercilessly, but it appears she also did so with some justification. When the viewpoint character begins behaving in a dangerously self-destructive manner in the final stages of the story, Catriona demonstrates a level of concern that is not in keeping with his earlier portrayal of her: in other words, he has vilified her and demonised her in his own mind, but his perception of Catriona is not entirely accurate.

The stories in *An Aghaidh Choimheach* encompass a wide range of emotions, styles and also subject-matters. Where despair dominates in 'Briseadh na Cloiche', shyness in 'An Gamhainn', the emotion vacillates between fear, excitement and horror in 'Feòil a' Gheamhraidh'. In 'An Dà Latha',[9] anxiety is to the fore, whereas 'Mòine Dhòmhnaill Agus Ordag 'an Bhàin' ('Donald's Peat and Iain Bhàin's Big Toe') focuses on capturing a sense of the humour, familiarity, and sometimes competitiveness, that bind a small community together in the necessary labours of survival. Although there are thus stories that focus on humour, happiness and social interaction, the most common emotion in the collection is loneliness. Aonghas Iain in 'An Aghaidh Choimheach' has returned to his family and first world after spending most of his life abroad, but he soon realises he can no longer fit in. Both Ailean and Mairi-Anna are lonely in 'Am Partaidh'. Both Cailean and Mairi, the widow, are lonely in 'An Gamhainn', although there is at least the potential that they will become the solution for each other's predicament. The focal character and Catriona both seem to be lonely in 'Briseadh na Cloiche'. In both 'An Dà Latha' and 'Oidhche Shathurna' ('Saturday Night'), we have main characters who waste themselves by seeking oblivion in alcohol: in both cases, at least partly because of loneliness.

Because of his grasp of characterisation, Moireach captures real life better than almost any other Gaelic writer, but he is also prepared to stray away from realism. 'Ignig Dannsair' ('Ignig the Dancer'), for instance, is a fable about mice. Although it is perhaps hinted at by the name *Ignig*, it is not immediately clear that the characters are mice until the story begins to develop. Ignig is a prodigiously powerful jumper and dancer of unparalleled skill among mice who are known for their jumping and dancing. He became famous for dancing on the back of a cow and was a great peace-keeper. The story is told within inverted commas, as if it is meant to represent some kind of oral tradition. The narrator is involved as a peripheral, observing character, and the story has the traditional Gaelic quality of *dùnadh*, in that it begins and ends with the same words:

'Cha robh mise ri mo shaoghal air tiodhlaigeadh cho mór' (45, 52)

('I was never in my life at such a big funeral')

Similarly, 'Gormadh an Fheòir' ('The Greening of the Grass') has an absurd plot that anticipates the style of some of Finlay Macleod's work, for example. 'Gormadh an Fheòir' has some of the most impressive and evocative imagery and metonymy in the whole collection. In some ways, it has echoes of the Welsh traditional tale of Blodeuwedd, in that it links people with the natural world and shows the two things are part of each other.

Pòl MacAonghais

The Pòl MacAonghais story mentioned above, 'An Gille Gallta', appears in his collected stories published in 1993, *An Guth Aoibhneach* ('The Joyful Voice').[10] Like *Bùrn is Aran*, *An Guth Aoibhneach* also includes a small amount of poetry, although, in this case, the poems are randomly interspersed with the stories, much as they might be in a literary magazine. It is not entirely clear if MacAonghais ever intended for the poems and stories to appear together, but it is, nevertheless, of benefit to the Gaelic reader to be able to access almost all of his short work in one source.

The title of the book is something of a misnomer, to an extent, as the stories are often not at all joyful. MacAonghais, also a playwright of some distinction, had a particular skill for creating sad and thoughtful ambiences. 'An Gille Gallta' carries this off beautifully, and is a perfect example of how to convey a bittersweet atmosphere: the tragic situation of the leading character is mitigated by the new relationships he forms and the learning and growing that he undergoes. Similarly, 'Cur As an t-Solais' ('Put Out the Light') is the heartbreaking account of a man's final illness and decline towards death. It is also an example of MacAonghais's fine ear for dialogue, which is so often one of the chief weaknesses in other Gaelic writers. The dialogue in this story is moving and believable, and each utterance clearly belongs with its speaker. The main character's thoughts and internal monologue structure the story and carry the reader along convincingly as he veers towards suicide. 'Air Feadh na Fìdhle' similarly shows MacAonghais's ability to convey anxiety, angst and sheer despair.[11] The main character, Floraidh, is harassed by a musician, Chisholm, as she carries out her work in the hotel where he is playing. She grows increasingly angry at his inappropriate behaviour and, as the main sentient centre of the story, paints a picture of a man who is unpleasant and uncaring. However, Floraidh accidentally breaks Chisholm's double-bass when she knocks down a hatch. Chisholm's reaction is one of such utter despair that she cannot help but feel terrible for him.

Cailein T. MacCoinnich

Cailein T. MacCoinnich was a particularly prolific writer of short stories, most of them involving far-fetched, outrageous or adventurous plots.[12] He produced three collections of tales: *Oirthir Tìm* (1969, 'The Edge of Time'), *Mar Sgeul a Dh'Innseas Neach* (1971, 'Like a Story a Person Tells'), and *Nach Neònach Sin* (1973, 'Isn't that Strange'). All three books feature stories that are heavily influenced by the pulp fiction of the 1950s and 1960s and earlier. *Oirthir Tìm* has several fantastical plots that involve travel through time or other dimensions. *Mar Sgeul a Dh'Innseas Neach* has several stories that almost belong to the detective genre, and others of a similar nature, featuring characters with peculiar and well-developed talents. *Nach Neònach Sin* focuses on the supernatural and draws on the folk traditions of the Highlands. Some of the stories are merely adaptations of folk tales.

The opening story in *Mar Sgeul a Dh'Innseas Neach*, 'Am Prìosan Sàile' ('The Sea Prison') features a character in the 'lovable outlaw' mould, who swears he can break out of any prison, and who has had plenty of experience in proving that to be true. The landlord makes one last attempt to imprison him by abandoning him on a remote island, and the rest of the story is about the character's various talents. He makes himself useful to the small community living on the island, but eventually sets his mind to escaping and succeeds. 'Deireadh an t-Saoghail' ('The End of the World') has an even more disreputable character, who is also charming and possessed of remarkable talents. He passes himself off as a prophet of the end of the world, then takes advantage of people's preparations for doom to go looting. Two of the stories, 'Crudha Eich' ('A Horse's Hoof') and 'Rud Nach Fhaic Sùil' ('A Thing an Eye Cannot See'), have characters and plotlines that seem to draw on the Sherlock Holmes tradition: the author published several similar stories in *Gairm* (see Chapter 3). In 'Crudha Eich', the first-person point-of-view character's friend, Diarmad, has unusual powers of deduction. He solves a murder that most people had considered an accidental death. He and the viewpoint character demonstrate a flexible attitude towards justice at the end of the story, where they decide they are in a position to judge whether or not the murderer should be punished. In 'Rud Nach Fhaic Sùil', there is, again, a first-person narrator who has an uncommonly-clever friend. His friend, Cathal, is a lawyer who enjoys solving mysteries for the fun of proving that no human mind can devise a conundrum he cannot untangle. He works out the cunning device by which an expensive bull has been stolen from a railway carriage, purely to prove to his friend that he can. As in 'Crudha Eich', the characters are more interested in solving the contrived puzzle than they are in law or justice. Other stories feature similar contrivances and cunning devices. 'An Dìleab' ('The Legacy') is a twist-in-the-tale inheritance story involving a riddle and a secret hiding place; 'A' Mhuc' ('The Pig') is about a lost pig worth more to the landlord than his wife, and about the clever gardener who works out what happened to the pig; and 'Guth na Cogais' ('The Voice of Conscience') is about a man who hatches a clever plot to kill his wife, gets away with it, but then is driven to his own death, apparently by his conscience.

These kinds of stories with clever twists form the bulk of the material in *Mar Sgeul a Dh'Innseas Neach*, but the final story in the book, 'Sgialachd Cheutain' ('Ceutain's Story') is much more like a traditional tale. The narrative is in the style of the folk tale, with extensive use of hyperbole and broad description. The plot involves the grandson of a king, who must deal with a curse, go on a quest for his throne, face magical challenges, receive unusual gifts and fight battles. 'Sgialachd Cheutain' prefigures some of the work of Donnchadh MacGillÌosa, in the way it draws on the Gaelic oral tradition, but it fails to make such good use of the resources as MacGillÌosa does. MacGillÌosa's collection *Tocasaid 'Ain Tuirc* is discussed in Chapter 6. The other main stories that draw on this tradition are Iain MacLeòid's 'Gruagach' stories that appeared in *Gairm* (see Chapter 3) and some of Fionnlagh MacLeòid's recent work.

Nach Neònach Sin (1973), MacCoinnich's first collection, is less interesting than *Mar Sgeul a Dh'Innseas Neach*. All eighteen stories are of supernatural events, almost all them based on folklore or on things that the author claims have happened to him personally or to his friends. In terms of style, the stories are all campfire yarns, based on the sorts of tales MacCoinnich would have heard at *cèilidhs* in his youth. They have a good deal in common with the 'readings' of Fionn, the early fiction works of MacCormaic and their respective contemporaries. For the most part, the motifs are lifted from traditional tales. All of the stories are told in the same narrative voice, and the narrator often intrudes to comment on events, agreeing or disagreeing with what protagonists have said or done. Because the focus of most of the stories is on a marvel of one sort or another, they can almost all be summed up in a one-line *précis*. For instance, as can be discerned from the title, 'Neul Mhór a dh'Fhianuisean' ('The Big Cloud of Predictions') features a cloud that tells the future. 'Ge b'e bhios air dheireadh' ('Whatever is behind') tells of how girls used to use supernatural means to find out who they would marry, until one woman saw something that disturbed her so much she soon died. In 'Taibhs' ('Ghost'), one protagonist apparently sees a ghost, and the narrator/author figure thinks he heard its footsteps. 'Claigeann Greannach Cruaidh' ('Mean, Hard Skull') tells of a strapping young man who journeys to a shinty match and is struck repeatedly by eerie human skulls on the way, perhaps leading to shinty being abandoned in the Western Isles. 'Cù Mór Cheann an t-Sruthain' ('The Big Dog of Ceann an t-Sruthain') is an effort at *dinn-sheanchas*, the traditional Gaelic lore of using tales to explain how places got their names. 'Rud Nach Fhaic Sùil' ('A Thing the Eye Cannot See') shares its title with a story from *Mar Sgeul a Dh'Innseas Neach*, but is entirely different: this one is about the difference between humans' and animals' perceptions of the supernatural. Several of the tales are, in fact, little collections of mini-tales that share a common motif: such as 'A Saoghail Eile' ('From Other Worlds') and 'Sop ás Gach Seid' ('A Miscellany').

Eilidh Watt

Eilidh Watt's two collections for adults were *A' Bhratach Dheàlrach* (1972) and *Gun Fhois* (1987). Despite the long delay between the books, Watt continued writing unabated during that period, and contributed many stories to the magazine *Gairm*, as discussed in Chapter 3. The metaphor in the title story of *A' Bhratach Dheàlrach* ('The Shining Banner') comes from a flashback in which the main character Sìne remembers her father talking about the courage of an old neighbour, Màiri. Sìne's father admired the precise neatness of Màiri's flowers, tended to carefully every year no matter what. He described this as her *bratach dheàlrach*. Sìne questioned him about this and he explained that Màiri's attention to detail in her garden was like an old warship that refuses to surrender to the enemy and keeps its flags flying high in order to signal this. Sìne did not understand at the time, but has come to understand her father's wisdom and her old neighbour's courage by the time the story reaches its present chronology. Màiri's defiance is not aimed at a human enemy but at time and old age: by forcing herself to tend her garden and keep it neat and beautiful, she signals that she is not yet ready to surrender to time. Sìne eventually comes to admire her courage and strength of character. Other stories focus on the interaction between members of families and their relationship with the land and the sea. In 'Litir an Lagha' ('The Letter of the Law'), a young man wins a substantial sum of money on the pools: the story explores the effect this has on his friendships. 'Ach 'na Dhùthaich Fhèin' ('But in his Own

Country') shows the importance of the link between the people and their animals in a rural setting.

Watt's other collection, *Gun Fhois* ('Without Rest'), points up her fascination with the idea of second sight. Indeed, the book carries a subtitle, *Sgeulachdan mun Dà Shealladh* ('Stories about the Second Sight'). Supernatural abilities, and the difficulties they cause, are ubiquitous throughout the volume. Indeed, there is such a sense of homogeneity throughout *Gun Fhois* that stories are not even titled: they are numbered instead. Ruaraidh MacThòmais noted that this was problematic when he reviewed the book in *Gairm* (MacThòmais 1987–8: 90). In fact, it results in rendering the stories more forgettable in their own right, and it would have been a successful device only if there was either a stronger sense of cohesion, as in a short story cycle, or else much greater diversity of style and subject matter. As it is, it is very difficult to keep the stories distinct in the memory even after a number of readings. This perhaps does Watt a disservice as her writing is at times engaging and entertaining.

Story 5 in *Gun Fhois*, for instance, features a likeable first-person narrator, whose troubles engage the reader's sympathy. She has the ability to see dead people, and only gradually comes to understand that she must not talk about this to her living friends and relatives. We appreciate the loneliness and pain this must cause her. The story then focuses on one incident where she sees the apparition of a living person who cannot possibly be present because he is away in the war. Story 6 has a structural innovation, in that it consists mainly of a character reading diary entries. The diary entries completely take over from the middle of the second page until the final short paragraph. The diary has been written by a character who is terribly troubled by visions. The phrase 'gun fhois' comes from this story, as the character recounts a day in which the visions and voices are unceasing. The story is one of Watt's more successful, largely because the ending is left ambiguous. Other stories can be structurally laboured or suffer from endings that are both predictable and uninteresting. Or, as in Story 3, the story tries hard to deliver a meaning or message, but ends up being laboured and contrived, with an explicatory ending. On the whole, *Gun Fhois* is not of the standard of some of Watt's best uncollected fiction, as discussed in Chapter 3, but it has some fine moments.

Conclusion

This chapter has surveyed some of the most important collections of short stories produced in Gaelic prior to the Ùr-Sgeul project being established, although constraints of space have meant that some notable books, such as Iain MacLeòid's *Sràidean is Slèibhtean* (1971), have been missed out (I hope to rectify this in an article currently in progress). The first point to note is that, even before Ùr-Sgeul was initiated, the short story was a relatively vibrant medium in the literature. Fionnlagh MacLeòid was probably justified in 1963 in his warning that there was a danger of the short story being skewed by one writer's prolific output when no one else was contributing to the canon. As this chapter has shown, many other writers did respond to the challenge, and that one writer, Iain Mac a' Ghobhainn, was admired but not directly emulated to any great extent. The styles and subject matters developed a certain diversity over time, although there remained a tendency among most of the writers to stay within established parameters in terms of setting, character types or storylines. The strongest writers from a literary viewpoint were undoubtedly Iain Mac a' Ghobhainn and Iain Moireach, as has long been known (Marner 2000). However, the short story genre on the whole harbours considerable quality. This is borne out by the several anthologies of stories that have been published over the years.

As the leading literary critic following the invention of the true short story in Gaelic, Donald John MacLeod (Dòmhnall Iain MacLeòid) was perhaps ideally placed to make a selection of stories for an anthology. His *Dorcha Tro Ghlainne* ('Through a Glass Darkly') was published by Gairm in 1970, and was accompanied by his useful introductory essay. The stories were selected from *Gairm* magazine, and most of them are discussed in Chapter 3. The authors were among those who received the most praise from MacLeod in his PhD work (MacLeod 1970).

Amannan ('Times/Occasions', 1979) came about as the result of a competition run by the Gaelic Books Council. The book contains ten stories written by seven different authors. The winning piece was Pòl MacAonghais's 'Droch Àm dhe'n Bhliadhna' ('A Bad Time of Year'), an evocative story that also appeared in his posthumous collection, *An Guth Aoibhneach*. Worth mentioning here are two stories by writers whose work is not dealt with elsewhere in this book: namely, Pòl Mac a' Bhreatunnaich and Donnchadh MacLabhruinn. Pòl Mac a' Bhreatunnaich's 'Leigheas Dhòmhnaill Alasdair' ('Donald Alasdair's Cure') is a light-hearted yarn about the practical jokes and other mischief that occupy young men in rural places. Some of the fun comes at the expense of the title character, whose laziness is exposed by the tricks of the young men. MacLabhruinn's 'Oran Gaoil' ('Love Song') is a very well constructed story about an ageing spinster, Miss Young, who befriends a younger man. Miss Young has learnt Gaelic very well: according to the story, she is more fluent than she realises. She meets a young Lewis man and becomes smitten with him. The story uses internal monologue to convey Miss Young's thoughts, marked as separate from the narrative by italics. This is unusual in Gaelic writing, and yet it is highly effective in this story.

Eadar Peann is Pàipear ('Between Pen and Paper', 1985), edited by Dòmhnall Iain MacIomhair, is a collection of stories previously published elsewhere. Stories in *Eadar Peann is Pàipear* were selected from a range of sources, including individuals' own collections, but the great bulk of the stories were harvested from *Gairm*. Many of them are discussed elsewhere in this book. In trying to explain his motivation for editing the collection, and justify his selections, MacIomhair wrote a short introduction giving his own thoughts about the short story in Gaelic. He himself was one of the leading lights in the development of the genre, and so it is appropriate to end this chapter by translating some of his words, by way of illustrating how literary fiction moved on between the 1960s and the end of the century:

> although it is a story, it is different in several ways from other modes of writing. The short story usually arises totally out of the imagination of the author himself, even though it might be based on something else. It stands on its own feet. It has a beginning, a middle and an end. It is not a segment of something longer.
>
> [. . .]
>
> The story can touch on life, on death, on love, on piety or on anything else that touches on the mind of a person, and indeed on the character of a person in general. (MacIomhair 1985: i–iv)

Chapter 6

Contemporary Fiction

Throughout most of the twentieth century, books of prose fiction were sparse in Gaelic. Those books discussed or mentioned in Chapters 4 and 5 of this volume represent the bulk of what was published in that time. Thus, there were fewer than twenty novels written for adults in the entire century, most of these coming in the 1970s and 1990s. The number of short story collections was similarly small, although short stories were at least appearing in magazines, as detailed in Chapter 3. Nevertheless, the advent of the Ùr-Sgeul[1] project has meant changes of seismic proportions in the publishing of Gaelic prose. Indeed, while it has long been acknowledged that there was need of a book like this present volume, the efforts of the Ùr-Sgeul project have provided further impetus, by necessitating the creation of a position statement before the current explosion in publishing goes much further. At the time of writing, Ùr-Sgeul has facilitated the publication of fifteen original novels, one novella, one translated novel, and seven books of short stories. In other words, the productivity of the past six years comes close to matching that of the whole preceding century (see Storey 2007). Furthermore, in spite of the apparent precariousness of the funding streams behind the venture, there is every sign that this project will continue for some time and that it has acted as a catalyst for the development of a new wave of Gaelic fiction writing. Most notably, although some of the books have been written by long-established figures such as Tormod Caimbeul, Tormod MacGill-Eain, Donnchadh MacGilllosa, Iain Mac a' Ghobhainn and Fionnlagh MacLeòid, others are by writers who are either new to prose or are altogether new to publishing Gaelic work. Several of the writers are what we might describe as young, which may prompt some optimism for the future within the wider Gaelic literary circles. And, for the first time, we have seen writers returning to print quickly, modulating between novel-writing and short story-writing in the same natural way that we expect in other languages. Thus, Aonghas Pàdraig Caimbeul, whose *An Oidhche Mus Do Sheòl Sinn* (2003, 'The Night Before We Sailed') was the first novel in the project, has already produced another three novels. Iain F. MacLeòid has contributed two novels, of very different types (with a third promising title published just too late for inclusion here), as has Màrtainn Mac an t-Saoir, who also published the first book of short stories under the Ùr-Sgeul banner, *Ath-aithne* (2003, 'Re-acquaintance'). Norma NicLeòid has begun the first series of novels the Gaelic language has ever seen, with her highly-effective *Dìleas Donn* (2006)[2] and its follow-up *Taingeil Toilichte* (2008), and a third in the set is anticipated soon. Ùr-Sgeul has also allowed for the publication of long-dormant works, such as Iain Mac a' Ghobhainn's *Am Miseanaraidh* (2006, 'The Missionary') and the same might be said of parts of Fionnlagh MacLeòid's *Dìomhanas* (2008, 'Idleness'): it appears the former was written in the 1970s and abandoned, while the latter includes stories written throughout MacLeòid's career.

In Chapter 3, it was shown how the short story was the main vehicle through which fiction was explored and allowed to develop in Gaelic during the second half of the twentieth century. By the time *Gairm* was ten years old, the short story was beginning to show signs that it could one day come to match poetry in terms of literary achievement in the language. By the end of *Gairm*'s run, it would be possible to argue that some of the short stories in the language were good enough to rank with the best of the modern poetry. Readers might have worried that the winding up of that remarkable magazine after fifty years would strike a fatal blow to these developments. Fortunately, however, at around the same time as Donald Meek stepped into the breach with *Gath*, the Gaelic Books Council-led Ùr-Sgeul project also came into being. In two fascinating papers read at conferences, and now available to access online, John Storey gives an insight into the processes and challenges facing the energetic project. Ùr-Sgeul has been responsible for the biggest single publishing initiative ever seen in Gaelic fiction. In fact, Ùr-Sgeul has almost exactly doubled the number of existing Gaelic novels, and has also contributed seven books of short stories. Some of these are single-author collections, but *An Claigeann aig Damien Hirst* (2009) is a collection of twenty-one stories by different writers. Although this includes long-established authors like Dòmhnall Iain MacIomhair and Alasdair Caimbeul, *An Claigeann aig Damien Hirst* also represents work by several writers who had little or no fiction published prior to the collection's appearance. The speed with which Ùr-Sgeul is approaching its thirtieth book, and the appearance of all these new writers, seems to suggest that Gaelic fiction is currently experiencing something of a golden age.

Màrtainn Mac an t-Saoir

The first of the books to come out as a result of Ùr-Sgeul was Màrtain Mac an t-Saoir's *Ath-aithne* (2003). *Ath-aithne* is a collection of eighteen stories, four of which are in English. Some of the concerns in the stories are flagged up immediately by their division into four sections, entitled respectively 'Cogaidhean is Cogaisean' ('Wars and Consciences'), 'Seachd Àraid na Seachadan' ('Most Especially the Seventies'), 'Thall no Bhos' ('Over There or Over Here') and 'Duais on Dè dhan Diugh' ('A Prize from Yesterday to Today'). In a review of Mac an t-Saoir's more recent novel, Raghnall MacilleDhuibh noted that *Ath-aithne* was: 'profound, supple, different, full of social conscience and the strong personality of the author and the characters' (MacilleDhuibh 2008). While this is true, and the stories are full of promise, there is a certain unevenness in the writing at times, as of a new author still finding his voice and learning to control his technique. In 'Cleas an t-Samhraidh' ('Trick of the Summer'), for instance, the ending is meant to be poignant, but loses much of its impact through being predictable. The execution of the ending is clichéd and not at the same level as some of the striking imagery throughout the rest of the story. However, on the whole, *Ath-aithne* is an impressive introduction to the short story mode for a relatively new writer. The promise that the book showed has further developed through Mac an t-Saoir's two subsequent novels, especially the more recent, *An Latha as Fhaide* (2008).

As the first book in the new series, and as the first of its kind in many ways, *Ath-aithne* (2003) deserves a dedicated study in its own right. Along with that book, Mac an t-Saoir's two novels, *Gymnippers Diciadain* (2005, 'Gymnippers Wednesday') and *An Latha as Fhaide* (2008, 'The Longest Day') have established him as one of the leading authors in the current drive to promote the writing of prose fiction. The first, *Gymnippers Diciadain*, is set primarily in Edinburgh in the year in which it was being written (2004), which gave it a strong air of contemporaneity when it was published, but threatens perhaps to date it quickly. The reader is constantly reminded about the date because the short inter-chapters often mention news items that were important at the time. This device helps to lend a sense of time passing to the book, as most of the chapters, especially in the first half, are very similar in content and presentation. The plot is very simple, which is why the inter-chapters are so important structurally. There are also really only two characters, although other people do make brief appearances. This is another deliberate device, as it serves to illustrate how important these two characters and their casual weekly meetings become in each other's lives: their Wednesday meetings at the Gymnippers establishment are isolated from the ups and downs of the rest of their lives, otherwise only hinted at in dialogue and in the inter-chapters.

The two characters are a Uist man, DJ (short for Donald James) and an urban Gael called Caroline. Caroline has grown up on the mainland but picked up Gaelic due to having family ties to Skye (not unlike Mac an t-Saoir's own background, although his own link is to Uist). DJ and Caroline meet when they begin taking their children to a weekly gym class, and they begin chatting because they recognise one another as Gaelic-speakers. The bulk of the novel is taken up with their long conversations in the gym cafe while their children play in the gym. They gradually become friends, and there is always a suspicion of an underlying romantic interest, which is, from the start, subject to the complication that both are married with children (which we, and they, know right from the beginning). Through the conversations, the reader gradually learns more about their respective families and backgrounds. This 'drip-release' technique is effective in gradually revealing why both of them convey an air of slight dissatisfaction with their apparently happy, normal lives. The second movement in the novel involves a trip to Uist. For DJ, this represents an opportunity for him to find out if he and Caroline can embark on a sexual relationship. Caroline also seems to entertain the possibility, but she resists the temptation and this immediately changes their friendship.

Gymnippers Diciadain works as a novel, albeit with some weaknesses. Some of these are features intrinsic to the novel itself and might not be regarded by all readers as negative: for instance, the use of the contemporary news items. Characterisation is stronger than in *Ath-aithne*, but Mac an t-Saoir's use of dialogue is still not always assured, especially when he moves into English. The English dialogue is, at times, poorly observed and corny, compared to the much-sharper Gaelic dialogue.

Màrtainn Mac an t-Saoir's second novel, and third contribution to the Ùr-Sgeul series, is, in many ways, his most accomplished work so far. Although the premise behind *An Latha as Fhaide* ('The Longest Day', 2008) is not entirely promising, the execution is admirable. Mac an t-Saoir gave himself even less to work with in this novel than he did in *Gymnippers Diciadain*, reducing from two main characters to only one. As a result, *An Latha as Fhaide* has considerable space for introspection and reflection. However, given that this 'longest day' is a period that the main character has set aside for just exactly that kind of reflection, the long internal monologues are an acceptable component of the piece. There are some parts of the novel where these internal debates go on for too long or are too repetitive, but on the whole they work well enough.

The main character is a man from Harris called Niall MacLeòid. Closing in on retirement, he has spent his career in the diplomatic service and has enjoyed considerable success, financial reward and a varied and apparently interesting life. The entire novel takes place within one day of his life (the 'longest day', as he keeps reminding us, and he has indeed chosen the summer solstice for the occasion). MacLeòid has recently had a major health scare and, without telling any friends or family, has had to come to terms with his imminent death. He has therefore planned a single, self-indulgent day, re-visiting places that were important to him in his youth and trying (without making any prior arrangements) to meet up with some of the people who were significant for him before he began his career. This lack of prior organisation threatens to derail his day several times, and it leads to him wondering repeatedly about the value of what he has done and about the appropriateness of the events that do take place.

When the novel opens, MacLeòid has just slept with his old sweetheart, Anna. This provides the first dramatic tension in the novel as he wrestles with the propriety of what he has done. He is not so concerned about having cheated on his wife (although he does briefly pick over that) as he is about the fact that this was not part of his plans and has, strictly speaking, taken place the night before his big day: surely his tryst with Anna deserves to be part of the 'longest day', he thinks. At this stage in the novel, there is a real danger of the gimmick of the 'longest day' taking over and becoming an unwieldy burden that will make the novel a stodgy and predictable read. However, MacLeòid's preoccupation with the rights and wrongs of Anna's place in the 'longest day' is soon replaced by some amusing and distressing incidents involving his mother and a neighbour of hers. Whenever the 'longest day' gimmick returns, though, it is problematic, flagging itself up as a contrivance.

The characterisation of Niall MacLeòid is central to the novel: this 'longest day' is, in essence, a microcosm of his life. His uncertainties, insecurities, compromises and betrayals are all played out, once more, in miniature. Like the novels of Aonghas Pàdraig Caimbeul and Norma NicLeòid, there is always a sense that religion is a strong influence on the book. Niall MacLeòid rejected faith early in his life, but it is clear that he is still bound by religious ways of thinking. This reveals itself in his absolutist philosophy of life, looking for significance in the trivia of his day. The characterisation of all the other personae in the novel is achieved through the perception of MacLeòid, who is the first-person narrator. Thus, we learn relatively little about everyone else and we are consequently as surprised by their actions as MacLeòid himself is. There are times in the novel where this is a particular strength, in that it mitigates against the predictability of the plot. There are, however, places where it threatens to subvert the novel entirely: the clearest example of this is in the ending, which is discussed later.

Among the questions MacLeòid finds he must confront during his reflective day is one that has been discussed elsewhere in this book and has been prevalent throughout Gaelic fiction: what constitutes a Gael? MacLeòid is a Gael who has turned his back on his home community in order to have a successful career. He has embraced the last remnant of the British Empire and become one of its agents, aspiring to join the most exclusive of its cliques. Throughout his career, it appears, he has resented both his origins for holding him back from full membership of these cliques, and the cliques themselves for holding his Highlandness against him: MacLeòid often thinks of how his father-in-law has always considered him a lower-class foreign interloper in a society that is too good for him. MacLeòid's wife Julia only visited Harris once, did not enjoy her experience, and vowed never to return. As a result, he himself has not been back to the island for some time, and he wonders if it is still his home. This question is relevant in a number of the recent Gaelic books, as an awareness of the alienation from the 'heartland' environment begins to make itself an integral motif: it is no longer merely the authors who are exiles, but their characters as well. MacLeòid finds himself being led by his mother into questioning various issues to do with home, identity, authenticity and attentiveness. He wonders if he is still a Gael after all these years, if he is a Scotsman, or if he is something else; and he also wonders what other people think he is. Looking for an essentialist understanding of these things, he tries to work out if his practices and place of residence define him. At length, these reflections lead him to feel guilt at abandoning the island: he wonders if he, and others like him, have left Harris and its language to die. Closely linked to this is his obsession with his own name. He has spent so long away from the Gàidhealtachd that he has had to get used to people mispronouncing it as if either 'Neil' or 'Nyall'. He habitually refers to himself by all three versions of his name, as if struggling to grasp hold of his identity: we might infer that 'Niall' is his name when he thinks of himself as a Gael, 'Neil' when he thinks of himself as a Glasgow-based Scotsman, and 'Nyall' when he takes his place among the Surrey and London society families to which he has become attached.

> 'S mathaid gur e seo latha cuideigin eile 's gun deach mise a thaghadh airson a chur seachad dha? Ach cò? Cò aige a bhiodh an latha sin? Neil, Nyall? Mgr Niall MacLeòid, LVO, CMG? (128)

> ('Maybe this is someone else's day and I was chosen to spend it for him? But who? Whose would that day be? Neil, Nyall? Mr Niall MacLeòid, LVO, CMG?')

On the other hand, some of the characterisation is lazy, such as the inclusion of MacLeòid's CV, which is designed to give a quick reference to his back-story, and the portrayal of his mother in rather stereotypical terms. MacLeòid's wife Julia is also only sketched in and, as the discussion below of the ending of the novel would suggest, this is a weakness in the book's structure.

An important theme in the novel is revealed by the minor characters who keep appearing, especially those who crop up unexpectedly. MacLeòid has become somewhat preoccupied by the notion that people drift in and out of each other's lives: they may seem important for a time and then less so, or they may even disappear altogether. Thus, characters like Anna, the neighbour Eòghann, and former flatmate Andaidh Rothach appear without warning, uninvited into MacLeòid's day, and he must find ways to cope with their presence. He must reconcile their present selves with the people he remembers, each time realising that they also represent the old Niall, the boy or young man he was when last he knew them. Some of these meetings are a little too contrived, such as encountering the brilliant and once-popular Andaidh who is now a down-and-out in Queen Street Station in Glasgow. However, the point is well-made, and is also shown from another perspective, when MacLeòid considers approaching a young couple he hears speaking Gaelic on a train. He thinks he should go and introduce himself and find out where the young man is from, as he is sure he hears a Harris accent in his Gaelic. He chooses not to drift in and out of their lives, however, and then wonders why he made that choice. Interestingly, MacLeòid seems to consider that going over and speaking to them in Gaelic would be 'doing the right thing', and he is upset with himself for not doing it:

> This is the time. This is the chance – it isn't often you get the like. The last time in Orly – an old lady from Islay visiting her daughter who had been in France for ten years. (130)

[. . .]

> It is past – the opportunity lost. (130)

[. . .]

> The words 'Who do you belong to in Harris?' come as they should have appeared a minute ago, but my lips are not willing to sound them, or else, maybe they weren't capable. (130)

[. . .]

> *There you are, Niall. Sometimes you do the right thing and sometimes you don't.* (131)[3]

Much of the middle section of the novel is concerned with MacLeòid's musings, and this serves to emphasise how the novel seems to lack a sense of tension or connection. Even MacLeòid himself later becomes aware of the lack of a plot and tries to create one by contemplating a suicide that will somehow give meaning to what has otherwise been a fairly dull and unsatisyfing day, at once both random and predictable.

The final movement of the novel deals with MacLeòid's return to his current 'home' in the south of England. He is invited to the graduation party of his son's talented girlfriend, Gerri. Gerri has completed her degree in medicine and MacLeòid is expecting her to marry his son Carl and help to encourage Carl to mature and take responsibility for himself. When he gets back to the south of England, Carl takes him to Gerri's party. The whole family behave oddly towards one another, but this may be partly explained by two things: Carl and Gerri are amicably splitting up to pursue different goals, and MacLeòid's daughter Sophie had a scare with her unborn child earlier in the day. MacLeòid is exhausted after his long and emotional day, and he ends up taking an unplanned nap on the bathroom floor. When he wakes up, he tells a long story from *seanchas* which seems to carry the moral of the novel in miniature.[4] His story has different effects on different people: some are disturbed, some are mortified, some fascinated. The story illustrates the idea that other people, even people close to you, are often too preoccupied with their own thoughts and problems to be able to give of themselves when you need them. His wife Julia is both mortified and angered by his behaviour. She then proceeds to behave very oddly for the next several hours. This behaviour is entirely unexpected for the reader, who has little knowledge of Julia, other than that she seems to be a confident, controlled individual, well suited to her situation and happy with her family and financial stability. In the final chapters, we encounter a slightly manic version of the woman. Sophie reacts negatively to both her parents, and MacLeòid himself feels cut off, too tired to react at all. When he eventually gets home, he contemplates killing himself, largely because of the anti-climax of having prepared to meet death, having said goodbye to his earlier lives, and then having come home to live for perhaps another twenty years before doing it all again. At the very end, the twist in the tale is that Julia in fact seems to have killed herself and MacLeòid tries to save her, probably in vain. This twist is, unfortunately, too well concealed throughout the novel and so it feels gratuitous and ineffectual, rather like the ending of *Na Klondykers*, which is discussed below.

Aonghas Pàdraig Caimbeul

The first novel to appear in the new series was Aonghas Pàdraig Caimbeul's[5] *An Oidhche Mus Do Sheòl Sinn* ('The Night Before We Sailed'), which was published in 2004. At 383 pages and over 100,000 words, it was roughly twice as long as any Gaelic novel that had ever gone before, apart from *Cailin Sgiathanach*, which weighs in at around 76,000 words. The sheer size of the novel must have been intended as a signal that Gaelic literature still had some life left in it even after the demise of *Gairm*. It seems likely that the packaging is meant to do that, too. The style of presentation of the Ùr-Sgeul books is modern, glossy, attractive, energetic, vibrant, and streetwise. They all share some common design features, which make them look like they belong to a single stable and form part of a strategy. But, they also have distinct styles of cover design. All of the covers to date have been created by the same designer, James Hutcheson, but they each have their own identity and they all signal the style of the individual books effectively. *An Oidhche Mus Do Sheòl Sinn*'s cover depicts a hand holding a skimming stone, ready to throw it into the water. This image is crucial within the book, as there are a number of instances of characters standing with skimming stones in their hands, trying to decide whether to throw them or not. The book is thus partly about existential choice and about decision-making.

An Oidhche Mus Do Sheòl Sinn is a saga that follows the lives of various members of a large South Uist family during the hundred-year period of 1913 to 2013. It also follows the fortunes of the island and of the Gaelic language during that time and deals with the changing influence of Roman Catholicism and religion more generally on people's lives during that century.

The language in the novel is very dense. Caimbeul has tried to use language to recreate the sense of a stronger Gaelic community that would have existed in Uist early in the twentieth century. Caimbeul reflects the largely-monolingual nature of the community, and its richer Gaelic vocabulary, not only in the dialogue but also in the narrative itself. Unfortunately, this makes *An Oidhche Mus Do Sheòl Sinn* a challenging read in the early chapters. Not only is the language overly dense, but the plot is also overly intricate and involved. The story follows so many different people in the family that it almost feels like a series of mini-novels; the narrative leaves individual characters for very long periods before returning to them – and sometimes their particular story has moved on a good deal in the intervening time, so that it can be difficult to work out who is who and what is happening to them, in the absence of a strong plot to link them.

The start of the novel is based just before the outbreak of the First World War and the early focus is on the impact that the two world wars had on the small Hebridean communities. Caimbeul depicts these globally significant events intruding into a rural idyll that has been able and content to go its own way up until that point. In some ways, this is an interesting counterpoint to MacCormick's *Gun D' Thug I Spèis Do 'n Àrmunn* (discussed in Chapter 1), which is set during the Napoleonic Wars: in that story the Hebridean communities are fully involved in and appraised of international news and politics. Caimbeul seems to be trying to perpetuate an Edenic myth about the Hebrides in his novels. In an interview with Peter Urperth for the Hi-Arts journal *Northings* in 2003, Caimbeul said:

> South Uist at the turn of the century did have a kind of golden hue and I feel that, in a sense, I was in touch with that, the dying remnants of it were there in my childhood. When I was born there was no electricity, there was no radio, and there was no television and no running water. It came when I was about ten years of age, so I feel as though I touched these things.

> As research for this work I read Dwelly and then I read Carmina Gadelica and I was awe struck by the fact that these were works from just over a hundred years ago and the depth of language and lyricism then was just remarkable.

Clearly, then, a major function in writing the novel was his attempt to reach out to this Uist of the past and rediscover the lost Gaelic community of the early days of the last century. His perception of the Uist of the past seems to be coloured by a poetic romanticism, which has led him to try to recapture some of the magic of childhood by delving into archaic language.

Aonghas Pàdraig Caimbeul's second novel, *Là a' Dèanamh Sgèil Do Là* (2004),[6] is so full of inconsistencies that it reads more like a debut novel. The main difficulty with the novel is the plot, which is highly fragmentary and poorly constructed. The writing is also uneven, capable of beautiful and sweeping imagery that threatens to transcend all earlier works of prose fiction, but also regularly descending into bathos, didactic rhetoric and tedious litanies. More than any of the other Gaelic novels, *Là a' Dèanamh Sgèil Do Là* deserved to undergo a much more rigorous editing process.

The main point-of-view character, who tells almost all of the story, is Seòras Stubbs, an Englishman who has settled in Skye and learnt Gaelic to a high level of fluency. Stubbs is, in fact, the only character who is developed adequately in the novel, and is the only who does not suffer from two-dimensionality. The main plot follows parts of his life, especially after he meets and falls in love with the woman who becomes his wife, Caitrìona. Much of the middle section of the novel is taken up with telling the story of their love, as she struggles to free herself from a previous abusive relationship. The failure to characterise Caitrìona credibly is one of the major shortcomings in the book, and it is almost impossible to relate to her as a character in any meaningful way. At one point in the novel (at least), Caitrìona is depicted as being angelic in nature, and this multifaceted perfection makes her too remote for her to be identifiable as a real character. It also makes it impossible to believe in her relationships, either with her first husband or with Seòras.

A secondary plot involves the old man who befriends Stubbs and his family at the beginning of the novel. The old man is Calum Lamont, who is known affectionately as Calum Winkles, since he spends his time gathering shellfish. Indeed, the shellfish become an important motif in the novel, and it is possible to imagine that they are supposed to evoke an image of Christ as the fisherman. Calum's story gets so much time on the page that the novel feels fragmentary and incoherent, especially as it takes so long to reveal what is actually important about his background: essentially, Calum Lamont is closely aligned with the figure of Christ, and becomes the evangelising influence in the novel.

Chapters 4 and 6 give some forewarning about the evangelical nature of the book. First, Stubbs is impressed by Calum's belief in a Christian God, and his conviction that God has revealed to him the day when he will die. Despite claiming to believe in neither religion nor superstition, Stubbs accepts Calum's pronouncement as fact. Indeed, one of the major themes of the book is ideology, and the narrator attempts to compare religions, superstitions and atheist morality, and demonstrate how the first of these is superior. This message is even clearer when Stubbs first describes Caitrìona. She is so perfect that he sees her as some kind of supernatural being who is more colourful than any normal person. Stubbs wishes he could believe in God so that he would have someone to thank for Caitrìona's creation. This desire to believe in God is key to his later development, and also enables Caitrìona's own radical conversion later in the novel. Both Stubbs and Caitrìona are, in effect, pseudo-atheists who desperately wish to believe in God without actually realising it. When Caitrìona does eventually convert, she does so with a zeal that turns her into even more of an angelic figure. From that point onwards, if not before, it seems inevitable that Stubbs, too, will change his view by the end of the book, and that that is really the point of the novel.

Aonghas Pàdraig Caimbeul's third novel, *An Taigh-Samhraidh* (2007) picks up some of the concerns that are nested within *Là a' Dèanamh Sgèil Do Latha* and develops them into the central theme. As he expresses it himself in the descriptive text on the back cover:

> Who owns a house? Just the most recent person to buy it, or are there other rights? And cultural heritage – who owns cultural heritage?
> Only the locals, or can others gain possession of it? And is the culture of the Gaels so different from many other cultures, or at all more valuable?

These are valid concerns, although the reader might well be suspicious about a novel that is so overt about expressing social and anthropological concerns. As it turns out, the author does not always succeed in controlling the temptation to intrude and insert opinions, and this has the effect of weakening the novel. The same themes are dealt with more convincingly in Fionnlagh MacLeòid's 'An Dachaigh' ('The Home') in *Dìomhanas*. The narrator in *An Taigh-Samhraidh* is, in general, conversational and intrusive. However, this works well for most of the book and only threatens to be problematic when it is too obviously didactic. In Chapter 8, the author is highly intrusive and instructive, explaining how events have got to the stage where a non-Gael can own a house with such a Gaelic history. The main narrator is a character in the novel, Ronnie Weaver. The tension for the plot is generated by a robbery which Weaver has perpetrated on a house owned by incomers to a *Gàidhealtachd* community. The narrative oscillates between first-person narration for telling about Weaver and third-person when the focus is on Tom and Rebecca, the couple who have been robbed. The theft has a profound effect on Rebecca, in particular, and strains her relationship with Tom beyond endurance. It is not initially obvious that Ronnie Weaver is the culprit, but this soon becomes clear as we gain an insight into his feelings about the community and his sense of historical ownership. In particular, when we learn about Seumas Dubh and the history of the house itself, it becomes clear that Weaver is uncomfortable with the economic realities of property ownership. His sense is that it is a kind of theft for non-locals to move into the area and buy a piece of the local cultural heritage – in this case, a house that has been in the area for generations. Weaver's chance to justify the theft, and indeed Caimbeul's chance to justify the plot of the novel, comes in Chapter 19. Neither Weaver nor the author take their chance, and this leaves the plot unsatisfying and directionless. The novel exhibits a postcolonial consciousness (pp. 78–84, 99–131 are obvious examples), and Ronnie Weaver struggles with a sense of 'otherness'. There is a strong sense, however, that the plot is building towards a confrontation of some sort. When that confrontation comes, the novel shies away from engaging with it. On page 213, Weaver stands up in court and explains his actions. Following in the tradition of the first Gaelic novelist, however, Caimbeul has this speech taking place off-stage, thereby losing all the impact of the moment and reducing the dénouement to anticlimax. The reader is expected to imagine a speech of great eloquence:

> I gave a great long speech about history and about land rights and language and so on, every bit as good as Tommy Sheridan himself, while the court sat attentively and patiently for me, as for a child kicking his legs on the floor, or crying in a shop for a toy he won't get. (213)

The judge then pronounces that the speech was entirely irrelevant in face of the legal realities. Because of the way the novel has been structured, the reader is left tending to agree with the judge rather than sympathising with Ronnie Weaver. As elsewhere, Caimbeul's writing is at its best when imagery is to the fore: 'between the pages and the outside world' (189). And, as is the case in much of the recent fiction, some of the least convincing writing is in English-language dialogue:

'Good God, Rebecca – listen to yourself! You sound like a spae-wife out of one of these women's magazines handing out obvious truths as if they were the pearls of Socrates! Your intelligence – and gender – deserves better.'

[. . .]

'Quite the philosopher, Rebecca. But then again, Moral Phil was one of your core courses in your medical Degree [*sic*], in that expensive – sorry, prestigious – place you went to. Cambridge, wasn't it?' (146)

Caimbeul's most recent novel, *Tilleadh Dhachaigh* (2009), is also his shortest to date. At only 119 pages, *Tilleadh Dhachaigh* ('Returning Home') is a return to the conventional length for Gaelic novels. The size is determined by the structure of the book, which is limited to the length of a single train journey, with only two main characters. The novel follows the first-person narrator as he goes west on the train from Aberdeen. During his journey, he gradually reveals that he is probably really a ghost and that the novel is not a single journey but an amalgam of the journeys he has witnessed on this same line since he died at the time of the First World War. Instead of haunting the battlefield or the trenches, he haunts the train journey between Aberdeen and Kyle of Lochalsh, which reminds us that he is a synecdoche for the huge Highland losses suffered in both world wars, and that his death marks the last of the major events that devastated the language and its culture (see Scholes 2010): after the First World War, Highland society was no longer able to sustain a population of monolingual Gaelic speakers, and migration into towns and cities reached a critical stage. The war, therefore, could be seen as a last watershed moment in the long, apparently inexorable decline for the language and its cultural community as self-sustaining entities.

The novel is told in dramatic monologue style, which is another reason why it had to be kept short: it would be difficult to sustain interest in a much longer book using that technique. As in *An Taigh-Samhraidh* and much of Caimbeul's other work, the sound of place-names dominates. It is clear that Caimbeul has a deep interest in the sound of Gaelic place-names and in their juxtaposition with names from languages other than Gaelic. In *Tilleadh Dhachaigh*, each chapter is named for a place, in most cases these being stops or landmarks on the train line. The text also includes litanies of place-names and some name definitions and discussions. Once again, Caimbeul reveals his fascination for Dwelly's Gaelic dictionary and for the whole lexicographical tradition, but the manifestations of this fascination often result in breaking down the narrative voice and creating an intrusive authorial voice. In a review of the book published in 2010, Des Scholes showed signs of despair that Caimbeul has written in his newspaper column that Gaelic is effectively a dead language and that he and others are maintaining a fiction by writing in it and conducting their business in it. It may be that these are not Caimbeul's views at all and that he was simply doing what all columnists do from time to time and trying to provoke a response. However, it could be that *Tilleadh Dhachaigh* represents his effort to come to terms with some of these issues through the medium of fiction. In any event, *Tilleadh Dhachaigh* is the best of Caimbeul's novels to date, perhaps because it is closest in form to the short story, which I would argue is his strongest medium as a writer (see Chapter 3).

Donnchadh MacGillÌosa

One of the highlights of the contemporary period is Donnchadh MacGillÌosa's *Tocasaid 'Ain Tuirc* ('The Hogshead of Iain Son of the Boar', 2004). MacGillÌosa published some stories during the last years of *Gairm*, as was mentioned in Chapter 3. These stories found their way into the collection, along with a number of others. According to the cover blurb, the book is a collection of stories that has recurring characters and is similar to a novel at the same time. If that description were accurate, we might designate the book a short story cycle and it would thus be the first and, so far, only short story cycle in the language. In fact, the situation is rather more complex than that. The main character in the book is known by the nickname of *An Tocasaid* ('The Hogshead'), and one of the stories describes in detail how he came by such a peculiar name. Unusual and creative nicknames are an integral part of the modern *Gàidhealtachd*, perhaps most evidently in Lewis. Some of the stories go to great lengths to convey the sense of how important naming traditions are on the island. Indeed, even a glance down the contents page will show that the titles of fifteen of the sixteen stories mention a character that appears in them (if we may describe talking shoes as 'characters'!). Of these, only two are conventional names and the others are descriptive by-names of one sort or another. In some of the stories, the account of the origin of a name eventually leads to a revelation of how this character knows or interacts with An Tocasaid or one of the others. Throughout most of the stories, there is an underlying love of the whimsical, and MacGillÌosa's gift with humour is prevalent. Along with the naming and considerable use of folkloric elements, this typically *Gàidhealach* humour marks *Tocasaid 'Ain Tuirc* as one of the most clearly Gaelic of the contemporary works of fiction. Some of the other books were clearly written with the intention of breaking with the conventions, as is suggested elsewhere in this chapter. This book subtly reaffirms its connection with those conventions while at the same time actuating a progressive movement in a direction that takes account of the hybridisation of contemporary Gaelic culture and yet emphasises the aspects that have been attenuating. This blend of different views of Gaelic cultural expression is extremely effective.

The character who gives the book its title is a man of remarkable talents. One of the first things the reader learns about him is that he wrote a successful book at the age of only twelve. When the narrative shortly thereafter delivers a comical version of Tormod's *sloinneadh*, we are able to discern much more about his character and exploits:

> Tormod Beag, Tormod Beag againn fhìn, Tormod Noraidh, Norman
> MacLeod One, in contradistinction to Norman MacLeod Two,
> alias Tormod Nell, mac Thormoid 'Ain Tuirc, an donas beag ud, am
> bastard na bids' ud, am balach gòrach, an dòlas duin' ud, a bhlaigeird
> air do chasan, a mhic an uilc, a mhic an diabhail, m' eudail-s' air a
> mhullach, the man himself, College Boy, Guga, a Thormoid a luaidh,
> a Leòdhasaich na galla, yon big teuchter, Desperate Dan, Plum
> MacDuff, that Scotch git, you great big fucking Paddy, my own dear
> darling, the Body, the Brain, sweetie-pie, Prof, Dead-Eye Dick, honey,
> Leg-over Len, Mac, wherefore art thou Romeo, Come-again Charlie
> – agus a bhàrr orra sin uile, quintessentially and perennially, an
> Tocasaid, agus Tocasaid 'Ain Tuirc. (18)

This is almost impossible to translate adequately, with the two languages so closely interwoven. Much of the humour relies on the relationship between the languages, and the irony consists in the invitation to the reader to identify which aspects of An Tocasaid's life relate to which of his many nicknames. The first few are simple enough: 'Little Norman', 'our own little Norman' and 'Norman son of Norrie'. 'Norman MacLeod One' undoubtedly comes from his school days, and 'that Scotch git' from his time in England. Several of the nicknames refer to his womanising ways, and all of these are in some version of English, suggesting that most of his womanising took place off the island. Some of the names point towards relationships with people from other parts of Lewis and from other parts of the *Gàidhealtachd*: 'Guga' (which is a young gannet, hunted as a delicacy by the men of Ness, but disdained by many other islanders), 'a Leòdhasaich na galla' ('son of a bitch Lewisman'). Some of An Tocasaid's characteristics are demonstrated in the other stories. For instance, 'Cock of the Walk' (the title is in English in the book) illustrates his physical prowess. An Tocasaid's abilities seem to owe much to the stock of Gaelic mythology, as he manages to leap over another boy and tie him up in the same movement. 'Na Brògan Donna' ('The Brown Boots') and several other stories recount the folklore An Tocasaid has heard from his grandmother. These stories seem to have had a major influence on his own development and on his perception of himself. The main character in the stories is a prince called An Sgeilbheag (which is a name for the forefinger), who comes to be partly identified with An Tocasaid himself as these stories-within-stories progress.

Tocasaid 'Ain Tuirc is more closely integrated than a short story cycle and yet has less cohesion than a novel. It lies poised between the two in an uneasy and brilliant tension. There is a marked main character, An Tocasaid, whose exploits and identity underpin most of the book. It is his relationships and development that drive the interest even in some of those stories in which he does not directly appear. On the other hand, there is no sense of linearity, far less a plot or a structure that could be indicative of a novel. It is an idiosyncratic and unique collection that will take its place as one of the classics in Gaelic fiction.

Iain F. MacLeòid

Iain F. MacLeòid, nephew of authors Norma NicLeòid and Fionnlagh MacLeòid (whose works are also discussed in this chapter), has published two novels under the Ùr-Sgeul banner, although he was an accomplished writer before taking to prose fiction. The first of the novels, *Na Klondykers* (2005)[7] is, in some ways, the stronger of the two, with gritty, witty, real-sounding dialogue and engaging characters who hold the reader's interest. MacLeòid's real talent, however, seems to be in writing action: in both novels, the action sequences are the most convincing passages. MacLeòid's description of action sequences in *Na Klondykers* is innovative: with a few notable exceptions, Gaelic novels since the 1970s tended to avoid action. The opening passage of *Na Klondykers*, depicting the horrific events of the Piper Alpha disaster from the viewpoint of a survivor, is entirely unlike anything that had appeared in a Gaelic novel before. The passage is set in the present tense and makes use of various techniques, such as the speeding up and slowing down of time, the restriction of sensory perception, and a sense of disembodiment, to convey the immediacy of the danger and fear. Although the rest of the novel never quite reaches the same heights in terms of tension or vividness, there are other passages that are also powerful. The strength of this opening sequence is slightly undermined, in some ways, by a failure to come to get to grips with its significance in relation to the rest of the novel. The main character, Dòmhnall, is the Piper Alpha survivor who provides the sentient centre for the opening passages. When he leaves the oilrigs to return home and take up fishing in the unnamed town that is so evidently Ullapool, Dòmhnall is haunted by his memories, but the novel keeps pulling in another direction and subverting the possible interest in exploring the effects on Dòmhnall's psyche. Instead, the plot oscillates between a love story involving Dòmhnall's brother Iain (who takes over as the main character, in many ways) and some underworld dealings that seem interpolated just to add to the sense of gritty modernity. As a result, the plot begins to unravel in the latter stages, and the ending is both corny and unnecessary. Aside from that, and an issue with language that I have discussed in an article elsewhere (Watson 2007), *Na Klondykers* is a successful debut novel.

Am Bounty (2008) is the second novel by Iain F. MacLeòid. Although similarly featuring a short, bilingual title, *Am Bounty* is a radical departure from *Na Klondykers*. This is the first Gaelic novel to be based directly on historical events. *An t-Ogha Mór* and the other early novels do rely heavily on a historical environment, and could be described as 'historical novels', but *Am Bounty* is the first Gaelic novel to focus on a known historical character and fictionalise his actual actions. While it may be a cause for initial concern that MacLeòid would choose such a well-trodden path for his historical novel, a path which has featured at least two Hollywood films and numerous other fictional treatments, MacLeòid avoids some of the problems of cliché by steering clear of any of the best-known protagonists in the *Bounty* mutiny.

The main character in *Am Bounty* is Seumas Moireasdan,[8] who tells the story as a first-person narrator. Structurally, most of the novel takes place in flash-back, so we know from the first that Moireasdan is a condemned man, waiting to be hanged for his part in the mutiny. MacLeòid makes use of the reader's expected knowledge of the broad story, and can thus focus on Moireasdan's own thoughts and feelings rather than trying to telescope out to a broader narrative view. This works well, for the most part, especially when he uses dramatic irony and foreshadowing. However, in one sense it falls flat: the ending is supposed to be a dramatically happy twist, like the dénouement of *Na Klondykers*, with its double-twist epilogue, but this merely results in the reader feeling cheated by a *deus ex machina* (much as the reader feels cheated in the other book, where the main character is not actually saved, but there is a sense that his 'spirit' is preserved). The ending might have been stronger, and thus the whole book better, if Moireasdan had revealed at the beginning that he had been saved from execution: the reader would then have wanted to read on to find out how. As the book stands, the ending suffers from similar narrative problems to those in Caimbeul's *Là a' Dèanamh Sgèil Do Là*. The frame narrative structure allows the story to move along quickly in places and more slowly elsewhere without losing momentum. However, where there are some portions leading up to the end of the novel that tend to drag and are over-long and episodic, the dénouement is then rushed and unsatisfactory. The narrative itself is generally well-paced and engaging, but the dialogue is stilted and unrealistic. It is clear that the author was trying to capture the spirit of the novel's time-setting, but this is unconvincingly executed and even perhaps anachronistic in places. The characters themselves then suffer from their dialogue and fail to elicit sympathy with the reader, and this is even true of Seumas Moireasdan himself, who has little to make him attractive as a hero, but is also not an engaging antihero.

There are two main sections in the book: the description of the voyage to Tahiti, the arrival there and the mutiny; and then the events following the mutiny, in which Moireasdan's relationship with the murderer Brown comes to the fore. The mutiny itself takes place almost entirely off-stage, with Moireasdan learning about it when he is dragged on deck along with the other members of the crew not directly involved. He is only kept on board the ship because there is not enough room for him on the captain's boat. Despite modern reconsiderations of the events surrounding the *Bounty*, Bligh is depicted as harsh and unnecessarily cruel, a man not capable of leading others or running a ship: in other words, his portrayal appears to owe something to Hollywood depictions of the Captain. Fletcher Christian, on the other hand, is shown in an equally-poor light, or even perhaps as a worse leader than Bligh. Moireasdan has no fondness for either of them, but is highly loyal to the Navy and to the King, despite the fact that he was press-ganged as a youngster. This is an interesting aspect of the novel and it might have been worthwhile for MacLeòid to have pursued it further. The portrayal of Moireasdan's youth is one of the most convincing parts of the novel, and it might have been interesting to see more of his early years in the Navy and watch him gradually lose his initial desperation to return home and look after his family. Moireasdan's mind-set throughout the novel gives a convincing and fascinating picutre of the power of the Empire in taking over the consciousness and beliefs of its conquered peoples.

When the mutineers leave the other members of the crew behind on Tahiti, they must work together to survive. At this point, Moireasdan becomes something of a leader among them. When Brown appears and integrates himself into their group, and into the native islanders' society as well, enmities begin to surface. Moireasdan's faction want to build a boat in order to get home and submit themselves to Naval justice, but Brown wants to stay on the island and avoid the Navy, knowing that he is a wanted man. The conflict eventually leads to all-out war between the factions, and many people are killed, before Brown and Moireasdan face off against one another. Before they end up killing each other, however, another Navy ship comes to the island and Moireasdan is captured. From this moment until the final few pages, Moireasdan believes he will be executed as a mutineer. The new ship meets with considerable bad luck, and is wrecked long before it can reach home. However, eventually, Moireasdan does reach England, and ends up dutifully awaiting his execution.

Some of the action in this second main section of the novel is highly engaging. However, as is so often the case with Gaelic fiction, the narrative yields to long, uninterrupted tracts of dialogue, and the dialogue is often clichéd or unconvincing. The following long extract may serve to illustrate all of these points (note that the dialogue here, as with much of the dialogue in this novel, is actually in English and has not been translated):

'Just the two of us now, Morrison. Not that I like that. But needs must. I know I've hated you in the past, and most likely you've hated me. But there's nothing for it but to bury the hatchet, and try and make the best of things.'

'We're not finished yet.'

'Aye, we are. And we'll soon be overrun if we don't wake up and make ready. They're outside realizing that most of the white men are ready dressed for the pot, and now might be a good time to get rid of the rest of them. That includes me. And you. I've been a good chief, but . . . there have been times when I've . . . maybe . . . made the most of my position. Nothing that a chief mustn't do but . . . well, some haven't seen my side of it.'

'You're the most despicable man I've ever seen, Brown.'

'Praise will get you nowhere, Morrison. This will.'

[. . .]

'You take the front, and if you see any of them coves too close with a bit of revenge in their eyes, don't hesitate to send them to their creator. Another few bodies won't matter much today. We've got to make them know that we're not sitting ducks, just yet.'

'You expect me to join with you, Brown, after everything?'

'Well, how shall I put it, mate. If you don't, you'll die.' (131–2)

Nevertheless, in spite of these shortcomings, *Am Bounty* holds up well as a cohesive and entertaining novel. It marks a point in the development of Gaelic fiction where the novel has come of age as a genuinely entertaining escapist artefact. If the market for Gaelic novels has, to date, relied largely on the fact that they are written *in Gaelic*, and therefore will be bought by the loyal Gaelic-reading public, *Am Bounty*, along with *Samhraidhean Dìomhair* and the *Dìleas Donn* novels, leads the way in the movement towards books people will buy because they are enjoyable and escapist reading.

Tormod MacGill-Eain

The comedian and media personality Tormod MacGill-Eain published two novels during the brief burst of productivity in the 1990s, both of which are discussed here in Chapter 4. His third, *Dacha Mo Ghaoil*, appeared in the Ùr-Sgeul series in 2005, and his fourth, *Slaightearan* ('Rascals') joined the series in 2008.[9] *Dacha Mo Ghaoil* is, in essence, a comic novel, although there are serious elements and the comedy gives way to darkness in many places. The novel centres around a group of islanders who are involved in legally questionable money-making schemes. The main character, Daibhidh MacÌosaig has graduated from university some time prior to the events in the novel, but has trouble deciding how to spend his life. He teams up with a scam artist called Donnchadh and a thug called Calum. Donnchadh wants their help in bringing to fruition a crazy plan he has involving ostrich-rearing and sexual trafficking. He wants, ultimately, to set up a mud-wrestling, lap-dancing club in Uist. Calum, meanwhile, invests his ill-gotten gains into establishing himself as a drug-dealer. Meanwhile, a lawyer called Mairead suspects that she knows what they are doing and determines to catch them out.

Dacha Mo Ghaoil is intended to be an entertaining diversion of a novel, less serious in some ways than *Keino*, although there are subtexts and subtleties at work even here. And, although some of the dialogue is vicious, the threats of violence are brutal, and a number of characters are genuinely unsavoury, there is a tongue-in-cheek quality to the whole piece that makes it an easy read.

Slaightearan (2008) is a return to the kind of issues and concerns that were central to *Cùmhnantan*, and it also marks a return to a very similar style of writing. The Ùr-Sgeul books usually carry a short 'puff'-style quotation on the front cover, sometimes extracted from a review by a critic. Both *Dacha Mo Ghaoil* and *Slaightearan* have tongue-in-cheek parodies of these snippets. *Dacha Mo Ghaoil* has '. . . anabarrach sgileil' ('tremendously skilful'), attributed to Vladimir Soloviev, and *Slaightearan* has '. . . tha mi air mo bheò-ghlacadh leis' ('I'm gripped by it'), which is attributed to

Seonag Tarantino.[10] This practice immediately alerts the reader to the fact that both books are intended to be treated as more light-hearted than some of the other Ùr-Sgeul volumes.

The main character in *Slaightearan* is Murchadh, who is similar in many ways to MacGill-Eain's other leading protagonists, especially Dòmhnall Caimbeul from *Cùmhnantan*. In a stylistic innovation – which seems to have been devised to cut down on description and any action not directly related to the plot – Murchadh introduces himself, in italics, at the start of the book. That is to say, he gives a short précis of his biography and hints at some of his motivations. This section (pp. 9–13) reads like an extended piece of stage direction and adds to the impression that *Slaightearan*, like all of MacGill-Eain's novels, could easily have been written as a script and might have suited that format better. Like the CV in *An Latha as Fhaide*, the italicised stage-direction device is too transparent as a short-hand way of conveying a lot of detail quickly, and it has the opposite effect to the one desired, in that it results in distancing the reader from the character. The same device is repeated for some of the other characters later in the novel. The main part of the novel is in third-person narration, but the stage-direction portions are in the first-person, from the point of view of the character being introduced. Despite the shortcomings of the device, the character differentiation is well executed.

Much of the novel is concerned with Murchadh's attempts to come to grips with his alcohol addiction and his wasteful tendencies, both of which echo the plot and motivations in *Cùmhnantan*. And, like Dòmhnall Caimbeul, Murchadh is a talented entertainer and sharp wit, who is attractive to much-younger women. The main premise of the novel is founded on a comedy tour Murchadh has undertaken with Raonaid, a young women he finds extremely attractive. He has wasted all the money they have made on the tour and she wants him to get it back before she will consider a relationship with him. Murchadh works up a scheme to con the money out of the other main character, Sam Wilson. Sam is known as 'Sam the Scam', and is a television executive when the action begins, although we already know from his stage-direction introduction that Sam will fall on much harder times. Perhaps because of Sam's nickname or perhaps because he is a television executive, the reader seems to be expected not to sympathise with him greatly and to accept that Murchadh's actions are appropriate.

Several of the chapters are almost entirely comprised of dialogue, with the result that the book is suspended somewhere between novel, *còmhradh*[11] and television script stylistically. The dialogue is often sharp and very often witty. Exhanges between pairs of characters can be quick-fire and funny, but the humour is sometimes used to disguise tenchant comments on more serious issues. For instance, in Chapter 5, MacGill-Eain explores islanders' anti-English reactions in the context of being tired of tourism and globalisation. Slightly later, there is a sharp attack on Catholic priests and their alleged sexual fondness for small boys. Then there is an attack on the followers of organised religion in general, aimed especially at Christians, who are seen as too stupid to remember a story from one week to the next and so they need to keep going back to church to hear it again. Others who suffer from MacGill-Eain's satire include people who have learnt Gaelic as adults and then use it on television, islanders who pretend not to be Gaels, and everyone involved in Gaelic broadcasting. At the same time, MacGill-Eain reveals a fascination with the question of Gaelic identity. From Suki's "Tha mise cho Gàidhealach ri fàd-mòna" (p. 81, 'I'm as Highland as a peat') to Murchadh's "Slàinte nan Gàidheal gasta . . . cac!" (p. 103, 'the Health of the noble Gael . . . shit!'), the novel wrestles with the question of whether the Gaels truly are a separate people with their own identity.

The plot works out in predictable fashion: indeed, it would have been predictable enough even without the ironic foreshadowing effected by the stage-direction introductions which are set several months later and look back on the events of the novel in hindsight. Nevertheless, MacGill-Eain's execution is, as always, enjoyable. Although we know Sam will get his comeuppance, and that Murchadh will succeed, and we even know how it will all happen, there is still enough in the writing to compel the reader to carry on with the book to the end. The epilogue is unusually structured, essentially taking the form of notes. It serves the purpose merely of tying up the loose ends and leaving the reader with a final impression of the lasting effects of the events of the novel.

Iain Mac a' Ghobhainn (Crichton Smith)

Tormod Caimbeul and Tormod MacGill-Eain were not the only long-established novelists to have had their work published as part of the Ùr-Sgeul project. Iain Mac a' Ghobhainn's *Am Miseanaraidh* ('The Missionary') was probably written in the 1970s. Like *An t-Aonaran*, *Am Miseanaraidh* echoes an English work of Mac a' Ghobhainn's,[12] but it is not at all clear why the Gaelic novella did not appear during his lifetime. Perhaps he was dissatisfied with it, as it is not on a par with *An t-Aonaran*; but, although his critical faculties were well regarded in relation to other writers, Mac a' Ghobhainn was not always the best judge of his own work. Indeed, in *Scottish Writers Talking 2*, Isobel Murray describes how Mac a' Ghobhainn gave her husband Bob Tait a box of his writing and invited him to winnow out any that was worthwhile and dispose of the rest (Murray 2002: 112). It may be that *Am Miseanaraidh* was simply forgotten about, written at a time when it was much more difficult to publish extended fiction in Gaelic.

In any case, it is one of the highlights of the Ùr-Sgeul publishing venture: as Aonghas Pàdraig Caimbeul has stated in a review:

> *Am Miseanaraidh* makes a very welcome addition to the now-growing body of contemporary Gaelic literature: the great name of Iain Crichton Smith adds gravitas to it, and the story itself adds depth and intelligence to the corpus. (Campbell 2006)

The novella features one main character, Dòmhnall Dubh, who is the missionary of the title. His name is a common nickname for the Devil, and it seems likely that Mac a' Ghobhainn was being deliberately ironic with this choice of name (Watson 2006a). At the beginning of the story, Dòmhnall Dubh is a minister in Scotland, but he quickly becomes dissatisfied with his lot and decides to emigrate to Africa, where he can really help people. I have suggested that the pacing at this part of the novella has not been well constructed (Watson 2006a): Mac a' Ghobhainn's usual economic style, which is so powerful in *An t-Aonaran* and *Na Speuclairean Dubha*, and which works well elsewhere in this novella, is a weakness in the brief opening chapter. Once Dòmhnall Dubh reaches Africa, the writing matches the action better. Dòmhnall Dubh finds his expectations challenged as soon as he begins his work. As Dòmhnall MacAmhlaigh (Donald MacAulay) has expressed it in his foreword to the book:[13]

> At first the Missionary struggles to impose his own control on the world in which he is, but everything goes against him, everything he believes he must do turns to loss. (6)

In fact, Dòmhnall Dubh's decision to go to Africa in the first place seems to be an exercise in trying to regain some control that he feels he has lost. He has been reduced to stammering and virtual muteness by his inability to impose his own understanding on the world around him. Letters to the newspapers and constant prayer have failed to bring people into line with his hopes for their behaviour, and his departure for Africa is a despairing attempt to spread his message to people he believes more likely to listen. Unfortunately for him, as soon as he begins his missionary work, he starts to realise that the Africans are no easier to control than his own people.

Raghnall MacilleDhuibh (Ronald Black) suggested in a review that the missionary finds himself when he gives up his collar (MacilleDhuibh 2006). In a sense, he also loses himself, at least inasmuch as he defines his identity by his adherence to his religious practices.[14] Unlike the Ministear Mór in *Dùn-Àluinn*, Dòmhnall Dubh throws off his coat and collar in despair, when all of his efforts to convert the people seem destined to failure. For both ministers, the removal of the costume signifies the beginning of their downfall: the Ministear Mór falls from being the one clergyman who champions the people to being an alcohol-soaked vagrant who lives in a cave; Dòmhnall Dubh falls from being the civiliser and missionary to being the bringer of more terrible violence than ever before. Caimbeul saw Dòmhnall Dubh's story as an exploration of how 'religious doctrine and practice is challenged once it is placed in a totally different context' (Caimbeul 2006). This is true, to an extent, but surely the purpose of the opening pages of the novella is to show us that Dòmhnall Dubh's religious faith has already failed him before he goes to Africa: his entire design in going there is to try to rediscover whatever elements of his being he felt he was losing at home; he goes to Africa in an effort to embrace his religion more closely. As Caimbeul has pointed out, the novella, like much of Mac a' Ghobhainn's other writing, hinges on a sense of dichotomies. Dòmhnall Dubh wishes to impose what he considers God's will on the world around him, but he does it by initially abhorring both nature and human nature. When he fails to control either of these things, he goes 'native' (MacilleDhuibh 2006) and becomes an extreme version of the tribespeople he had thought to control. MacilleDhuibh considered *Am Miseanaraidh* to be the most 'Christian' of the works Mac a' Ghobhainn wrote, and speculated that that was why he never published it himself (MacilleDhuibh 2006).[15] That may be so, but the portrayal of religion is not altogether positive: indeed, Dòmhnall Dubh's faith repeatedly lets him down, and it is his adherence to his religious doctrines (at least, as he sees them) that leads to most of the tragedy in the novella.

Norma NicLeòid

Until 2008, no Gaelic novel had ever been graced with the existence of a sequel. Norma NicLeòid's *Dìleas Donn* was always intended to be the first book in a trilogy, and, at the time of writing, we await the appearance of the third in the series. *Dìleas Donn* is well-written and convincing. Although the plot is relatively simple, it is well-structured and controlled. Because the characters are rounded and have believable concerns, dilemmas, aspirations and short-comings, the plot coheres well. Characterisation is strong with the main characters, but the minor characters lack the same sure touch, including those who seem to spend more time on the page than is justified by their role or their roundedness. The only other shortcoming in the writing is in the way that point-of-view can sometimes shift without warning. It may be that the shifts are done deliberately, but they feel uncontrolled and have the effect of distancing the reader.

There are three main characters in *Dìleas Donn*, and their backstory and relationships form much of the interest in the novel. The central character is Bellann, an islander who left Scotland in her youth, married in Canada and was widowed young. She became successful as a nurse and returned to Scotland. In the novel's present chronology, she is living in Aberdeen. She is attending a psychiatrist, in the hope of understanding some of the issues that have arisen in her life, especially in relation to the abortion she had when she was younger. The father of the unborn baby was Ailig Iain, who is the second of the three main characters. Ailig Iain and Bellann were married when they were young, but, when he became more deeply religious, his faith came between them and they divorced. Ailig Iain believes he cannot have children as his second wife Muriel has never conceived and he is unaware of Bellann's aborted child. Muriel is the third of the main characters. She was a keen musician in her youth, but gave that up in order to be with Ailig Iain when he divorced Bellann. She convinced herself that she shared his faith because she was so keen to be with him. During the course of the novel, she comes to realise that her faith is based on self-deception.

The main plot points can be summarised briefly. Bellann is appointed to a role overseeing nursing care in Aberdeen. This takes her regularly to care provision policy meetings in Edinburgh. When she arrives at one such meeting, she discovers that the Western Isles' representative is Ailig Iain. Surprised, and yet pleased, to see each other, Bellann and Ailig Iain quickly become infatuated with one another all over again. They begin spending time together after their meetings and, although they both remember the reason they separated in the first place, Ailig Iain's early-conversion zeal has faded, and they are both aware of this. Meanwhile, the reader begins to understand that there was a strong bond between Ailig Iain and Bellann's father. Whenever Bellann returns to Aberdeen, she visits her psychiatrist, who begins to suspect she wants to take her relationship with Ailig Iain further. Meanwhile, Ailig Iain does not tell Muriel about Bellann at all, which, in turn, hints to the reader that he, too, secretly wants to pursue a relationship with Bellann. In the end, they inevitably do sleep together. This causes Ailig Iain extreme religious angst, and also places great strain on his marriage. Bellann is at first pleased, but then realises she has fallen pregnant. After Muriel finds out about the pregnancy, Ailig Iain has a break-down. Bellann's father dies and leaves Ailig Iain a considerable amount of money. Muriel keeps in touch with Bellann and returns to her music, considering getting back with her old band. By the time Bellann has the baby, whom she names Melanie, the three main characters are able to discuss the future together rationally. Muriel believes that Melanie should not be an only child, and she suggests that Ailig Iain and Bellann should try to conceive another child.

This is where the novel ends, and it would be a satisfying and complete enough ending even if there was no prospect of a sequel. However, several areas for development open up during the course of the book, especially in the final third or so, and the reader is left wanting to know more about what will happen to Melanie and her unusual trio of parents. The second volume, *Taingeil Toilichte*, is set twenty years later. At the end of *Dìleas Donn*, Muriel has made the unexpected and outrageous suggestion that Ailig Iain and Bellann should try to conceive another child so that Melanie would not have to grow up alone. Muriel would go on a long tour with the band, Dìleas Donn, and leave them the time and space to do just that. As soon as *Taingeil Toilichte* begins, we understand that this is exactly what happened. Melanie, who is now graduating with a degree from Aberdeen University, has a brother, Dòmhnall. This peculiar family situation is one of the central issues in the novel, and it seems that it was one of Melanie's main motivations in studying Psychology at university. Melanie's other main reason for her choice of degree was the desire to understand her father's faith, her mother's antipathy towards it, and Muriel's ability to mitigate between the two and tread a middle path.

The two new characters, Melanie and Dòmhnall, are well-conveyed. Each has inherited physical or emotional characteristics from the three older adults who shared their upbringing. In the main, though, their attitudes reflect Bellann and Muriel more than Ailig Iain. Melanie and Dòmhnall are contrasting characters, although they also have much in common. She is cerebral and curious, whereas he is domestic and contented with his lot. Melanie's non-Gaelic name symbolises the different kind of attachment she has to the community, compared to her brother, whose name is rooted in the Lewis naming tradition. Dòmhnall has no desire to leave the island or try out Higher Education, even though there is no indication that he is in any way less intelligent or capable than his sister. He wants to settle on crofting land, drive a bus for his daily income and play in the band: that is the extent of his ambition.Other characters who made fleeting appearances in *Dìleas Donn*, such as Mobà and Heins, Muriel's bandmates, are brought much more to the fore in this second novel. Ailig Iain plays a much less significant part in events, relegated to being a source of concern and guilt for Melanie for much of the book, although he does enjoy a trip to Glasgow and London, which is discussed briefly below. A third new character, Doris, looks like she may be going to feature prominently in the forthcoming third volume in the series, as do one or two other members of the island community.

It was already clear in *Dìleas Donn* that Norma NicLeòid writes well, and this is confirmed in *Taingeil Toilichte*. She avoids many of the awkwardnesses, gimmicks and contrivances of some of the other contemporary authors, and she has perhaps the best ear for natural-sounding dialogue of any current fiction writer in Gaelic. Significantly, however, her novels rely on dialogue less than many of the other works of extended fiction in Gaelic of the period considered in this book, although there is still an imbalance in favour of dialogue at times. The narrative voice has a sure and confident touch, moving easily between different levels of description and explication without ever getting too bogged down in detail or expounding back-story. Thus, the first few chapters quickly and naturally fill in much of what has taken place in the twenty years between volumes without detracting from the current novel. There is a strong sense that there is a destination in mind and that the reader is being moved along towards it subtly.

Like *Dìleas Donn*, *Taingeil Toilichte* has a relatively simply plot, mainly based on the development of the relationships of the unusual family that was created in the first novel. Melanie wants to embark on a PhD to study the psychological effects of religion within her home community in Lewis. Although her supervisors try to talk her out of it, knowing what a traumatic experience it is likely to be for her, and how vulnerable it will leave her, Melanie is determined to pursue this course of study and gets her own way (which illustrates a characteristic she has inherited from Bellann). Melanie and her supervisors decide she must pretend to be converting to Free Church Christianity so that she can better integrate into the local religious community and gain a fuller insight into their language and ways. This seems rather unethical and the reader might question the likelihood of a university now approving this kind of deliberate and elaborate deception for the sake of a research project, especially in his/her home community. Nevertheless, this is the premise as it stands. Melanie's supervisors are aware of the potential problems and undertake to engage a psychiatrist to help her with any personal issues that arise out of the work. Coincidentally (although likely enough, considering his background), the psychiatrist that they ask to work with her is none other than Dr MacCumhais, who treated Bellann during her time in Aberdeen in *Dìleas Donn*.

Much of the novel is taken up with Melanie interviewing members of the community over a period of several months; perhaps even a year or more. This causes a rift with her mother, who always brought her up to think critically and never expected her to embrace the Free Church dogma, but it is a source of joy for her father, who always prayed his children (especially Melanie) would become Christians. While Melanie is busy attending sermons and prayer-meetings and interviewing family and acquaintances for her thesis, a second plot begins to develop. This plot initially centres on Muriel. She continues to enjoy her time with the band and they arrange a tour to the southern islands of the Western Isles. Dòmhnall goes with the band, temporarily replacing Mobà. This affords Muriel the opportunity to think how much things have changed in the twenty years since the great personal crises of *Dìleas Donn*. She thinks about how greatly the church has changed in the time, opening up much more to new ideas, encouraging young people to take part in sports (the opposite of how the church was a generation previously), and becoming much less dogmatic in its general demeanour. Nevertheless, it is, in essence, still the same old church, and she finds it does not compare favourably with some of the older Gaelic mythology that preceded it. Muriel also thinks a great deal about her family, and how Dòmhnall seems much closer to her than Melanie: she understands that this is because she specifically wanted him to be born.

Muriel's story fleshes out her character more than was permitted in the first volume. We see the fun-loving and resentful sides of her personality, and we become aware of her own insecurities and doubts. We even see her flirtatious side, when she encounters Dr MacCumhais, who is on holiday back in his home community. Coincidentally, MacCumhais's granddaughter Kathleen begins a relationship with Dòmhnall after one of the band's performances, and this brings MacCumhais back into things.

Tormod Caimbeul

Tormod Caimbeul, author of the acclaimed *Deireadh an Fhoghair*, finally published a second novel in 2006. Along with *Gormshuil an Rìgh* (which is discussed briefly below), Caimbeul's *Shrapnel* (2006) is one of the most challenging and formidable of the recent books of fiction. It is set in Edinburgh, where Caimbeul himself studied and worked, and it focuses on the seedy side of life in the city. Commentators have been tempted to compare the novel with *Trainspotting*, and there are indeed some comparisons to be made. As far as subject matter and atmosphere are concerned, crime, violence and vice are at the heart of the book. Further, Caimbeul intersperses the Gaelic with Scots or Edinburgh demotic in the novel, and some of the dialogue would not be out of place in one of Welsh's novels. In common with a number of the urban Scottish writers of the past two decades, Caimbeul avoids using quotation marks to flag up dialogue. Instead, he uses indented dashes, as in the quotation below. This results in the text looking fragmented and disjointed, an effect that echoes the shifting sense of focus in the narrative. Like *Deireadh an Fhoghair*, *Shrapnel* is a difficult read. Even though the two novels are different in almost every other way, they share this feature of an elusive sense of narrative focus, which leaves the reader struggling sometimes to gain purchase on the text.

The title character is Walter Watson, whose nickname 'Shrapnel' again hints at the sense of fragmentation that underpins the novel. Watson is a retired detective with a violent past that returns to cause him problems during the course of the novel. There is a sense of underlying violence throughout the novel, and both major and incidental characters are fascinated by it:

— Vengeance is mine, saith the Lord! Ach gur h-ann leis-san a bha
an dioghaltas – cha robh say aig an Tighearna ann – agus dh'fhan e
gu foighidneach fad bhliadhnachan a' faire air mac an diabhail gus an
d'fhuair e mu dheireadh an cothrom. (111)

[. . .]

— See him, killed a fuckin' polisman like me, like . . . (112)

(Vengeance is mine, saith the Lord! But vengeance was his – no
Lord had a say at all – and he waited patiently for years watching the
bastard until at last he got the chance.)

Caimbeul has a gift for dialogue, especially humorous, ironic or cynical
dialogue. At times, he almost loses control of this, but there is always a
sense that he is deliberately pushing at boundaries to see what the text can
sustain. An example that illustrates all of these points appears on page 32,
and the reader here will immediately see that this device can be demanding:

— 'Eil thu air tron oidhche, Mavis?

— Tha, fad na seachdain. 'Eil thu fhèin?

— Tha . . . well, fhad 's tha esan ann.

— Bidh e greis mhath ann. Chaidh a phronnadh.

Thàinig iad na b' fhaisge, mo chluasan fosgailte.

— 'Eil e na chadal?

— Tha.

— Cinnteach?

— Tha.

Guthan ìosal.

— Fad na h-oidhche?

— Fad na seachdain.

— Agus mise.

— Mura fàs e nas fheàrr.

— Mavis?

— Mm?

— Dhomh do làmh.

— Des!

— Bruidhinn air fàs . . .

— Crikey!

— 'Eil thu . . . ?

— Chan eil! Tha!

— Cà 'n tèid sinn?

— Far nach tèid breith oirnn.

— . . . in flagrante delicto!

— In the sluice, Willie, arsa Mavis. (32)

This long quotation shows the quickfire nature of much of the dialogue in the novel. It is reminiscent of drama, in the way that the dialogue itself is used to suggest the action that is taking place. This extract traces a comical seduction that is overheard in a hospital. There is irony in "Eil e na chadal?' ('Is he asleep?'), when the character in question is not asleep and is the sentient focus of the scene. There is comedy in 'Bruidhinn air fàs' ('Talking about growing') followed by 'Crikey!' (and, as elsewhere, Caimbeul also relies on switching between the languages to create extra comic effect). The whole extract shows how hard Caimbeul is willing to make the reader work at following the interactions.

Like the novels of Tormod MacGill-Eain, *Shrapnel* represents a major step in terms of genre development in Gaelic fiction. It is to be hoped that the wait between *Shrapnel* and Caimbeul's next novel will not be as long as that between his first two.

Màiri Anna NicDhòmhnaill

Màiri Anna NicDhòmhnaill is the author of the novel *Cleas Sgàthain* (2008).[16] Like Catrìona Lexy Chaimbeul, whose *Samhraidhean Dìomhair* is discussed below, NicDhòmhnaill has experience of writing for children, but this is her debut novel for an adult readership. Like *Samhraidhean Dìomhair*, *Cleas Sgàthain* is aimed at the entertainment side of the novel-reading market and, again like the other book, it is engagingly written. While, on first appearances, *Cleas Sgàthain* would also appear to be appealing to the 'chick lit' market, the plot, characterisation and dialogue nudge it more in the direction of 'kiddult' literature. The plot is utterly contrived and this is clear from the first pages to the end. However, the writing is appropriate to the kind of scenario thus created, and the novel succeeds in entertaining.

The main characters are twins, aged about twenty-nine. One lives in London and the other has stayed at home in Uist. The sister in London, Iseabail, has just received a big promotion at work. She has gone to get a beauty treatment to celebrate and ended up with a bad rash all over her face. Unwilling to go to her new job in that condition, she prevails on her sister, Catrìona, to take her place for the first few days. The novel opens halfway through their conversation, with Iseabail pleading with her sister – the dialogue immediately feels infantile and more in keeping with the conversation of twelve-year-olds than twenty-nine-year-old professional women. Catrìona agrees to the swap, against all likelihood (and, one would imagine, against all likelihood of success, if Iseabail's promotion was in any way earned). Luckily, and coincidentally, their parents are away on a holiday (for an unspecified amount of time), so there is no chance of anyone spotting the swap, as (again pushing the bounds of likelihood, given that they are twenty-nine), their parents are the only ones who can tell them apart. The novel is meant to be about how the two women cope with taking each other's places, but is quite unbalanced, with most of the focus on Iseabail trying to come to terms with living back in Uist. The London-based passages tend to feel hurried, sparse and unconvincing. Considering that Catrìona is in a much more difficult situation than Iseabail (who, after all, knows the environment and people of Uist), it seems to make more sense to focus more on her efforts to survive in London and in the professional situation. The theme of duplicity is maintained elsewhere in the novel, and other characters are not quite what they seem (although their reasons for their various deceptions are not always clear or explored). There is a very heavy reliance on dialogue throughout the novel, not just in the form of face-to-face speech itself, but also in epistolary form, involving email, phone conversations and text messages. This is innovative and one of the strongest aspects of the book, but is sometimes gratuitous or evasive. At times, the lack of narrative becomes problematic. In general, *Cleas Sgàthain* is an enjoyable and unchallenging read.

Fionnlagh MacLeòid

Along with Donnchadh MacGillÌosa, the other contemporary virtuoso of the short story in Gaelic is Fionnlagh MacLeòid. MacLeòid is the husband of Norma NicLeòid, author of *Dìleas Donn* and *Taingeil Toilichte*. Although the pair share an interest in psychology, which shows up in their work, their writing has little else in common. The one other thing that makes them comparable is that MacLeòid and Norma NicLeòid are two of the best writers producing Gaelic fiction today. NicLeòid's writing is engaging and entertaining, and MacLeòid's is challenging and thought-provoking.

Dìomhanas (2008) is, perhaps surprisingly, Fionnlagh MacLeòid's first book of short stories. He published the *tour-de-force* 'An Cluaisean' in the 1960s, then a few other stories in *Gairm* and *Gath*, but did not follow these up with a collection. Those who read *Dìomhanas* may now consider that fact a loss to the literature that has finally been repaired. *Dìomhanas* contains twenty-four stories, most of which are around eight or so pages long. There is a strong tendency towards first-person point-of-view, to the extent that the occasional story that has a third-person perspective comes as a surprise. In several of the stories, the viewpoint character turns out to be female, and it is fair to say that MacLeòid writes convincingly from a female perspective. He is also convincing with a range of different kinds of characters, from different ages to different backgrounds and motivations. Ultimately, though, the bulk of the stories are set in Lewis or places similar to Lewis and feature characters who are Gaels – at least inasmuch as these things can be discerned. The stories range from the realistic to the surreal and bizarre, some of them reminiscent of the work of Alasdair Gray in various ways. Further, in 'Triùir Nighean an Rìgh agus Mac na Banntraich' ('The King's Three Daughters and the Widow's Son'), MacLeòid shows that, like Donnchadh MacGillÌosa, he is willing and able to draw on the rich store of traditional tales from the Gaelic oral culture as a source of inspiration.

'An Cluaisean'[17] was a well-known and popular story long before *Dìomhanas* appeared, but it was a good choice to include it in this collection, as it is full of ideas that underpin much of MacLeòid's other writing. First and foremost, 'An Cluaisean' is a story clearly inspired by MacLeòid's training in Psychology, in which subject he gained a PhD from Aberdeen University. MacLeòid's particular interest was in bilingualism, which feeds directly into 'An Cluaisean', as well as several of the other stories. The 'Cluaisean' of the title is a boy who has had an operation to remove his tonsils but which has inadvertently severed his corpus callosum.[18] This procedure (performed deliberately) was evidently of considerable interest in the field of Psychology during MacLeòid's studies, and the entire story is devised as a comical exploration of the ideas of identity and unity and their link to the integrity of the brain. When the 'Cluaisean' wakes up from his operation, he is initially able to hear only Gaelic, and can speak only through his ear. Later, when he has recovered further, he can hear English and speak that language through his other ear. However, the two halves of his brain remain effectively separate consciousnesses, neither one able to remember or even understand what the other has said or experienced. He is then able to read English and Gaelic texts simultaneously, although only one half of his personality will be aware of each. Comically, the head of An Comunn Gaidhealach thinks that this is the solution to the increasing use of English at Mòds and throughout An Comunn's activities: he believes it will cure people of their tendency to codeswitch and mix the languages, and he immediately advocates a regime of tonsilectomies followed by bizarre methods of disposal of the offending tonsils.

In some ways similar to 'An Cluaisean', the story 'Ùrachadh' ('Renewal') again considers the extent to which body parts are part of human identity. Although rather tongue-in-cheek again, like 'An Cluaisean', this story is based on the age-old mind-body dualism debate which also underlies the former story. The chief protagonist has a heart transplant, and this results in changes to her character. Eventually, the professor in charge of the procedure reveals that he now believes that the heart may rule feelings and emotions as people used to believe.

'An Cluaisean' is not the only story about a strange relationship with language. The closing story 'Tiop' ('Chip') features a chief protagonist who learns Gaelic by having a chip implanted in his brain. His mother finds it difficult to understand why he should choose to have a language of such limited utility implanted when he could have opted for a much more widely-known language instead. This is a reference to the whole issue of transmission of Gaelic in an age when the language is no longer a communicative necessity. MacLeòid has had a long interest in bilingualism, going back to his own research and then stretching through his career in education. Learning a language by having a chip implanted is shown as being effortless (although presumably involves a dangerous operation), and this must be taken as a cipher for learning a language in the home environment. The mother's question, however, remains valid, even where the learning is straightforward and simple: why would the character choose Gaelic over other languages? The answer seems to be couched in terms of identity and culture. Much of the rest of the story contains little snippets from other stories in the book, as the character starts to become aware not only of the morphology, syntax, phonology and vocabulary of his new language, but also acquires a cultural awareness. In effect, he begins to turn into a slightly different person. MacLeòid's point here is a well-worn one in linguistics, which has been debated many times over the past few decades: that knowledge of a language has an effect on the way a person perceives and understands the world (see also p. 99 in the story 'An Ceum' and p. 118 in 'Ist! 'Eil e ach an leth-uair co-dhiù?').[19] The implication is that knowledge of a second language therefore gives a person two slightly different ways of perceiving the world (or, possibly, a third, hybrid way which is not quite the same as how a monoglot speaker of either of the languages would view things). This is not so noticeable to someone who grows up with two languages, but it comes as a shock to the main character in this story, who suddenly has the entire cultural baggage of a new language to deal with.

Very many of the stories in *Dìomhanas* are in first-person perspective, and there is considerable use of internal monologue, which sometimes slips into stream-of-consciousness. Sometimes, the reader is deceived into thinking that the perspective is other than what it is, as several stories take the form of well-disguised frame tales or even seem to shift perspective as the action progresses. 'A' Chùil' ('The Nook') is an example of this. It begins with a long, vivid description of a man the narrator sees, and appears to be a third-person perspective. The narrator then turns out to be a character. This perceptual shift is related closely to the plot and theme of the story, however, and the device is very effective. The man who is seen at a distance, Murchadh, turns out to be a native of the village where the narrator, a boy of eleven, Anthony, now lives. The village is in Lewis and no longer has any natives. Anthony, uniquely, has learned Gaelic to a good level of fluency and so is excited to speak to Murchadh. Murchadh, in turn, is both glad to speak to the boy and at the same time horrified that his community has so completely died. The story explores the ideas of community and the link between people, the land and their language. It also perhaps allows for the possibility that new kinds of links can be forged. Related to this are stories such as 'An Dachaigh' ('The Home') and 'Dùsgadh' ('Awakening'), which both explore the link between cultural history and place. In 'An Dachaigh', the characters have moved from Sheffield to a croft (in Lewis, most likely) and they are amazed by the beauty of their new surroundings. Soon, though, the female character finds a picture of people who used to live there when it really was a croft, and she begins to wonder about the people and the place. She finds old Bibles and recordings of Gaelic singing. She wonders what the bay is called and imagines that people probably drowned there in the past: in other words, the place begins to fill in its own story for her, when she goes seeking for the stories. All of this is ironic, considering that MacLeòid so often avoids giving his characters names and tends to avoid being specific about where the stories are set, too. Similarly, 'Dùsgadh' considers the tension that is created by people moving away from where they 'belong'. The main protagonist goes to retrieve his grandfather from New Zealand after a fifty year absence because he wants him to see his mother once before she dies. As the story progresses, we begin to understand that the reason this grandfather has never met his own daughter (i.e the main character's mother) is because the community religion made a pariah of him: in other words, he moved away because he no longer 'belonged'. The theme of conforming to local social expectations is prevalent throughout the collection, but this is the story that develops it most fully.

The next story in the collection, 'Latha Eile' ('Another Day'), has a similar start, in that the narrator is again on the beach. This story introduces the theme of worthiness, which recurs frequently throughout the collection and is a common idea in modern Gaelic fiction in general, most clearly treated, perhaps, in Iain Mac a' Ghobhainn's 'An Fhìrinn'. Here, the narrator wonders about whether she is worthy of pity or forgiveness or if people deserve what they get. The narrator is descending rapidly into a mental and physical illness which a Calvinist-influenced mindset seems to be telling her she probably deserves. The reader is aware of events only through a stream-of-consciousness internal monologue, which is intercut with Biblical allusions. Religion, faith, superstition and tradition are further explored in 'A' Dùsgadh Chlach' ('Raising a Stone').[20] Some men are digging up boulders in order to build a barn. One of the boulders appears to have a name written on it. This quickly gives rise to a cult, which turns into a religion. People become very excited about it, but the initial excitement gradually passes into custom and tradition.

There are some stories that are deliberately not realistic – even more so than 'An Cluaisean' and 'Ùrachadh'. These include the aforementioned 'Triùir Nighean an Rìgh agus Mac na Banntraich', which follows the traditional tale formula to some degree and then becomes a peculiar mixture of folktale and parody on folktale collectors. These stories also include 'Cùil Lodair' ('Culloden') and 'Na h-Ailbhein Gaoithe' ('The Wind Elephants'). In 'Cùil Lodair', the infamous battle is reimagined as a modern-day event, with lads going on the Stornoway-Ullapool ferry to attend. The BBC even sends out a van to do outside broadcast coverage. In 'Na h-Ailbhein Gaoithe', the people of a village come to believe there will be a great deluge, comparable to the Biblical Flood. To save themselves, they get hold of inflatable rubber elephants that one man has been making. They fill these with helium and launch themselves into the sky to try to survive the coming water. Again, this story pokes fun at the way religion and faith are spread and maintained, highlighting the fact that they rely so heavily in stories and on a suspension of one's natural state of disbelief.

'A chàirdean, cà'il am bàr?' ('Friends, where is the bar?') is a slightly longer story than most of the others. The unusual style of title mirrors that of 'Ist! 'Eil e ach an leth-uair co-dhiù?', which was mentioned briefly above. In common with many of the stories in the book, 'A chàirdean, cà'il am bàr?' is a first-person narrative. The main character – indeed the only one who is allowed to be humanised – is a writer who is struggling with his sense of himself and is evidently suffering alcohol-related problems. He is teaching a summer writing course to try to earn some money, as he is also in financial difficulties: he clearly does not want to be doing the course. His lack of enthusiasm, and his lack of engagement with the outside world and other people, is symbolised by his naming of the students as C1–5, based on which computer they are occupying. The use of language is an important theme in the story, as it explores the way that modern technologies are leading to an ever-increasing colloquialisation and fragmentation of language. At the same time, the story acknowledges the backlash effect, with one of the students representing the tendency to become ultra-conservative in an effort to preserve obsolescing aspects of speech. These issues are highly relevant in the Gaelic context, with Gaelic now beginning to have a much wider internet presence and with ever more efforts to encourage people to develop texting and blogging registers for the language. And, like one of the characters in this story, there are some – perhaps especially among those who learn Gaelic as adults – who try to retain old sayings, idioms and proverbs, and so they pepper their speech with them, even in slightly inappropriate contexts. MacLeòid extends this parody to the often-discussed existence of multiple Gaelic-promotion groups:

> nì sinn b-litir le b-eachd, mar plana-na-g 's gheibh sinn
> airgeadteachdasteach ann an cladhan dhan choimhearsnachd-
> choimhearsnachd-choimhearsnachd vo v-nag no vo c-nag no g-nag;
> g-nag? ainm a' feitheamh ri buidheann. (162–3)[21]

The writer-character finds himself increasingly isolated from his students, as their enthusiasm does not match his own understanding. He can sympathise with neither the desire to tear language apart nor the desire to conserve it, as represented in the two extremes among his students. He is stuck in the middle in the struggle between traditionalism and modernity and he can see no way out. He seeks solace at the bar, realising that 'words will not do on their own' (162).

Fionnlagh MacLeòid's other book to date in the Ùr-Sgeul series is an allegorical novel, *Gormshuil an Rìgh* (2010, 'Gormshuil the King's Daughter'). *Gormshuil an Rìgh* owes much to both the Gaelic traditional story and the Norse saga. Like 'Triùir Nighean an Rìgh agus Mac na Banntraich', it is set in a world where kings and heroes can encounter fabulous creatures with unlikely abilities. The novel begins *in medias res*, and there is never an attempt to set the scene or explain anything. Characters' names are all folkloristic and fantastical (e.g. 'Nathair-Bheumnach, Gribh-Ìneach, Nathair-Nimhe [and] Leòmhainn-Bheucach': 71). The opening pages rely heavily on dialogue, and so there is not much in the way of world-building. As a result, meaning is uncertain and a Beckett-like quality begins to formulate. Characters often end up fighting, sometimes in highly magical ways. There is a good deal of declaiming as well, which is related to the fighting. Some parts of the book are made of several mini-stories, and the whole is somewhat fractured and unresolved. In a forthcoming review, Ashley Powell notes the wide range of literary techniques employed in the novel, especially the repeated use of anthropomorphism and pathetic fallacy (Powell forthcoming). Powell also points out that two of the major themes in the novel are connectivity and rebirth. This is where we may see the allegorical side of the novel: as Powell hints, it is possible to read it as a partial allegory on Gaelic and the Gaelic community. *Gormshuil an Rìgh*, like *Dìomhanas*, suggests that Fionnlagh MacLeòid is going to become a major figure in Gaelic fiction in the near future.

Catrìona Lexy Chaimbeul

Catrìona Lexy Chaimbeul[22] produced her debut novel for adults in 2009, having already been writing for children. Her *Samhraidhean Dìomhair* ('Secret Summers') gives the overall impression of being a very success-ful piece of writing. Chaimbeul's style is polished and accomplished and, although there are weaknesses in the book, *Samhraidhean Dìomhair* is one of the most promising novels to come out under the Ùr-Sgeul aegis, espe-cially considering that the author is very young, and it may be hoped that she has many other books to write in future. It should be noted at this point that Ùr-Sgeul exists not primarily to create high-brow, 'literary' literature: it exists to create a body of prose fiction for adults to read in Gaelic, as such a thing has never existed before and has often been considered a loss. With that in mind, *Samhraidhean Dìomhair* fits in perfectly. The plot structure is complex, which is necessary, as the plot itself is so simple that it requires a device to hold the reader's attention for some 172 pages. In a review of the novel by Raghnall MacilleDhuibh,[23] he considered the plot structure confusing and bemoaned the lack of some sort of signposting to help the reader along. In fact, the plot structure is one of the most effective devices in the novel, as it allows the author to encapsulate the fragmentation of the characters' thought-processes and friendships within a metaphorical and metonymic framework.[24] The structure is handled very competently by the author, marking Chaimbeul as one of the most disciplined of the new writers.

There are five main characters in the novel, each of whom has point-of-view scenes. It may be that this is too many point-of-view characters for such a short book, as the characterisation is one of the weaker aspects of the novel, especially in terms of balance. All of the characters do have credible aspects in their make-up, but there is a tendency to stray towards archetypes and MacilleDhuibh's comparison with a television soap opera is astute. These main characters are Stevie, Màiri-Ellen, Iain (-Alasdair), Chrissie and Mona. They are young adults at the time of the book's 'present' chronology, but the significant event that changed all of their lives hap-pened when they were at the end of their school careers a few years earlier. It is quickly clear that they were a group of close friends who have become separated, but it is not at all clear at first how they came to be friends when they seem to have little in common, and the bulk of the novel is taken up with slowly releasing the story of both their coming-together and also their parting. Although all five are point-of-view characters, their time on-page is not equal: we seem to see less of Màiri-Ellen than of any of the others, and Stevie is absent for much of the early part of the book. Furthermore, Chrissie takes up a good deal of the story, especially in the middle section, and it would be tempting to see her as the author's favourite character, offering, as she does, the opportunity to write about lifestyles and situations that have not really appeared in Gaelic before. Unfortunately, this sustained focus on Chrissie tends to give the book the impression of being rather light-weight at times, with the details of her life reading as if they come from a celebrity magazine. Chrissie is potentially an interesting character, and she certainly develops during the course of the novel, but many of the episodes in her life are too far from the ambience of the rest of the novel for cohesion; of course, this is deliberate, designed to show how far she has run away, both geographically and emotionally, but it does not always work. The other character who is given the chance to exhibit some interesting characteristics is Iain. Although some of his back-story could seem hackneyed, it is nevertheless integral to the plot of the novel, and it does raise some questions in the reader's mind whenever Iain is the focus.

Iain lived with his Granny following the deaths of his parents. When she was too old to look after him, they swapped roles, and he looked after her, thus avoiding being taken into care. This resulted in significant freedom for him, as a schoolboy running his own household. We soon realise that this is a large part of the motivation for the five friends coming together: some of them were attracted by Iain's freedom and the fact that they could behave as they pleased in his house. When Iain's Granny dies, she leaves him with a box of film, and it is made very obvious that this film has great significance; by the time the reader learns of it, it is evident that the box holds the key to understanding what happened to destroy the five's friendship.

Stevie's main role in the novel is to bring all of the characters back together at the end, by travelling to Skye with his bride-to-be in preparation for his wedding. As Mona's brother, he was also the main instigator behind the fatal accident that leads to the friends growing apart. When we first encounter Stevie, he gives the impression of being a highly damaged individual, and indeed the later revelations of the plot elements bear this out, but he undergoes a significant character change when he meets the new love of his life, and thereby also loses much of his appeal as a character.

Màiri-Ellen is still in love with Stevie even during the novel's 'present' chronology, and she has failed to move on from the first of the 'secret summers' referred to in the novel's title. Like Chrissie and Stevie, she is trying to run away from the past, by moving to Edinburgh and taking a succession of lovers. By keeping all her relationships at arms'-length, however, she is as stuck in the past as Iain.

Mona is the one character who has tried to stay at home and settle into a home life, caused by her young pregnancy and the birth of her daughter Peigi. Unfortunately, she has found herself trapped in a loveless marriage, and she regrets the absence of her brother Stevie and their friends. Peigi subverts her step-father's no-Gaelic rule by teaching the language to her twin half-brothers when she thinks no one is paying attention. When Mona finds out, she is both horrified and gratified, and this is the catalyst that perhaps will push her into moving on with her life.

The novel builds suspense well, and uses irony and foreshadowing successfully, if a bit obviously from time to time. There is a good balance of narrative and dialogue compared to other recent Gaelic novels. The final section's pace increases well and pushes the reader along towards the dénouement. The weaknesses here are simply in the hackneyed way in which the five friends all get back together at the end for the final climactic moment; Iain's sudden epiphany and the way he changes instantly (the character change is too radical to be believed, considering how enormous Chrissie has been in his life up to that point); and the way credibility is stretched towards the end. However, the double-twist in the ending is satisfying and works in a novel of this type.

Alison Lang

Alison Lang's debut, *Cainnt na Caileige Caillte* (2009) mainly focuses on characters and settings that are not 'Gàidhealach', although stories like 'Oidhche gun Ùrnaigh' and 'Beul gun Phutan' are deliberate attempts to fit into the long-standing conventions in Gaelic fiction. In 'Oidhche gun Ùrnaigh' ('A Night without a Prayer'), the characters are urban Gaels, attending prayer meetings in Edinburgh. The hybridisation of Gaelic culture is metonymised in the names of the two principal characters: Diana and Aonghas. Diana's romance with Aonghas leads her to question her religious practices. Sin and guilt are the central themes. 'Beul gun Phutan' ('A Mouth without a Button'), on the other hand, has no such weighty themes. It is a simple tale of a family cooking together. Other motifs in Lang's stories include failing relationships, loneliness, cats and futility. 'Latha Eile san Fhactaraidh' ('Another Day in the Factory') incorporates a number of these motifs and owes much to the Greek myth of Tartarus. The main character retreats into an introspective inner world to escape the tedium of the quotidien, which is a metonym for the pointlessness of all life. Both 'An Tèile' ('The Other Woman') and 'Faileas' ('Reflection') consider the effects of promiscuity and the way that sexual relationships actuate interpersonal dynamics that are utterly different from any other kinds of relationships or friendships. In 'A Dh'innse na Fìrinn' ('To Tell the Truth') and the title story, 'Cainnt na Caileige Caillte' ('The Language of the Lost Girl'), various senses of the concept of truth are explored. On the whole, *Cainnt na Caileige Caillte* is a deft and polished debut collection from someone who promises to contribute much to the literature.

Conclusion

It is clear that Gaelic fiction is currently enjoying its period of greatest productivity and, in some senses, its period of greatest success. Indeed, before this current book is even published, there will be at least two more books of fiction in print that are not discussed here. Further, in addition to those books which have been mentioned in this chapter, and elsewhere in this book, there are additional markets which have not even been explored here. For instance, there are more short novels and story books for children and teenagers than were ever available before. Some of these are translations and others are original works.[25] In some cases, they have been written by authors who also contribute to the adult markets. Authors like Tormod Caimbeul and Norma NicLeòid translate children's story books into Gaelic, while Catrìona Lexy Chaimbeul and Màiri Anna NicDhòmhnaill write original works. Iain Mac a' Ghobhainn wrote perhaps the first original Gaelic novel for children and then supplemented it with several others. Other established writers, such as Maoilios Caimbeul, followed suit. Like the books that are written for adults, the children's story books and novels are now being published with high-end production values, so that they look and feel just as modern and attractive as any English-language book available to children. From a sociolinguistic perspective, this is evidently an important thing, but it may also be important from a literary perspective, as the literature becomes less 'marked' and more mainstreamed: taking on the hallmarks of normality, as perceived by an English-dominant bilingual audience, a Gaelic book has more chance of being appreciated on its own merits and not merely for the sake of being a 'Gaelic book'.

In the past few years, another new initiative has seen the launch of four books aimed at the 'adult learner' market. This is long overdue and will surely be welcomed by the thousands of adults who are learning the language. The publisher, Sandstone Press, has invested in creating high-quality products that match the effort that has gone into writing them. The four titles that are in print at the time of writing are *Litir à Ameireagaidh* (2005, 'Letter from America') by Flòraidh NicDhòmhnaill, *Sgeulachdan an Dà Shaoghail ann an Ceithir Litrichean* (2007, 'Stories of the Two Worlds in Four Letters') by Michael Newton, *Cleasan a' Bhaile Mhòir* (2009, 'City Tricks') by Catriona Lexy Campbell/Catrìona Lexy Chaimbeul, and

Cogadh Ruairidh (2009, 'Ruairidh's War') by Iain MacLean/Iain Mac Ill Eathain. Notably, the last two texts have their authors' names in English on the cover and then in Gaelic on the title page inside. All four books have English descriptions on the back cover and English information about the series and author inside the cover. In the first two books, this information includes a description of the purpose of the series:

> The Sandstone Meanmnach Series is aimed at Advanced [*sic*] Gaelic learners as well as accomplished readers. Recognising that most readers come from an English language background, they open with an introduction from the author that will contextualise and lead into the story. Other English language aids will appear as best fits. These stories are of novella length and so less daunting to the developing reader of Gaelic. They should serve as an intriguing introduction to longer works such as those published for the Gaelic Books Council under the Ùr-Sgeul colophon.

For the most part, the English language aids amount to a short *précis* in English before each chapter and a Gaelic-English glossary at the end of the chapter. This current book is perhaps not the place for suggesting further developments, but it might be that the publisher could explore other options for enhancing the utility of these texts. For instance, they might consider incorporating voice recordings, difficulty-graded series based on restricted vocabulary and structures,[26] the use of images to avoid over-reliance on glossaries, and recurring characters so that readers can follow an established text world as the language and structures become more difficult. Undoubtedly, many other suggestions will be forthcoming from the readership. In any case, Sandstone's initiative is greatly to be welcomed. Perhaps the most significant thing to note about these first four books is that the writing itself is of a good standard. In terms of literary merits, they would not have been out of place being discussed in the main body of this chapter: however, for reasons of space constraints here, their target audience excluded them. The authors of the Sandstone books could easily go on and contribute to the non-learner market for fiction, as Catrìona Lexy Chaimbeul has already done.

At the beginning of the twentieth century, Gaelic prose fiction was only starting to appear. As the opening chapters in this book have shown, writers struggled to establish style and genre in the first half of the century. There were undoubtedly some highlights, but these were the exception and they failed to inspire a movement that in any way came close to matching the refulgent poetry renaissance that took place from the 1930s onward. Fiction came into its own, as Derick Thomson has quite rightly said, within the pages of *Gairm* magazine; and, as I have argued in Chapter 4, most especially during the 1960s. This led to a resumption in novel-writing between the 1970s and 1990s, but, despite a brief flurry between 1993 and 1996, production was never more than sporadic. As this chapter has shown, the Gaelic Books Council's Ùr-Sgeul project has changed the scene dramatically. For the first time, readers of Gaelic fiction can expect to see several books published within a calendar year, all of them finished in the same quality as books in English. Also for the first time, there is a real move towards the development of genres within the literature. Several of the recent books have deliberately moved away from the 'literary' mode or else from realism or the settings so familiar to readers of Gaelic fiction for most of the past century. All of these developments can only be welcomed, albeit with the caution that the term 'genre fiction' must not be allowed to become a tag to excuse poor writing or editing. If the short story came into its own during the *Gairm* years, it may be that scholars of the future will say that prose fiction in general came to dominate the literary scene during the Ùr-Sgeul years.

Notes

Introduction

1. Donald John MacLeod (1977: 198) commented that 'the rich Gaelic oral prose literature of tales and sermons would require a paper in its own right' when electing not to include these matters in his seminal article about Gaelic prose. In fact, the tradition he was talking about deserves rather more than a paper, but work on this area is well in hand. Scholars of Irish have already begun trying to trace the link between folklore and modern literature. According to Pádraig Ó Snodaigh, 'of itself folklore did not evoke great literature' (1987: 5), but he does see it influencing some of the literary developments in some measure, and accepts Alan Titley's earlier argument that the modern literature is a modern continuation of the imaginative process that had existed for centuries in both oral and written form. See also Denvir and Ní Dhonnchadha (2000).

2. Gaelic writers and critics may wring their hands in dismay that, of all figures in the Gaelic milieu, Macpherson is the one who continually attracts attention – as always, for all the wrong reasons.

3. The first edition was published in 1984 as a single volume, but the second edition in 2006 stretched to two 400-page volumes.

4. The magazine *Gath* was established almost immediately when *Gairm* came to the end of its run. So far, however, *Gath* has not appeared on a regular basis: since 2003, only nine numbers have appeared, and there have been long hiatuses; notably the most recent gap of over two years between issues. *Gath* is discussed alongside *Gairm* in Chapter 3.

Chapter 1: The Origin of Gaelic Fiction

1. Another reason for the late development of a prose fiction may be similar to that identified by Philip O'Leary in relation to the similar slow progress of fiction in Irish: O'Leary argues that the novel failed to emerge because access to the press was so dominated by the authors of religious works. According to O'Leary, the novel in Irish showed signs of emerging via the prose romance tradition that came down through the myths, legends and folk tales (O'Leary 1994).

2. Carswell's *Foirm na h-Urrnuidheadh* (1567) is often called a translation, but its relationship with the source text is rather more complex than what a

contemporary audience might understand by that term: the term 'version', therefore, seems more appropriate.

3. Throughout the book, the translations are my own, except where specified. In many cases, I have not quoted the Gaelic at all, if a translation can convey the point perfectly well on its own. In some cases, I have not translated to English, as the translation would be unlikely to clarify the point being made.

4. More literally, he says something like 'He's nothing but a wooden block with no intelligence', but the phrase is commonly used in this way.

5. 'Fionn' literally means white or fair, and is undoubtedly a play on words with his surname. Whyte was certainly also invoking the legendary figure of Fionn MacCumhail, at a time when the fashion for the old Gaelic and Celtic heroes was very popular. I refer to Whyte as 'Fionn' from now on, in order to keep matters clear when cross-referring with his brother John. Because of the predilection among the early prose writers for using pen-names, I have used the English versions of many of their names in the opening chapters here, in the hope of avoiding confusion between the various versions of nicknames and so on. In several cases, these writers had their work published under the English version of their names anyway.

6. John's pen-name, Iain Bàn Òg ('Young Fair John'), might mislead the reader into thinking he was the younger brother, but the nickname comes from his sharing their father's name. Henry and John were cousins of the prolific writer and translator, Katherine Whyte Grant, who published *Aig Tigh na Beinne* (1911).

7. John Whyte's pen-name was 'Iain Bàn Òg'. 'Iain' is, of course, the Gaelic equivalent of the name John. The second element, 'Bàn', fair, may refer to his hair colour, or could be another play on the name Whyte, much like Henry's 'Fionn'. The third element, 'Òg', means young. Very often, John would sign off his writings simply as 'I.B.O.' He also used the pen-name MacMharcuis. See Meek 2007c for a discussion of the roles of the Whyte brothers in the land agitation at the end of the nineteenth century.

8. This practice was by no means unique. For instance, in Ireland, the Oireachtas (a loose equivalent of An Comunn Gàidhealach's Mòd) hosted competitions to foster the development of literature. Indeed, the language promotion bodies in the various Celtic countries shared these ideas with one another. Pádraig Ó Snodaigh (1987) traces the evolution of literature in Irish, seeing the same kind of deliberate efforts as were being undertaken on behalf of Gaelic literature at the beginning of the twentieth century.

9. Note that there is a deliberate echoing in the sound of 'cadal nan seachd seachdainean' (p. 60), adding to the dreamlike quality of the story.

10. The numbers three and seven are significant in Gaelic folktales, as they are elsewhere.

Chapter 2: The Early Novels

1. The full title is quoted earlier in the text, but the novel will be referred to by the short version from now on. The short version, *Dùn-àluinn*, is the name of the estate where the main action takes place, and is therefore also the name of the landlord. The subtitle, *an t-Oighre 'na Dhìobarach* ('the Heir in Exile'), reminds us that the hero of the novel is meant to be Cailean Òg.

2. Ruaraidh Erskine translates the passage: "My coat!' cries the minister, and he stripping himself of his black frock, and flinging it across a chair-back. 'If my coat it is that's coming 'twixt thou and me—yon thou hast it! ... Minister! Stay thou there till big Donald Stewart deals with Dùn-àluinn!" This appears in his short collection of pieces translated from Gaelic, *The Old Tribute*, published in London by The Mandrake Press in 1929 (p. 58).

3. The full title is *An t-Ogha Mór: no Am Fear-Sgeòil air Uilinn*, but (as with the other early novels) it will be referred to throughout by its main title here. The phrase *fear-sgeòil* literally means 'man of the story', and *air uilinn* is the Gaelic idiom for 'downcast' or 'disheartened', although it can also just mean 'resting on his elbow'.

4. It is probably safe to refer to the narrator as 'he', as there is not much in the text to distinguish him from the author, and he seems to identify with the male characters and the male storytellers who have passed on the various fragments of the plot.

5. Although, see Iain Ruairidh's assertion of just that on page 87: "Ged is uasal a h-uile Gaidheal, cha mhór" ('Although almost every Gael is noble').

6. Throughout their exchange, as often elsewhere in the book, it is not entirely clear that the word 'Gall' is being used for Lowlander, as its primary meaning was, until recently, foreigner. The word essentially means someone who is not a Gael, and thus came to apply to Scots who did not know Gaelic. However, there are suggestions throughout the novel that the word is usually used for Lowlander.

7. This echoes a Gaelic proverb: 'Tìr Gun Chànan, Tìr Gun Anam': 'A Land without a Language is a Land without a Soul'.

Chapter 3: Periodical Fiction

1. Somhairle MacGill-Eain, the leading figure in twentieth-century Gaelic literature, also published a short story, but it was clear that his skill lay in poetry.

2. MacThòmais had a co-editor, the well-known writer Fionnlagh I. MacDhòmhnaill (Finlay J. MacDonald) until 1964 (MacDhòmhnaill ceased to be co-editor between issues 46 and 47). Between issue 56 in 1966 and issue 96 in 1976, MacThòmais's one-time student and then colleague at Glasgow University, Dòmhnall Iain MacLeòid (Donald John MacLeod), joined him as assistant editor. For the 31st ssue, Alasdair Iain MacAsgaill replaced MacThòmais and MacDhòmhnaill, while they enjoyed what they described as a well-earned holiday; incredibly, this was the only issue that

MacThòmais overtly took no part in editing. In 1980, only three issues of the magazine appeared; however, the summer issue appeared as a double-number (111/112), allowing *Gairm* to preserve its record of four numbers per year.

3. This is a bad translation. The expression *seachd sian* is difficult to translate. Literally, it means 'seven storms' or 'seven elements', but it is used as a description of the worst and most extreme weather imaginable. The number seachd, is also an intensifier.

4. *An Cabairneach* was a magazine produced by Portree Comunn na h-Òigridh, and which Donald John MacLeod considered to be one of the highlights of Gaelic literary writing in the twentieth century. Finlay J. MacDonald (Fionnlagh I. MacDhòmhnaill), joint founder and co-editor of *Gairm*, was the first editor of *An Cabairneach* (MacLeod 1977, 215).

5. This bears comparison with the similarly-titled story by Cailein T. MacCoinnich, which appears in his *Nach Neònach Sin*, discussed in Chapter 5.

6. MacDhòmhnaill was joint editor of *Gairm* and was an acclaimed author in English as well.

7. Rarlon Seixias was later revealed to be the nom de plume of Dòmhnall Dòmhnallach. Some of his other writing is discussed later in the chapter.

8. 'Lowlanders' is an inadequate translation of the word *Goill*, which essentially means 'foreigners'. The word has come to be used most commonly to mean 'lowlanders' in modern Gaelic, although it may also be thought of as meaning 'those who are not Gaels'. Given the context of the story, in which Gaelic has risen to a position of some prominence far outside its twentieth century heartland, it would be reasonable to consider the word as signifying something like this here.

9. A red soldier is, of course, a 'red-coat', a member of the British Army during the decades when parts of the Highlands were effectively at conflict with the British establishment.

10. Because this line essentially puns the verb, it is not easy to translate. Literally, it says 'and she takes the trolley and her feet with her'. The Gaelic idiom of taking one's feet with one is equivalent to something like 'clearing off' in English. It is very commonly used.

11. Sometimes, his name is recorded as 'Aonghas Phàdraig Caimbeul'.

Chapter 4: The Second Wave of Novels

1. Máire Ní Annracháin (2006) writes about how small the numbers of texts are: 'Readers of this publication need no reminding of how few novels there are in Scottish Gaelic, arguably fewer than thirty, depending on where the boundaries of the genre are placed.' (141). This point about boundary placement is an important one that needs to be addressed, although it is one I am cautiously avoiding throughout most of the present book.

2. In fact, contemporary evidence seems to suggest that the books probably were well-received, albeit by audiences who disagreed with one another.

3. The translation first appeared in serialised form in *Gairm*.

4. Even now, after the first seven years of Ùr-Sgeul, and other fiction appearing outside of that banner, it is still the norm for characters to have a Gaelic background or for the story to be set in the Highlands, or both.

5. Briefly: Deirdre is so beautiful that she has been promised as bride to the King, Conchobair. However, she herself predicts she will marry a man who has black hair, white skin and red cheeks. When she meets such a man, Naoise, she falls for him at once. The two of them elope, fleeing Ireland for Scotland with Naoise's brothers and warriors. Conchobhair does not dare follow them to Scotland, so he sends messengers to pardon them and invite them back to Ireland. The leader of the messengers, Fergus, is one of the greatest of all legendary warriors, and Naoise trusts him completely. However, when they return, Fergus is obliged by a magical taboo to be elsewhere. Conchobhair seizes his opportunity and kills Naoise and his brothers and captures Deirdre. Deirdre kills herself in despair.

6. Like his brother, he is often best-known colloquially with the epithet *a' Bhocsair* (both brothers receiving this nickname in recognition of their father's fighting ability).

7. This is another title which is hard to translate, as it relies on ambiguity in the word *Meadhanach*, which can mean 'middle' (as in Murchadh's place in the family, as the middle brother of three), but can also mean 'mediocre' and is a euphemism for 'unwell' (both of which can also describe Murchadh). The title can be read as 'The Middle One'.

8. *Dùnadh* literally means 'closing' and refers to the fact that, in much of the Gaelic tradition, poets would begin and end a poem with the same word or line. Originally probably introduced to signal where one poem began and ended, it became a technical device that was used for effect, and is still seen occasionally in Gaelic poetry today.

9. A *sloinneadh* is a version of a person's name which also describes aspects of his/her background, especially in terms of the family: a kind of genealogical nickname that is a shorthand way for people to explain their family and kinship connections when they meet. Although not used to the same extent today as it was in the past, it is still common for people to be known by a *sloinneadh* that would include the names of father and grandfather: e.g. Calum Sheumais Dhòmhnaill, meaning 'Calum, son of James, son of Donald'. Because of the small stock of first names and surnames in many Gaelic communities, this *sloinneadh* often gives people a more accurate identification than using their full, registered name.

10. A small loch in the north-west of Lewis, in the approximate area of Ness.

11. Note that the expression *a' tilleadh dhachaigh* is often used as a euphemism for 'dying'. It appears from time to time in the work of Iain Mac a' Ghobhainn, as well.

12 . Derick Thomson, for many years Professor of Celtic at Glasgow University, published as 'Ruaraidh MacThòmais' whenever writing in Gaelic, even his scholarly work.

13. 'Portrona' is an old name associated with Stornoway.

14. Michelle Macleod is preparing an edition of his plays for publication with Acair.

15. Notice the fascination with words, and also the fact that characters within the novel are themselves archetypes: instead of being known by names, they are known by stereotyping nicknames: Scouser, Padaidh ('Paddy'), etc.

16. This is Tormod Calum Dòmhnallach.

17. Her short fiction is also impressive, as discussed in Chapter 3.

18. 'Keino' is the name of a proposition-bet game that is played in the novel.

19. This is rather like saying in English 'The Campbelly one', but is not disparaging and is a common way of referring to people.

20. An exception to this general rule is *Am Bounty*, which is a straight pulp-fiction, action-based historical novel. *Am Bounty* is discussed in Chapter 6.

Chapter 5: Collected Stories

1. 'Am Bocsair' should not be confused with his brother, also called Aonghas Caimbeul, who was known as 'Am Puilean' and was also a poet and prose writer of some significance.

2. Usually known simply as 'Dòmhnall Alasdair'.

3. Six of the stories have one of the Gaelic words for 'and' in their titles, which is one of the most obvious ways in which Mac a' Ghobhainn points towards contrasts.

4. These stones, often referred to as *Tursachan* in Gaelic, are huge standing stones that reside on a hill in the west of Lewis.

5. The English version of 'An Còmhradh', titled 'The Conversation', appears in Smith's (i.e. Mac a' Ghobhainn's) *The Village* (1976).

6. Mac a' Ghobhainn was influenced by his reading of Hume and Kierkegaard here. Kierkegaard's *The Sickness Unto Death* was a particular influence both here and elsewhere in *An Dubh is An Gorm*.

7. Cox (1992: 199, fn. 5) noted that the titles of 'Pickering' and 'Air an Trèin' should be exchanged.

8. I am not sure that there is textual evidence to identify the city, but a student of mine was convinced that it is meant to be Edinburgh. This would make some sense, as Moireach studied there himself.

9. Literally, 'An Dà Latha' means 'The Two Days', but the phrase implies a big change in someone's life. In the phrase 'thàinig an dà latha', for example, it would be equivalent to the English 'it's changed days' or 'it's a different world'.

10. MacAonghais died in 1987, having published stories in *Gairm* and in some of the anthologies also mentioned in this chapter. He collected his

stories shortly before his death and left them in the care of the Gaelic
Books Council, which allowed for *An Guth Aoibhneach* to be published.
Although fairly well-regarded, he is probably one of the more underrated
Gaelic writers, perhaps partly due to the fact that fiction was so long
considered the literary poor relation to verse. He was also a successful
dramatist.

11. The title is almost impossible to translate adequately. It is broadly
    equivalent to the English idiom 'to put the cat among the pigeons', but this
    does not really convey the correct sense in which it is used in this story.
    The idiom is also used as a (weak) pun here, as it contains the Gaelic for the
    word 'fiddle' and the main antagonist plays a double-bass.

12. He usually published as 'Cailein T. MacCoinnich', although slightly different
    versions of his name did appear from time to time.

Chapter 6: Contemporary Fiction

1. Ùr-Sgeul is an initiative that has been brought into effect by the Gaelic
   Books Council, in response to a demand for there to be more books for
   adults to read. A number of manuscripts had been submitted to the Books
   Council, and so the decision was taken that they would make an effort to
   bring these to the public domain (Storey 2007).

2. The title is difficult to translate neatly. It comes from a song, which acts as a
   psychological backdrop to the whole novel, without ever really appearing.
   The line is 'Mo Chailin dìleas donn', 'My faithful brownhaired girl.' The
   title of *Taingeil Toilichte* is similarly difficult to translate neatly, and draws
   on the same cultural tradition and the same song: *taingeil* is 'grateful' and
   toilichte is 'happy'.

3. The text appears in italics on the page, in Gaelic, to mark the character's
   inner voice.

4. *Seanchas* is the word used in Gaelic to describe the folk process: learning
   from older people in the community. The tradition-bearer, the village
   story-teller, is the *seanchaidh*.

5. The title of the novel is based on the words of a popular song that is
   significant to the characters.

6. His name appears as 'Aonghas Pàdraig Caimbeul', but he is also sometimes
   known colloquially as 'Aonghas Phàdraig', with lenition of the second
   name, in the style of a patronymic. The title of the novel is translated as
   'Day Speaketh Unto Day', which immediately points towards the highly
   evangelical and rhetorical nature of much of the book.

7. The translation is 'The Klondykers', referring to the fleets of large East
   European (often Soviet/Russian) fish-factory ships that regularly anchored
   off the west of Scotland in the 1980s and early 1990s and became a feature
   of the port town of Ullapool.

8. Seumas Moireasdan is based on a historical figure, who was from the island
   of Lewis and who did sail on the Bounty's fateful voyage.

9. The title *Dacha Mo Ghaoil* is deliberately difficult to translate, as it is a play on words. It makes use of the Russian word dacha, meaning a kind of country or exurban villa, and its similarity to the Gaelic word dachaigh, meaning 'home'. Thus, it means something like 'My Love's Country Retreat'.

10. Soloviev (1853-1900) was a highly influential Russian poet, philosopher and critic. The phrase '...anabarrach sgileil' is one that genuinely appeared on the cover of *Là a' Dèanamh Sgèil Do Là*, attributed to Wilson McLeod.

11. See Chapter 1.

12. 'The Missionary', which was packaged as a short story.

13. MacAulay wrote the foreword in Gaelic and, following the common practice, therefore published under the Gaelic version of his name: Dòmhnall MacAmhlaigh. He is also widely known by the English version of his name, being a well-published Celtic scholar and former Professor of Celtic at Glasgow University. He is also a leading poet, and his poetry usually appears under the Gaelic version of his name.

14. Black published as 'Raghnall MacilleDhuibh', but, as a leading Gaelic scholar, is also widely known by the English version of his name.

15. I have suggested elsewhere that Mac a' Ghobhainn was not anti-faith, as such, but that he was an opponent of the sort of dogma that is most commonly associated with religion: especially, as Campbell has identified it, religious fundamentalism, in its many forms (Campbell 2006). Indeed, there are suggestions in some of Mac a' Ghobhainn's personal interviews and various places in his work that he admired faith in some ways and certainly did not denigrate an individual's right to believe in a supernatural God, even though he himself could not share that belief.

16. The title is a pun, as the word *cleas* can mean both a trick and also like (similar to). Thus, the title may be read as 'A Mirror Trick' or 'Like a Mirror'.

17. It is not easy to translate this word, but it refers to the title character's reliance on his ears and power of hearing. Literally, it means something like 'the eary one'.

18. In reality, a corpus callostomy does cause a perceptual schism, in that most patients shown an image in the left half of their visual field are not able to name what they see: this is because the speech-control functions are, for most people, in the left side of the brain, and the image on the left side of the visual field goes to the right side of the brain.

19. 'An Ceum' is 'The Step' (but also means 'degree'), and 'Ist! 'Eil e ach an leth-uair co-dhiù?' is a rather colloquial usage but may be translated as 'Now! Is it only the half-hour?'

20. The word *dùsgadh* literally means 'rousing' or 'waking up', but it also has religious connotations: it is used, as here, of religious revival.

21. Because of the play on words, a translation here would not be satisfactory. In this Joycean passage, MacLeòid makes fun of the text-language tendency

to use single letters to stand for syllables, which is linked to, but usually independent of, the contemporary predilection for abbreviation, truncation and acroyms. This predilection has found much favour among Gaelic groups, to the extent that most Gaelic bodies are known by initialisms or acronyms. The repetition of the word choimhearsnachd, which means community, surely draws attention to two things: the focus of Gaelic promotion groups has not always been on the language as a community language; and the Gaelic community itself is now, if it was ever otherwise, extremely diverse, both geographically and demographically. The letter 'v' does not exist in Gaelic, but it appears in text language to represent 'bh': so, *vo v-nag* is *bho BhnaG*, 'from Bòrd na Gàidhlig'. The passage ends with the non-existent initialism *g-nag*, but the story caustically suggests that it will not be long before it is claimed by a group of its own: 'cha bhi fada aige ri feitheamh'. The other existent initialism is *c-nag*, which is CnaG, Comunn na Gàidhlig.

22. Her name also appears as 'Catrìona Lexy Campbell' on her novel, *Cleasan a' Bhaile Mhòir*, which is briefly discussed at the end of the chapter. She is the daughter of Tormod Caimbeul, the author of *Deireadh an Fhoghair* and *Shrapnel*.

23. The review appeared on the 29 October 2009 in *The Scotsman*.

24. MacilleDhuibh goes on to suggest that *Samhraidhean Dìomhair* is one of the best of the Ùr-Sgeul books.

25. And indeed, as noted elsewhere, translated works are ignored in this book.

26. Perhaps based loosely on European Framework levels.

Primary Texts

Amannan (1979), Edinburgh: W. and R. Chambers.

An Claigeann aig Damien Hirst (2009), Inverness: CLÀR.

Caimbeul, Alasdair (1990), *Trì Dealbhan Cluiche*, Sleat: Clò Ostaig.

Caimbeul, Alasdair (1999), *Lìontan Sgaoilte*, Sleat: Cànan.

Caimbeul, Aonghas Pàdraig (2003), *An Oidhche Mus Do Sheòl Sinn*, Inverness: CLÀR.

Caimbeul, Aonghas Pàdraig (2004), *Là a' Dèanamh Sgèil Do Là*, Inverness: CLÀR.

Caimbeul, Aonghas Pàdraig (2007), *An Taigh-Samhraidh*, Inverness: CLÀR.

Caimbeul, Aonghas Pàdraig (2009), *Tilleadh Dhachaigh*, Inverness: CLÀR.

Caimbeul, Tormod (1979), *Deireadh an Fhoghair*, Edinburgh: W. and R. Chambers.

Caimbeul, Tormod (1992), *Hostail agus sgeulachdan eile*, Stornoway: Roinn Foghlaim Comhairle nan Eilean.

Caimbeul, Tormod (1994), *An Naidheachd Bhon Taigh*, Sleat: Cànan.

Caimbeul, Tormod (2006), *Shrapnel*, Inverness: CLÀR.

Chaimbeul, Catrìona Lexy (2009), *Samhraidhean Dìomhair*, Inverness: CLÀR.

Dunn, Catrìona (1995), *Cha Sgeul Rùin E*, Stornoway: Acair.

Dòmhnallach, Dòmhnall Alasdair (2001), *Sgeulachdan Dhòmhnaill Alasdair*, Stornoway: Acair.

Lang, Alison (2009), *Cainnt na Caileige Caillte*, Inverness: CLÀR.

Mac a' Ghobhainn, Iain (1960), *Bùrn is Aran*, Gairm, Glasgow, 1960; 2nd edn 1974, excluding verse; 3rd edn 1987.

Mac a' Ghobhainn, Iain (1969), *An Dubh is an Gorm*, Glasgow: Oilthigh Ghlaschu (first published 1963).

Mac a' Ghobhainn, Iain (1966), *A' Chùirt*, Inverness: An Comunn Gaidhealach.

Mac a' Ghobhainn, Iain (1970), *Maighsteirean is Ministeirean*, Inverness: Club Leabhar.

Mac a' Ghobhainn, Iain (1973), *An t-Adhar Ameireaganach is sgeulachdan eile*, Inverness: Club Leabhar.

Mac a' Ghobhainn, Iain (1979–80), 'Murchadh', *Gairm*.

Mac a' Ghobhainn, Iain (1976), *An t-Aonaran*, Glasgow: Roinn nan Cànan Ceilteach Oilthigh Ghlaschu.

Mac a' Ghobhainn, Iain (1989), *Na Speuclairean Dubha*, Glasgow: Gairm.

Mac a' Ghobhainn, Iain (1991), *Na Guthan*, Glasgow: Gairm.

Mac a' Ghobhainn, Iain (2005), *Am Miseanaraidh*, Inverness: CLÀR.

Mac an t-Saoir, Màrtainn (2003), *Ath-aithne*, Inverness: CLÀR.

Mac an t-Saoir, Màrtainn (2005), *Gymnippers Diciadain*, Inverness: CLÀR.

Mac an t-Saoir Màrtainn (2008), *An Latha as Fhaide*, Inverness: CLÀR.

MacAonghais, Pòl (1993), *An Guth Aoibhneach*, Edinburgh: Saltire Society.

MacCoinnich, Cailein T. (1969), *Oirthir Tìm*, Glasgow: Gairm.

MacCoinnich, Cailein T. (1971), *A' Leth Eile*, Glasgow: Roinn nan Cànan Ceilteach, Oilthigh Ghlaschu.

MacCoinnich, Cailein T. (1971), *Mar Sgeul a Dh'innseas Neach*, Glasgow: Roinn nan Cànan Ceilteach Oilthigh Ghlaschu.

MacCoinnich, Cailein T. (1973), *Nach Neònach Sin*, Glasgow: Roinn nan Cànan Ceilteach Oilthigh Ghlaschu.

Mac Cormaic, Iain (1908), *Oiteagan O 'N Iar*, Paisley: Alexander Gardner.

Mac Cormaic, Iain (1908), *Gun D' Thug I Spéis Do 'N Àrmunn*, Stirling: Aonghas Mac Aoidh.

Mac Cormaic, Iain (1911), *Seanchaidh na h-Àirigh*, Stirling: Aonghas Mac Aoidh.

Mac Cormaic, Iain (1911), *Seanchaidh na Tràghad*, Stirling: Aonghas Mac Aoidh.

Mac Cormaic, Iain (1912), *Dùn-Aluinn: no an t-Oighre 'na Dhìobarach*, Glasgow: Alasdair Mac Labhruinn 's a Mhic.

MacGill-Eain, Tormod (1996), *Cùmhnantan*, Glasgow: Clò Loch Abair.

MacGill-Eain, Tormod (1998), *Keino*, Glasgow: Clò Loch Abair.

MacGill-Eain, Tormod (2005), *Dacha Mo Ghaoil*, Inverness: CLÀR.

MacGill-Eain, Tormod (2008), *Slaightearan*, Inverness: CLÀR.

MacGillÌosa, Donnchadh (2004), *Tocasaid 'Ain Tuirc*, Inverness: CLÀR (Ùr-Sgeul).

MacIomhair, Dòmhnall Iain (1982), *Camhanaich*, Stornoway: Essprint Earranta.

MacIomhair, Dòmhnall Iain (1985), *Eadar Peann is Pàipear*, Glasgow: Gairm.

MacIomhair, Dòmhnall Iain (1993), *Cò Rinn E?*, Glasgow: Gairm.

MacLeòid, Dòmhnall Iain (ed.) (1970), *Dorcha Tro Ghlainne*, Glasgow: Gairm.

MacLeòid, Fionnlagh (2008), *Dìomhanas*, Inverness: CLÀR.

MacLeòid, Fionnlagh (2010), *Gormshuil an Rìgh*, Inverness: CLÀR.

MacLeòid, Iain (1971), *Sràidean is Slèibhtean*, Glasgow: Gairm.

MacLeòid, Iain F. (2005), *Na Klondykers*, Inverness: CLÀR.

MacLeòid, Iain F. (2008), *Am Bounty*, Inverness: CLÀR.

MacLeòid, Seumas (1923), *Cailin Sgiathanach: no Faodalach na h-Abaid*, Glasgow: Alasdair MacLabhruinn 's a Mhic (this edn reprinted by Volturna and Marlsand, 1978).

MacMhaoilein, Calum (1990), *A' Sireadh an Sgadain*, Glasgow: Gairm.

MacMhaoilein, Calum (1993), *Seonaidh Mòr*, Glasgow: Gairm.

MacPhàidein, Iain (1902), *Sgeulaiche nan Caol*, Glasgow: Archibald Sinclair.

MacPhàidein, Iain (1921), *An t-Eileanach*, Glasgow: Alasdair Mac Labhruinn 's a Mhic.

Moireach, Iain (1993), *An Aghaidh Choimheach*, Glasgow: Gairm (first published 1973).

NicDhòmhnaill, Màiri Anna (2008), *Cleas Sgàthain*, Inverness: CLÀR.

Nic Gill-Eain, Màire M. (1971), *Gainmheach an Fhàsaich*, Inverness: Club Leabhar.

NicLeòid, Norma (2006), *Dìleas Donn*, Inverness: CLÀR.

NicLeòid, Norma (2008), *Taingeil Toilichte*, Inverness: CLÀR.

Smith, Iain Crichton (see also Mac a' Ghobhainn) (1970), *Survival Without Error and Other Stories*, London: Victor Gollancz.

Smith, Iain Crichton (see also Mac a' Ghobhainn) (1971), *My Last Duchess*, London: Victor Gollancz.

Smith, Iain Crichton (see also Mac a' Ghobhainn) (1973), *The Black and the Red and Other Stories*, London: Victor Gollancz.

Smith, Iain Crichton (see also Mac a' Ghobhainn) (1976), *The Village*, Inverness: Club Leabhar.

Smith, Iain Crichton (see also Mac a' Ghobhainn) (1993), *Thoughts of Murdo*, Nairn: Balnain.

Smith, Iain Crichton (see also Mac a' Ghobhainn) (2001), *Murdo: The Life and Works*, Edinburgh: Birlinn.

Watt, Eilidh (1972), *A' Bhratach Dheàlrach*, Inverness: Club Leabhar.

Watt, Eilidh (1987), *Gun Fhois*, Edinburgh: Macdonald Publishers.

Whyte, Henry ('Fionn') (ed.) (1885), *The Celtic Garland*, Glasgow: Archibald Sinclair.

Whyte, Henry ('Fionn') (ed.) (1898), *Leabhar na Cèilidh*, Glasgow: Gilleasbuig Mac-na-Ceàrdadh, Eanraig Mac'Illebhain; Edinburgh: Iain Grannda, Tormod MacLeòid; Oban: Eòghann Domhnullach, Tòmas Boyd.

Bibliography

Arnold, Matthew (1910), *On the Literature of the Celts*, London: J. M. Dent and Sons.

Bateman, Meg (2007), 'The Autobiography in Scottish Gaelic', *The Edinburgh History of Scottish Literature Volume 3: Modern Transformations: New Identities (from 1918)*, ed. Ian Brown, Thomas Owen Clancy, Susan Manning and Murray Pittock, Edinburgh: Edinburgh University Press, 225–30.

Bhabha, Homi (1990), *Nation and Narration*, London: Routledge.

Bhabha, Homi (1994), *The Location of Culture*, London: Routledge.

Black, Ronald (Raghnall MacilleDhuibh) (2007), "Alasdair mac Mhaighstir Alasdair and the New Gaelic Poetry", in *The Edinburgh History of Scottish Literature Volume 2: Enlightenment, Britain and Europe (1707–1918)*, ed. Susan Manning, Ian Brown, Thomas Clancy and Murray Pittock, Edinburgh: Edinburgh University Press, 110–24.

Blackie, John Stuart (1876), *The Language and Literature of the Scottish Highlands*, Edinburgh: Edmonston and Douglas.

Brown, Ian, Clancy, Thomas Owen, Manning, Susan and Pittock, Murray G. H. (2006), *The Edinburgh History of Scottish Literature*, 3 vols, Edinburgh: Edinburgh University Press.

Brown, Terence (ed.) (1996), *Celticism*, Amsterdam and Atlanta: Rodopi.

Bruford, A. J. and MacDonald, D. A. (eds) (2003), *Scottish Traditional Tales*, Edinburgh: Birlinn (1st edn 1994).

Byrne, Michel (2008), "'A Moment of History": Iain Mac a' Ghobhainn agus "Dàin do Eimhir" Shomhairle MhicGill-Eain', *Caindel Alban; Fèill Sgrìobhainn do Dhòmhnall E. Meek: Scottish Gaelic Studies* Vol. XXIV, 97–114.

Campbell, Angus Peter (see Aonghas Pàdraig Caimbeul in Primary Texts) (2006), Review of *Am Miseanaraidh*, *West Highland Free Press*, available on http://www.ur-sgeul.com/?s=home&m=news&c=view&news_id=38.

Campbell, Donald (1862), *The Language, Poetry, and Music of the Highland Clans*, D. R. Collie and Son: Edinburgh.

Chapman, Malcolm (1978), *The Gaelic Vision in Scottish Culture*, London: Croom Helm, London and Montreal: McGill-Queen's University Press.

Clerk, Archibald (ed.) (1910), *Caraid nan Gaidheal: The Friend of the Gael: a Choice Selection of Gaelic Writings*, Norman MacLeod, Edinburgh: John Grant, 1910 (first published 1867).

Cox, Richard (1992), 'Uirsgeul Mhic a' Ghobhainn: Iain Smith's Gaelic Fiction', *Iain Crichton Smith: Critical Essays*, ed. Colin Nicholson, Edinburgh: Edinburgh University Press, 190–9.

Craig, Cairns (gen. ed.) (1987–9), *The History of Scottish Literature*, Aberdeen: Aberdeen University Press.

Craig, Cairns (1996), *Out of History*, Edinburgh: Polygon.

Craig, Cairns (1999), *The Modern Scottish Novel: Narrative and the National Imagination*, Edinburgh: Edinburgh University Press.

Denvir, Gearóid and Ní Dhonnchadha, Aisling (2000), *Gearrscéalta an Chéid*, Indreabhán: Cló Iar-Chonnachta.

Fanon, Frantz (1967), *White Skin, Black Masks*, New York: Grove Press. First published in French (*Peau Noire, Masques Blancs*) in 1952.

Frater, Anne (1993), Review of *Clann Iseabail*, *Gairm* 163, 283–5.

Gillies, William (2006), 'On the Study of Gaelic Literature', in *Litreachas & Eachdraidh: Rannsachadh na Gàidhlig 2, Glaschu 2002 / Literature & History: Papers from the Second Conference of Scottish Gaelic Studies, Glasgow 2002*, ed. Michel Byrne, Thomas Owen Clancy and Sheila Kidd, Glasgow: Roinn nan Cànanan Ceilteach, 1–32.

Grant, Katherine Whyte (1911), *Aig Tigh na Beinne*, Oban: Macdonald.

Hale, Dorothy J. (ed.) (2006), *The Novel: An Anthology of Criticism and Theory 1900–2000*, Malden, Oxford and Victoria: Blackwell Publishing.

Kidd, Sheila M. (2000), 'Social Control and Social Criticism: the nineteenth-century *còmhradh*', in *Scottish Gaelic Studies* Volume XX, 67–87.

Kidd, Sheila M. (2002), 'Caraid nan Gaidheal and "Friend of Emigration": Gaelic emigration literature of the 1840s', *Scottish Historical Review* 81(1), 52–69.

Kidd, Sheila (2006), 'The Forgotten First: John MacCormick's *Dùn-Àluinn*', *Scottish Gaelic Studies* XXII, 197–219.

Lindsay, Maurice (1992), *History of Scottish Literature*, London: Robert Hale, (1st edn 1977).

Mac a' Ghobhainn, Iain (see Iain Crichton Smith) (1983), 'Ath-Sgrùdadh (4) Sùil Gheur: Sgeulachdan Iain Mhoirich', *Gairm* 122, 170–3.

MacAonghuis, Pòl (1972), Review of *A' Leth Eile*, *Gairm* 80, 377–9.

MacAulay, Donald (1983), Review of *Deireadh an Fhoghair*, *Scottish Gaelic Studies* 14, 138–40.

MacCurdy, Edward (1949–50), 'Norman MacLeod – "Caraid nan Gaidheal"', in *Transactions of the Gaelic Society of Inverness* Volume XXXIX–XL, 229–42.

MacDonald, Kenneth D. (2007), 'Glasgow and Gaelic Writing', *Glasgow: Baile Mòr nan Gàidheal/City of the Gaels*, ed. Sheila Kidd, Glasgow: Roinn na Ceiltis Oilthigh Ghlaschu, 186–215.

Macdonald, Norman M. (1979), Review of *Deireadh an Fhoghair*, *Books in Scotland* 5, 29–30.

MacilleDhuibh, Raghnall (Ronald Black) (2003), Review of *Dùn-àluinn*, *The Scotsman*, 5 December.

MacilleDhuibh, Raghnall (Ronald Black) (2006), Review of *Am Miseanaraidh*, *The Scotsman*, available on http://www.ur-sgeul.com/index.html?s=home&m=news&c=view&news_id=43.

MacilleDhuibh, Raghnall (Ronald Black) (2008), Review of *An Là as Fhaide*, *The Scotsman*, 11 October.

MacilleDhuibh, Raghnall (Ronald Black) (2009), Review of *Samhraidhean Dìomhair*, *The Scotsman*, 29 October.

MacInnes, John (2006), 'The Gaelic Literary Tradition', *Dùthchas nan Gàidheal: Selected Essays of John MacInnes*, Edinburgh: Birlinn, 163–83.

MacKinnon, Kenneth (2010), 'The Gaelic Language-Group: Demography, Language-Usage, -Transmission, and -Shift', *The Edinburgh Companion to the Gaelic Language*, ed. Moray Watson and Michelle Macleod, Edinburgh: Edinburgh University Press.

MacKinnon, Lachlan (ed.) (1956), *The Prose Writings of Donald MacKinnon 1839–1914, the first Professor of Celtic in the University of Edinburgh*, Edinburgh: Oliver and Boyd for the Scottish Gaelic Texts Society.

MacLean, Donald (1912), *The Literature of the Scottish Gael*, Edinburgh and London: William Hodge and Co.

Maclean, Magnus (1904), *The Literature of the Highlands*, Glasgow and Dublin: Blackie and Son Ltd.

MacLeod, Donald John (1970), 'Twentieth Century Gaelic Literature: a Description, Comprising Critical Study and a Comprehensive Bibliography' unpublished PhD thesis, Glasgow University.

MacLeod, Donald John (1987), 'Gaelic Prose', *The History of Scottish Literature Volume 4: Twentieth Century*, ed. Cairns Craig, Aberdeen: Aberdeen University Press, 331–5.

MacLeod, Donald John (1977), 'Gaelic Prose', *Transactions of the Gaelic Society of Inverness*, Vol. XLIX: 1974–6, Inverness, 198–230.

Macleod, Michelle (1999), '*Cianalas* Redefined', unpublished PhD, University of Aberdeen.

Macleod, Michelle (2007), 'Gaelic Prose Fiction in English', in *The Edinburgh Companion to Contemporary Scottish Literature*, ed. Berthold Shoene, Edinburgh: Edinburgh University Press, 149–56.

Macleod, Michelle (2007), 'An existential reading of the short stories of Iain Crichton Smith', *Northern Scotland* 26 (no page numbers).

Macleod, Michelle (2010), 'Language in Society: 1800 to the Modern Day', *The Edinburgh Companion to the Gaelic Language*, ed. Moray Watson and Michelle Macleod, Edinburgh: Edinburgh University Press, 22–45.

Macleod, Michelle and Watson, Moray (2007), 'In the Shadow of the Bard: the Gaelic Short Story, Novel and Drama since the Early Twentieth Century', *The Edinburgh History of Scottish Literature: Volume 3: Modern Transformations: New Identities (from 1918)*, ed. Ian Brown, with Thomas Owen Clancy, Susan Manning and Murray Pittock, Edinburgh: Edinburgh University Press, 273–82.

MacLeòid, Domhnall Iain (Donald John MacLeod) (1972), Review of *Gainmheach an Fhàsaich*, *Gairm* 79, 283.

MacLeòid, Iain (1994–5), Review of *An naidheachd bhon taigh*, *Gairm* 169, 93–5.

MacNeill, Nigel (1892), *The Literature of the Highlanders: A History of Gaelic Literature from the Earliest Times to the Present Day*, Inverness: John Noble.

MacThòmais, Ruaraidh (Derick Thomson) (1981), Review of *Deireadh an Fhoghair*, *Gairm* 114, 187.

MacThòmais, Ruaraidh (Derick Thomson) (1987–8), Review of *Gun Fhois*, *Gairm* 141.

MacThòmais, Ruaraidh (Derick Thomson) (1993), Review of *Am Fear Meadhanach*, *Gairm* 163, 285–6.

Marner, Suzanne (2000), 'Coimeas Eadar Teamanan Sgeulachdan-ghoirid Iain Mhic a' Ghobhainn agus Iain Mhoirich', *Gairm* 191, 252–4.

May, Charles E. (2002), *The Short Story: The Reality of Artifice*, New York and London: Routledge.

May, Charles E. (ed.) (1994), *The New Short Story Theories*, Athens: Ohio University Press.

Meek, Dòmhnall E. (Donald Meek) (1983), 'Ath-Sgrùdadh (5): Cailein T. MacCoinnich', *Gairm* 123, 237–47.

Meek, Donald E. (Donald Meek) (ed.) (2003), *Caran an t-Saoghail: The Wiles of the World*, Edinburgh: Birlinn.

Meek, Donald E. (2007a), 'The Literature of Religious Revival and Disruption', in *The Edinburgh History of Scottish Literature Volume 2:*

Enlightenment, Britain and Europe (1707–1918), ed. Susan Manning, Ian Brown, Thomas Clancy and Murray Pittock, Edinburgh: Edinburgh University Press, 360–70.

Meek, Donald E. (2007b), 'Gaelic Literature in the Nineteenth Century', in *The Edinburgh History of Scottish Literature Volume 2: Enlightenment, Britain and Europe (1707–1918)*, ed. Susan Manning, Ian Brown, Thomas Clancy and Murray Pittock, Edinburgh: Edinburgh University Press, 253–66.

Meek, Donald E. (2007c), 'Radical Romantics: Glasgow Gaels and the Highland Land Agitation, 1870–90', *Glasgow: Baile Mòr nan Gàidheal/City of the Gaels*, Glasgow: Roinn na Ceiltis Oilthigh Ghlaschu.

Moireasdan, Uilleam (1973), Review of *An Aghaidh Choimheach*, *Gairm* 85, 92–6.

Murchison, Thomas M. (ed.) (1960), *Prose Writings of Donald Lamont*, Edinburgh: Oliver and Boyd for the Scottish Gaelic Texts Society.

Ní Annracháin, Máire (1989), '*Deireadh an Fhoghair*', *Litríocht na Gaeltachta*, *Léachtaí Cholm Cille* 19, 168–91.

Ní Annracháin, Máire (2006), 'Television and the Novel: *Cùmhnantan* and *An Claíomh Solais*', *Litreachas & Eachraidh: Rannsachadh na Gàidhlig 2, Glaschu 2002 / Literature & History: Papers from the Second Conference of Scottish Gaelic Studies, Glasgow 2002*, ed. Michel Byrne, Thomas Clancy and Sheila Kidd, Glasgow: Roinn nan Cànanan Ceilteach, 138–47.

Ní Annracháin, Máire (2007), 'Shifting Boundaries: Scottish Gaelic Literature after Devolution', in *The Edinburgh Companion to Contemporary Scottish Literature*, ed. Berthold Shoene, Edinburgh: Edinburgh University Press, 88–96.

NicFhionghuin, Catrìona (1961), Review of *Bùrn is Aran*, *Gairm* 35, 279–82.

NicLeòid, Michelle (see Michelle Macleod) (2007), '*Puer Aeternus*: a' chiad phearsa ann an trì nobhailean Gàidhlig', *Léann* 1, 37–45.

Ó Baoill, Colm (2010), 'A History of Gaelic to 1800', *The Edinburgh Companion to the Gaelic Language*, Moray Watson and Michelle Macleod (eds), Edinburgh: Edinburgh University Press.

O'Connor, Frank (2004), *The Lonely Voice*, Hoboken: Melville House (first published 1962).

O'Leary, Philip (1994), *The Prose Literature of the Gaelic Revival, 1881–1921: Ideology and Innovation*, Pennsylvania: Pennsylvania State University Press.

Ó Snodaigh, Pádraig (1987), *Modern Literature in Irish: Survival, Revival, Arrival*, London: Connolly Association.

Powell, Ashley (forthcoming), Review of *Gormshuil an Rìgh*, *Causeway/ Cabhsair* 2.

Reid, Ian (1977), *The Short Story*, London and New York: Methuen.

Scholes, Des (2010), Review of *Tilleadh Dhachaigh*, *Causeway/Cabhsair* 1.

Smith, Iain Crichton (1989), 'The Double Man', in *The Literature of Region and Nation*, ed. R. P. Draper, Basingstoke: Macmillan Press.

Smith, Iain Crichton (1986), *Towards the Human*, Edinburgh: MacDonald Publishers.

Storey, John (2007), 'Ùr-Sgeul: Ag Ùrachadh Litreachas is Cultar na Gàidhlig . . . Dè an Ath Cheum?' available at http://www.arts.ed.ac. uk/celtic/poileasaidh/20Mar07_UrSgeul.pdf: last accessed 10.8.10.

Storey, John (2009), 'Ùr-Sgeul: ceistean agus cothrom / Challenge and opportunity for Gaelic prose in the twenty-first century', available at http:// www.ur-sgeul.com/index.html?s=home&m=news&c=view&news_ id=113: last accessed 20.8.10.

Thomson, Derick S. (1990), *An Introduction to Gaelic Poetry*, Edinburgh: Edinburgh University Press (1st edn 1974).

Thomson, Derick S. (ed.) (1994), *The Companion to Gaelic Scotland*, Glasgow: Gairm (1st edn 1983).

Thomson, Derick (1951), *The Gaelic Sources of Macpherson's 'Ossian'*, Edinburgh: Oliver and Boyd.

Thomson, Derick S. (2007), 'Scottish Gaelic Literary History and Criticism in the Twentieth Century', in *Aiste: Rannsachadh air Litreachas Gàidhlig: Studies in Gaelic Literature* Volume 1, 1–21.

Trevor-Roper, Hugh (2009), *The Invention of Scotland: Myth and History*, New Haven and London: Yale University Press, 2009 (first published 2008).

Watson, Moray (2002), 'Iain Crichton Smith's Perception', unpublished PhD, University of Aberdeen.

Watson, Moray (2004), 'Iain Crichton Smith: exile, sparseness and the Clearances', *Studies in Scottish Literature* 33, 15–29.

Watson, Moray (2006a), 'Dualchasan a' bualadh ri chèile', *Gath* 2, 40–4.

Watson, Moray (2006b), '"Dh'fhiosraich mi Céitean"', *Cànan & Cultar / Language & Culture: Rannsachadh na Gàidhlig 3*, ed. Wilson McLeod, James E. Fraser and Anja Gunderloch, Edinburgh: Dunedin Academic Press, 129–36.

Watson, Moray (2007), 'Language in the Development of the Gaelic Novel', *Northern Scotland* 26.

Watson, Moray (2008a), 'Argyll and the Gaelic prose fiction of the early twentieth century', in *Caindel Alban: Fèill-sgrìobhainn do Dhòmhnall E. Meek: Scottish Gaelic Studies* Volume XXIV, ed. Colm Ó Baoill and Nancy R. McGuire, 573–88.

Watson, Moray (2009), 'Iain Crichton Smith', http://www.litencyc.com/php/speople.php?rec=true&UID=4117.

Watson, Moray (2010), 'Language in Gaelic Literature', *The Edinburgh Companion to the Gaelic Language*, ed. Moray Watson and Michelle Macleod, Edinburgh: Edinburgh University Press, 63–89.

Watson, Moray (forthcoming a), 'Monologue, rhetoric and dialectic: how Caraid nan Gaidheal structures a *còmhradh*'.

Watson, Moray (forthcoming b), 'Cuirp Ghleansach Dhubh: an saoghal ann an uirsgeul na Gàidhlig', in *Sùil air an t-Saoghal*, ed. Niall O'Gallagher and Peter Mackay, Clò Ostaig.

Watson, Roderick (2006), *The Literature of Scotland*, Basingstoke: Palgrave Macmillan (2 vols; 1st edn, single vol. 1984).

Watson, William J. (1915), *Rosg Gàidhlig: Specimens of Gaelic Prose*, printed for An Comunn Gaidhealach by Glasgow: Alexander MacLaren and Sons (2nd edn 1929).

Watson, William J. (1918), *Bàrdachd Ghàidhlig: Specimens of Gaelic Poetry 1550–1900*, Inverness: An Comunn Gaidhealach.

Whyte, Christopher (2006), 'Sorley MacLean's "Dàin do Eimhir": new light from the Aberdeen holdings', in *Litreachas & Eachdraidh: Rannsachadh na Gàidhlig 2, Glaschu 2002 / Literature & History: Papers from the Second Conference of Scottish Gaelic Studies, Glasgow 2002*, ed. Michel Byrne, Thomas Owen Clancy and Sheila Kidd, Glasgow: Roinn nan Cànanan Ceilteach, 183–99.

Whyte, Henry ('Fionn') (1885), *The Celtic Garland*, Glasgow: Archibald Sinclair (1st edn 1881).

Index

Printed and bound by CPI Group (UK) Ltd, Croydon, CR0 4YY

03/02/2025

01830791-0005